A HISTORY OF THE WORLD

Designed with

Google™ earth

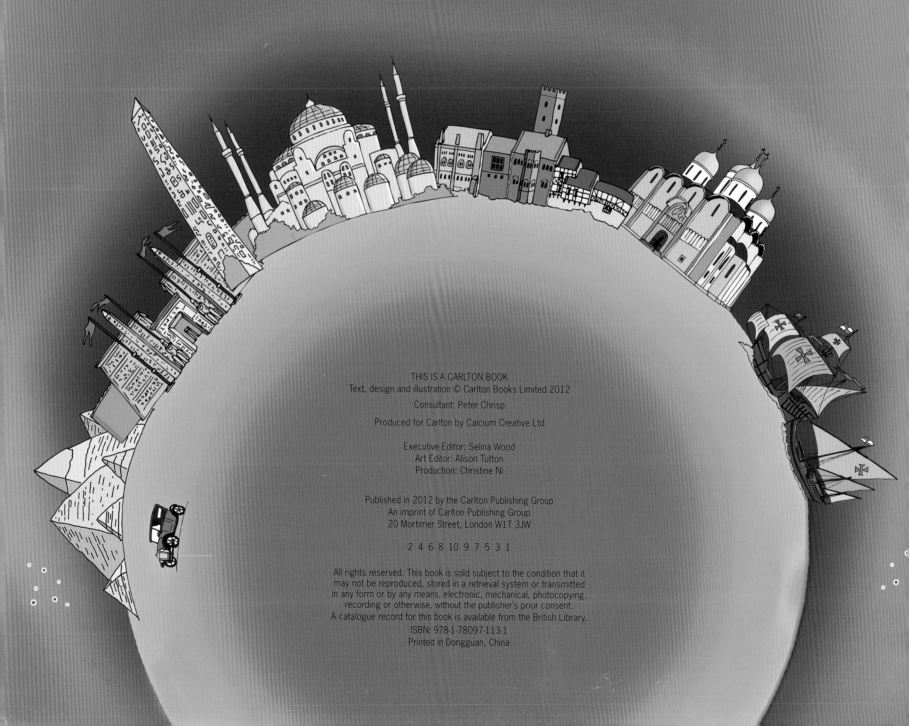

THIS IS A CARLTON BOOK

Text, design and illustration © Carlton Books Limited 2012

Consultant: Peter Chrisp

Produced for Carlton by Calcium Creative Ltd

Executive Editor: Selina Wood
Art Editor: Alison Tutton
Production: Christine Ni

Published in 2012 by the Carlton Publishing Group
An imprint of Carlton Publishing Group
20 Mortimer Street, London W1T 3JW

2 4 6 8 10 9 7 5 3 1

ISBN: 978-1-78097-113-1
Printed in Dongguan, China

A HISTORY OF THE WORLD WITH GOOGLE EARTH

Written by
Penny Worms

Illustrated by
William Ings

HOW TO USE THIS BOOK WITH GOOGLE EARTH...™

GOOGLE EARTH BRINGS HISTORY TO LIFE!

Read all about some of the most important places in history, then go online and look at the Google Earth website to explore what they look like today. There are puzzles to solve along the way to uncover a secret destination. So, are you ready for your time-travelling adventure?

The Pyramids, Egypt   View on Google Earth

INTRODUCING GOOGLE EARTH

Google Earth is a special computer program made from thousands of photographs of the Earth from space. You can fly from one continent to the next, across oceans and mountain ranges. Then zoom in to see almost everywhere up close. The world has never been so easy to explore!

DOWNLOADING GOOGLE EARTH

Google Earth can be used on most computers (see the back of this book for more details). It is free to download – just go to www.earth.google.com or search for Google Earth on the Internet. Click the download button and follow the online instructions to get started.

When you run the program, you will see a main image of the Earth (or part of it) and a search panel, which is usually found on the left.

MOUSE CONTROLS

By clicking on the main window, you can use your mouse to spin the Earth. If your mouse has a scroll wheel, roll the wheel forward to zoom in closer to the Earth's surface.

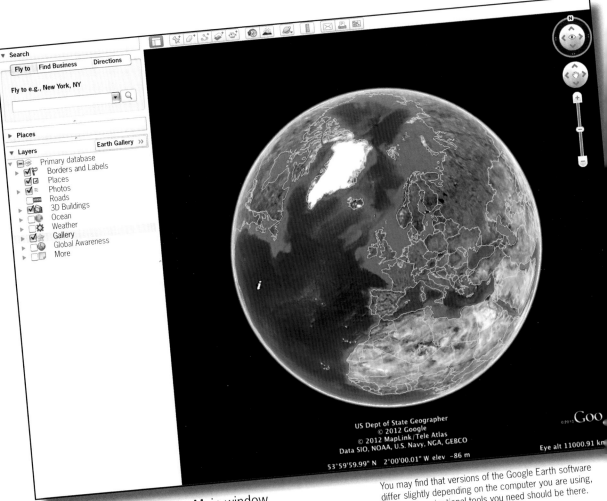

Search panel   Main window

You may find that versions of the Google Earth software differ slightly depending on the computer you are using, but all the navigational tools you need should be there.

THE 'FLY TO' BOX

At the top of the search panel is a 'Fly To' box. Type in the name of the place you want to visit or its co-ordinates. The co-ordinates are a string of numbers and compass points that will take you to a specific destination somewhere in the world. Always be careful to enter the co-ordinates as they are printed. Click on the magnifying glass and Google Earth will take you there in no time.

In this book, you are given the co-ordinates to some amazing places. Type in these co-ordinates exactly as they are printed, using all the spaces, full stops and letters, or you might end up in the ocean when you should be in the desert!

To check that your co-ordinates are working, try this test location **41 53 25.00 N 12 29 32.43 E** and click on the magnifying glass. Can you see the Colosseum in Rome, Italy?

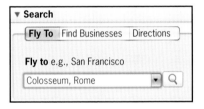

The Colosseum in Rome, Italy

NAVIGATION CONTROLS

Look at the top right of the main window. Can you see these navigation tools (see right)? If not, go to the View menu, click on 'Show Navigation' and select the 'Automatically' option.

Look Joystick

This controls your viewpoint. Using your mouse, click on the 'N' (north) and rotate your viewpoint. Use the inner wheel to raise or lower your viewpoint. Try it out on your view of the Colosseum.

Move Joystick

This moves you around the Earth in any direction. Click your left mouse button on any arrow to travel a short distance, or hold the button down to keep moving.

Zoom!

Click on the plus or minus signs (or drag the slider up and down) to zoom in or out.

Tilt!

You can also use the Zoom slider to view the Earth from different angles. Instead of looking at the Earth as if you are in a helicopter hovering overhead, you can look at buildings or mountains as if you were on the ground. Zoom in close using the zoom slider (not your mouse), and Google Earth will tilt automatically. You can also use the up arrow of the Look Joystick to tilt your viewpoint. Change your position if you need to, using your mouse.

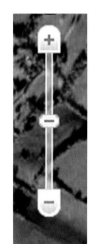

Rotated and tilted view of the Colosseum

Street View

The little yellow man is Google's Street View. Street View is made up of millions of photographs taken from a car moving along the road. Drag and drop the little yellow man anywhere on your site and you will find yourself at ground level viewing a 360 degree photograph of the exact spot where history was made. In some places, you can travel along a path by clicking onto the yellow lines ahead. You can use the other navigation controls to look up and down, turn left or right or to turn round completely. Please note though, Street View is not yet available everywhere on the planet.

EXPLORING HISTORY WITH GOOGLE EARTH™

GOOGLE EARTH has some amazing features that can help you view famous places from the past and explore them in detail. Get to know these tools first before you start your journey through time!

Layers

Wherever you go on Google Earth, you should know how the Layers feature works. Look back at the search panel on the previous page. Can you see the column on the left-hand side of the page called 'Layers'? There are lots of boxes here to tick and untick. These are choices you can make to view a location to get the information you need. Where a box has a black line beside it, you can click to see more options. For this book you need the following boxes ticked:

• Borders and Labels
• Places
• Photos
• 3D Buildings
• Gallery
  • 360Cities

Borders and Labels, Places

These give you placemarks and labels for the sites you are viewing.

Photos

To explore a place in detail, make sure you tick Photos. When this is ticked, photographic icons will appear on the screen. Open them and you will see close-up photos of the site you are viewing taken by people who have actually been there.

3D Buildings

If you tick this box you can see many building as 3D models. This is an important box that really shows what the buildings look like as reconstructions rather than just photos.

Gallery

There are lots of options in the Gallery menu to help you have fun viewing sites.

Make sure 360Cities is ticked so you can see red 360 icons on your screen. Click on these and you see amazing panoramic (all-round) views as if you are actually there! There are other interesting options in the Gallery, such as YouTube, where you can watch videos of the sites!

Historical Imagery

Another way to go back in time on Google Earth is to click the blue/green clock at the bottom left of the screen. This shows you the site you are viewing at an earlier date – for instance in 2002. You can see how the place has changed. At some cities, such as London you can go back as far as 1945!

▼ Layers	Earth Gallery ››
▼ ⊟⬨ Primary database	
▶ ☑⚑ Borders and Labels	
☑▢ Places	
▶ ☑◱ Photos	
☐▭ Roads	
▶ ☑⬚ 3D Buildings	
▶ ☐◉ Ocean	
▶ ☐✿ Weather	
▶ ☑★ Gallery	
▶ ☐◉ Global Awareness	
▶ ☐▢ More	

360Cities

3D Buildings

Photos

The Palace of Versailles, Paris, France

YOUR PUZZLE CHALLENGE

Now you are ready to take your history tour challenge. By opening the pages of this book you will travel back in time to eleven of the most important places and events in history. Look at the illlustrations to see how they would have looked in the past and then view how they look today on Google Earth.

You will be be asked to find people, places and objects in the picture and also:

– spot an historical misfit (something that's from the wrong time)

– spot a geographical misft (an object, animal or person that's in the wrong place or country)

– spot animals to rescue

– solve some puzzles

Throughout this book, some of the answers to the puzzles and searches are numbers that make up a co-ordinate to a final, secret destination.

Make a note of the numbers here as you work them out, then use them in the activity on the "Where in the world?" page at the back of the book. We've filled in a couple already to get you started.

FINAL DESTINATION

1st	2nd	3rd	4th		5th	6th	7th	8th
☐☐	☐☐	☐☐.☐☐	N	☐☐☐	☐	☐☐.☐☐	W

The Kremlin in Moscow, Russia

Good luck! See you when you get to the present day!

PS: All the answers are at the back of this book.

Google

ANCIENT EGYPT

Karnak, Egypt, 1250 BC

We start our tour of history at the beginning of human civilization. Before 9500 BC, many people were nomads – they didn't live in one place, but travelled around, hunting for food. Eventually, when people discovered how to farm land, they began to settle, building houses and villages in which to live. These grew into cities and some later became great civilizations. The ancient Egyptians were one of the greatest of all the ancient civilizations and they built these amazing temples at Karnak.

Nile river

Temple of Khonsu

Ram-headed Sphinxes

THE KING OF THE GODS

The pharaohs (rulers of ancient Egypt) created the great temple complex at Karnak to honour their gods. It included several temples. The biggest is the temple of Amun-Re, king of the gods. Every year, a religious celebration called the Opet festival took place. The statues of Amun, his wife, Mut, and their son Khonsu, were then taken in a procession down the Nile river to Thebes, the capital city. The ancient Egyptians believed that during the ceremony, Amun's power flowed into the pharaoh, confirming his right to rule Egypt.

Can you spot...
- A golden boat with Amun's statue inside
- The pharaoh (wearing a false beard and a blue crown)
- Two trumpeters announcing the pharaoh?

ANIMAL RESCUE
There were thousands of sacred animals kept in the temple building, including cattle, geese and rams. Can you find a captured lion?

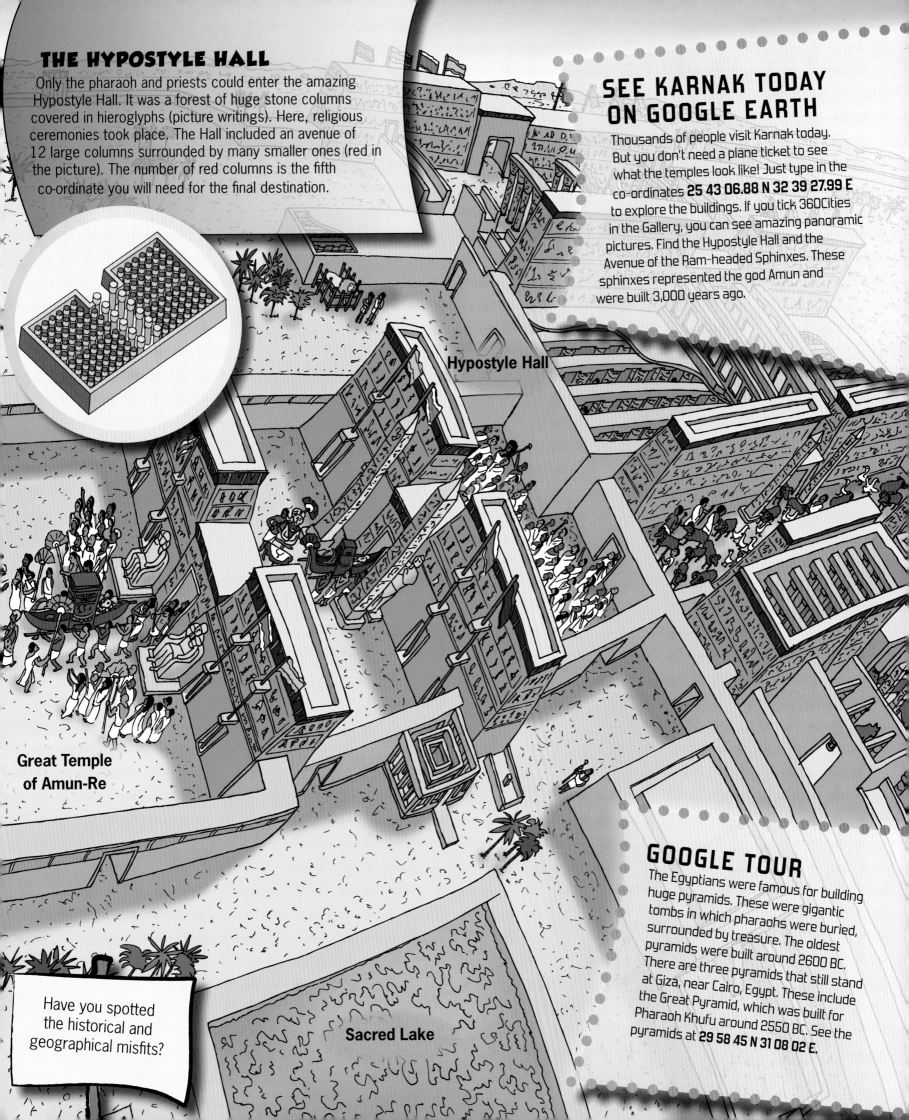

THE HYPOSTYLE HALL

Only the pharaoh and priests could enter the amazing Hypostyle Hall. It was a forest of huge stone columns covered in hieroglyphs (picture writings). Here, religious ceremonies took place. The Hall included an avenue of 12 large columns surrounded by many smaller ones (red in the picture). The number of red columns is the fifth co-ordinate you will need for the final destination.

Hypostyle Hall

Great Temple of Amun-Re

Have you spotted the historical and geographical misfits?

Sacred Lake

SEE KARNAK TODAY ON GOOGLE EARTH

Thousands of people visit Karnak today. But you don't need a plane ticket to see what the temples look like! Just type in the co-ordinates **25 43 06.88 N 32 39 27.99 E** to explore the buildings. If you tick 360Cities in the Gallery, you can see amazing panoramic pictures. Find the Hypostyle Hall and the Avenue of the Ram-headed Sphinxes. These sphinxes represented the god Amun and were built 3,000 years ago.

GOOGLE TOUR

The Egyptians were famous for building huge pyramids. These were gigantic tombs in which pharaohs were buried, surrounded by treasure. The oldest pyramids were built around 2600 BC. There are three pyramids that still stand at Giza, near Cairo, Egypt. These include the Great Pyramid, which was built for Pharaoh Khufu around 2550 BC. See the pyramids at **29 58 45 N 31 08 02 E.**

GOOGLE EARTH CO-ORDINATES: 40 45 00 N 14 29 06.18 E

THE ROMAN EMPIRE
Pompeii, AD 79

Your next stop on your whistlestop tour of world history is to Pompeii, a Roman town during the first century AD. The Romans had a huge empire that circled the Mediterranean from Britain to Turkey and the north coast of Africa. Many of their inventions, such as their legal system, alphabet, language and calendar, have been passed down through the ages and are still used in some form today.

Mt Vesuvius

Temple of Jupiter

A ROMAN TOWN

Pompeii was a thriving harbour town and a popular holiday retreat for wealthy Romans. The Forum, at its heart, was the centre for the government buildings, law courts and temples, such as the Temple of Jupiter (dedicated to the supreme ruler of the gods). Beside the Forum was the bustling Macellum (market) where traders sold goods such as wine, bread, oil and fish.

Can you spot....

· A fish seller holding up his catch of the day

· A statue of a Roman chariot

· A Roman sundial (used to tell the time)?

Forum

ANIMAL RESCUE

There were many dogs in ancient Pompeii, kept as pets and as guard dogs. Can you find a stray with two puppies to take home with you?

SEE POMPEII TODAY ON GOOGLE EARTH

The bustle of Pompeii stopped dead in AD 79 when Mt Vesuvius, only a short distance away, blew its top, burying the city and killing thousands of people. Much of the town has been excavated and you can see its remains on Google Earth. Tick Street View to travel along the very same streets that the ancient Romans did. Then type in the co-ordinates **40 49 19.04 N 14 25 23.77 E** to travel to the killer volcano, Vesuvius, to see its huge crater. Mt Vesuvius has not erupted since 1944 but it remains a danger to those who live nearby.

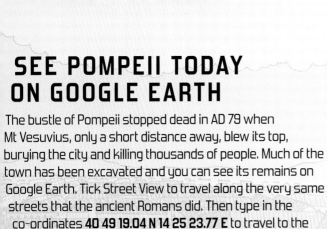

WHAT'S THE TIME?

Look at this picture of a Roman sundial. Can you tell what time it is by checking where the dark shadow falls? If you don't know your Roman numerals, here's a big clue:

1	=	I	6 =	VI
2	=	II	7 =	VII
3	=	III	8 =	VIII
4	=	IV	9 =	IX
5	=	V	10 =	X

Macellum

Have you spotted the historical and geographical misfits?

GOOGLE TOUR

Continue your Google Earth tour by taking a look at the Forum and Macellum. Zoom in to the Macellum. Look to the top left of the Macellum area (if you are facing north) and under a roof in the corner you will find two grim display cases (make sure you have ticked the 3D Buildings box). These bodies are among hundreds found of people and animals engulfed by scalding gases, rocks and lava during the volcanic eruption. It is their discovery and that of objects, equipment, frescos and food that have given us great insights into the lives of ordinary people at Pompeii.

THE BYZANTINE EMPIRE
Istanbul, Turkey, AD 532

Welcome to the city of Constantinople (now called Istanbul, in Turkey). A Roman emperor (ruler) named Constantine created this city, which later became the capital of the Eastern Roman Empire (which we now call the Byzantine Empire). Constantinople has always been an important city because it is on the border of Asia and Europe. Merchants would travel through this city, taking their goods between east and west.

Hagia Sop...

BEAUTIFUL BUILDING

During the sixth century, the Byzantine Empire was ruled by Emperor Justinian I. The people of Constantinople were mostly Christians – they no longer believed in the traditional Roman gods of previous years. When the city's main church, Hagia Sophia, was destroyed by fighting in AD 532, Justinian asked two men to rebuild it – Anthemius of Tralles and Isidore of Miletus. They built the most magnificent building the world had ever seen.

Can you spot...
- Justinian studying Anthemius's building plans
- A wine merchant selling wine
- Soldiers leaving the city to go to war?

ANIMAL RESCUE
Byzantine people loved to watch chariot-racing. But one of the horses has escaped with its chariot! Can you find it?

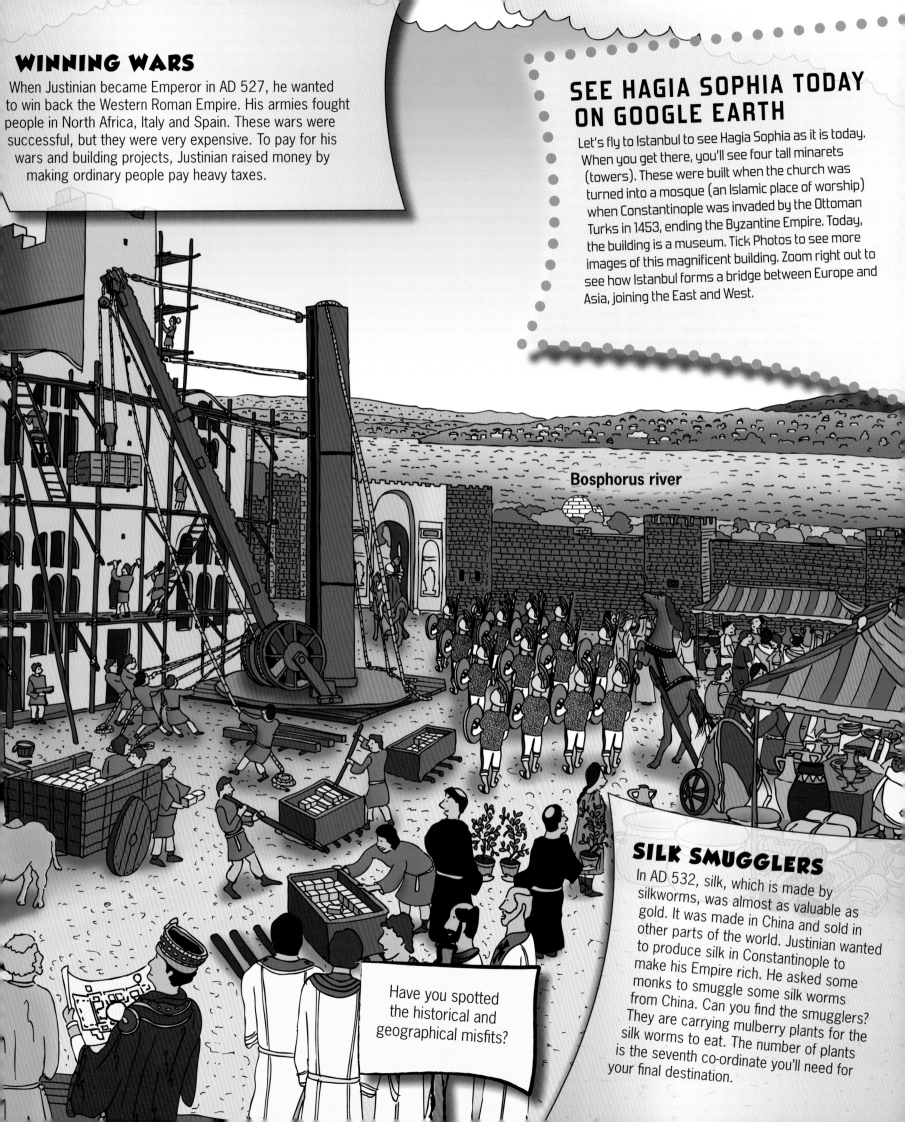

WINNING WARS

When Justinian became Emperor in AD 527, he wanted to win back the Western Roman Empire. His armies fought people in North Africa, Italy and Spain. These wars were successful, but they were very expensive. To pay for his wars and building projects, Justinian raised money by making ordinary people pay heavy taxes.

SEE HAGIA SOPHIA TODAY ON GOOGLE EARTH

Let's fly to Istanbul to see Hagia Sophia as it is today. When you get there, you'll see four tall minarets (towers). These were built when the church was turned into a mosque (an Islamic place of worship) when Constantinople was invaded by the Ottoman Turks in 1453, ending the Byzantine Empire. Today, the building is a museum. Tick Photos to see more images of this magnificent building. Zoom right out to see how Istanbul forms a bridge between Europe and Asia, joining the East and West.

Bosphorus river

Have you spotted the historical and geographical misfits?

SILK SMUGGLERS

In AD 532, silk, which is made by silkworms, was almost as valuable as gold. It was made in China and sold in other parts of the world. Justinian wanted to produce silk in Constantinople to make his Empire rich. He asked some monks to smuggle some silk worms from China. Can you find the smugglers? They are carrying mulberry plants for the silk worms to eat. The number of plants is the seventh co-ordinate you'll need for your final destination.

MEDIEVAL EUROPE

Wartburg Castle, Germany, AD 1206

We are now heading to Germany during the Middle Ages (500–1500 AD). At this time, Germany was ruled by an emperor. Noblemen such as kings, dukes and counts helped the emperor to rule and fought for him in wars. In return, the emperor allowed noblemen to own lots of land. To show off their power, many noblemen built and lived in huge castles. This is Wartburg Castle in an area called Thuringia in central Germany. In the thirteenth century, it was the home of a nobleman called Count Hermann I.

Great Hall

Tapestry, a woven wall hanging

PARTY TIME

Count Hermann I is thought to have loved music and great parties. He held banquets in the Great Hall of the castle and invited musicians and singers to perform. Incredible dishes such as stuffed peacocks and roasted pigs were served at these feasts.

Can you spot...

- A stuffed peacock
- Count Hermann
- Six musicians playing ancient instruments such as the lute and pipe?

Top table, the most important people sat next to the count

ANIMAL RESCUE

Can you find four of the count's prized greyhounds? Greyhounds were used widely in the Middle Ages for hunting.

THE FEUDAL SYSTEM

The system of allowing noblemen to keep their land in exhange for loyalty was called the 'feudal' system. As part of this system, noblemen gave some land to their knights. The knights also had to fight for the emperor. Noblemen and knights let poor people called peasants live on their land and grow their own food. In return, the peasants had to work for the noblemen and knights.

King

Lords

Knights

Peasants

HOW MANY PEASANTS?

Here's a puzzle. If seven of Count Hermann's knights each gave a strip of land to 11 different peasants, how many peasants in total would be able to grow their own food? This is the fourth co-ordinate that you'll need for your final destination.

SEE WARTBURG TODAY ON GOOGLE EARTH

Take a tour to see Wartburg as it is today. It is built on a steep hill, so visiting it means a hard climb. Luckily, with Google Earth, it's easy! The castle has been rebuilt over many years, but the original twelfth-century building still stands. This is where the Great Hall is located. It is a long building in the southeast of the castle called the Palas. Click on 3D Buildings, Photos and 360Cities to explore the castle.

GOOGLE TOUR

Continue your tour by visiting the northern part of Wartburg Castle. Can you find the black-and-white building next to the castle's entrance? In 1521, it was here that a famous church writer and speaker called Martin Luther hid away and wrote the New Testament of the Bible in German. Luther's version is still used today.

Have you spotted the historical and geographical misfits?

GOOGLE EARTH CO-ORDINATES: 39 54 56 N 116 23 29 E

THE MING DYNASTY

Beijing, China, AD 1420

From medieval Europe, let's head to China during the great Ming Dynasty in the fifteenth century. The Ming emperors had total power in China and were the people behind some of the most incredible building projects the world has ever seen, including the Forbidden City in Beijing, pictured here. They also built up a great army and navy to defend their empire.

SEE THE FORBIDDEN CITY TODAY ON GOOGLE EARTH

Tour the Forbidden City on Google Earth and see it as it is today. Visit the places few Chinese people would have seen during the Ming Dynasty. Use the navigation tools to change the angle of your viewpoint to find each area of the City that you can see in the picture. Look out for the city's huge outside wall and moat, which were built to keep people out. Anyone found trying to enter without permission was killed on the spot!

Hall of Supreme Harmony

Hall of Central Harmony

THE FORBIDDEN CITY

The Chinese government ran the country from The Forbidden City for over 500 years. The inner court of the City included the royal palace and gardens, where only the Ming emperor's family, servants and guards were allowed. The outer court included the large Hall of Supreme Harmony, where the emperor held meetings with important members of the government, and the Hall of Central Harmony, where the emperor rested before and after these ceremonies had taken place.

Can you spot...

- The emperor on his throne
- Five of the emperor's children playing in the garden
- An ancient Chinese football game?

ANIMAL RESCUE

Can you find a Qilin, or Chinese mythical unicorn? Here's a clue, it looks a bit like a lion!

Outer Cou

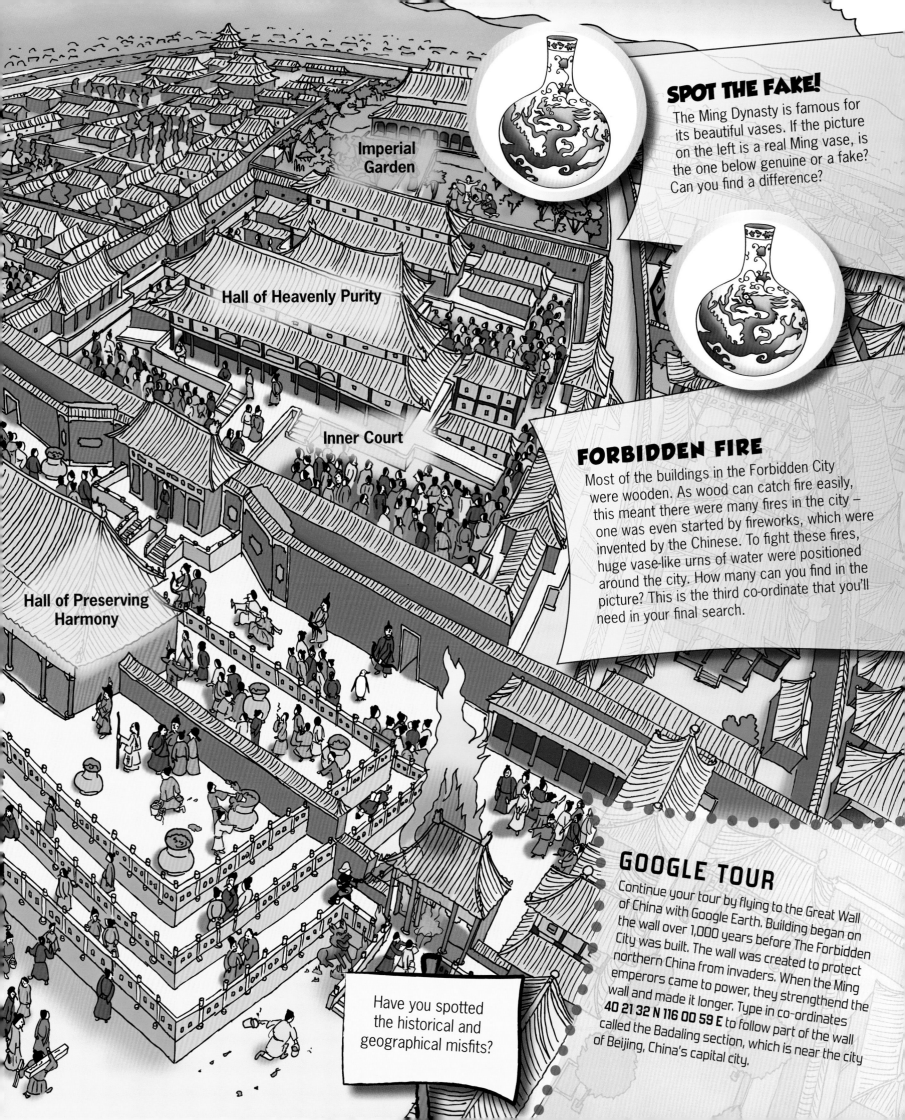

Imperial Garden

Hall of Heavenly Purity

Inner Court

Hall of Preserving Harmony

SPOT THE FAKE!

The Ming Dynasty is famous for its beautiful vases. If the picture on the left is a real Ming vase, is the one below genuine or a fake? Can you find a difference?

FORBIDDEN FIRE

Most of the buildings in the Forbidden City were wooden. As wood can catch fire easily, this meant there were many fires in the city – one was even started by fireworks, which were invented by the Chinese. To fight these fires, huge vase-like urns of water were positioned around the city. How many can you find in the picture? This is the third co-ordinate that you'll need in your final search.

GOOGLE TOUR

Continue your tour by flying to the Great Wall of China with Google Earth. Building began on the wall over 1,000 years before The Forbidden City was built. The wall was created to protect northern China from invaders. When the Ming emperors came to power, they strengthend the wall and made it longer. Type in co-ordinates **40 21 32 N 116 00 59 E** to follow part of the wall called the Badaling section, which is near the city of Beijing, China's capital city.

Have you spotted the historical and geographical misfits?

THE NEW WORLD

San Salvador Island, Caribbean, AD 1492

The fifteenth century was a time when European explorers went on voyages of discovery. One of the greatest explorers was Christopher Columbus, who sailed from Spain in his ship the Santa Maria. On 11 October 1492, he reached an island that he believed to be near Japan, in the Far East. However, Columbus was nowhere near Japan – he had landed in the Americas! These lands, unknown to Europeans at that time, came to be known as the New World.

Caribbean Sea

NINA

PINTA

SANTA MARIA

A NEW ROUTE

Explorers like Columbus were trying to reach the Far East to buy goods such as spices. These were popular in Europe, where they were sold for a lot of money. Sailors had previously tried to sail from Europe to the Far East on a long and dangerous route around the coast of Africa, but each voyage had failed. Columbus decided to sail westwards instead, believing it would be an easier route. But instead of reaching the Far East, his course had taken him to a Caribbean island near what is now the USA.

Can you spot....

- A group of dolphins
- Christopher Columbus carrying a flag and kneeling to salute the natives
- An islander with a gold ring through his nose?

ANIMAL RESCUE

Can you find a pair of West Indian whistling ducks? Rescue them before they are added to the pot!

SEE SAN SALVADOR TODAY ON GOOGLE EARTH

Travel to the Caribbean island of San Salvador, the place at which Columbus probably landed. Then type in **36 05 05.46 N 138 22 10.25 E** to travel to the island of Japan where Columbus thought he had landed. The world was a lot larger than Columbus thought!

THREE SHIPS

Columbus made his journey with three ships. Can you find the names of the three ships in this puzzle?

```
F I T X A O P L D S D
C G M V E X I A E B X
H B O N X F N L Z R G
B L A I L E B U E F W
S O N T A M T W A A J
K A N B P X R Y I F S
E L N S W F N H C R Q
```

BRINGING DISEASE

It is thought that when Colombus and his men first reached the Caribbean the natives were friendly and happy to trade goods, such as weapons and food. However, the explorers also brought diseases with them that were new to the native people. With no resistance to these diseases, many natives later died after coming into contact with the Europeans.

Have you spotted the historical and geographical misfits?

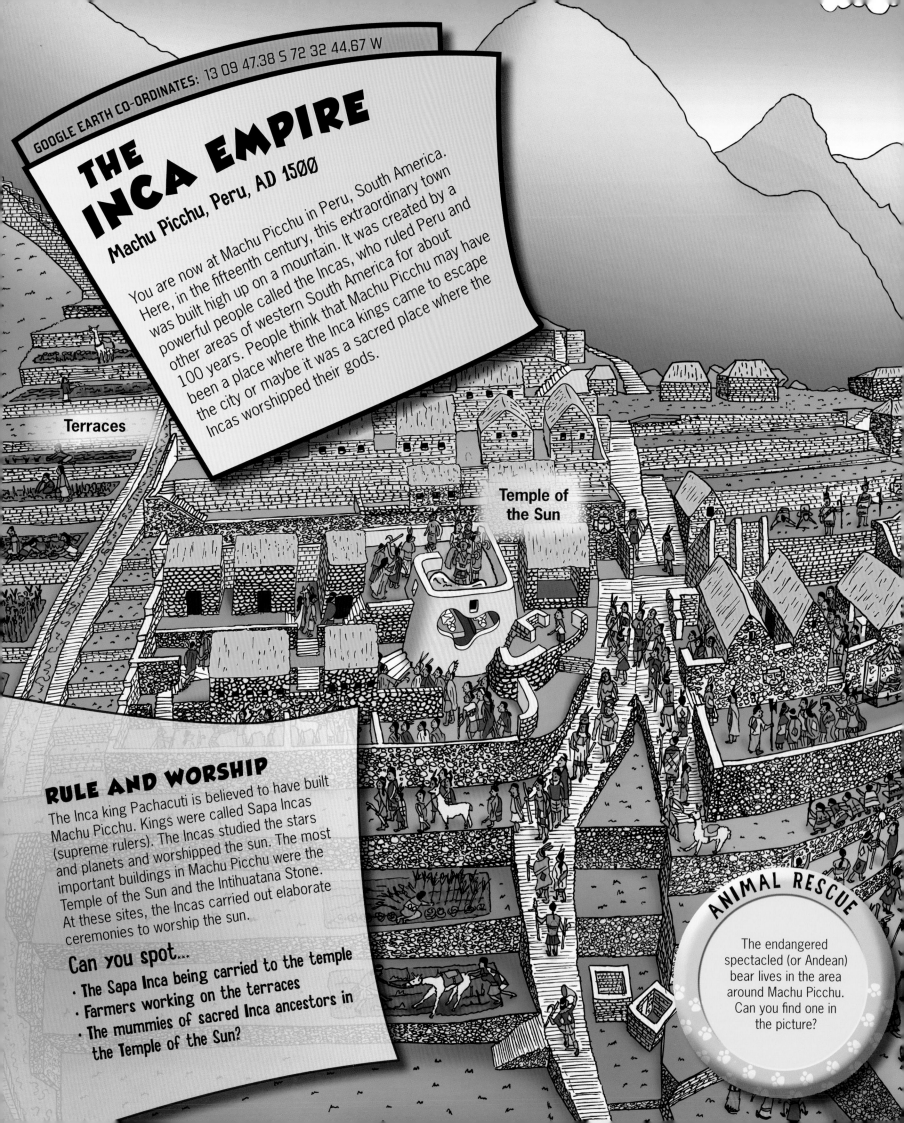

THE INCA EMPIRE

Machu Picchu, Peru, AD 1500

You are now at Machu Picchu in Peru, South America. Here, in the fifteenth century, this extraordinary town was built high up on a mountain. It was created by a powerful people called the Incas, who ruled Peru and other areas of western South America for about 100 years. People think that Machu Picchu may have been a place where the Inca kings came to escape the city or maybe it was a sacred place where the Incas worshipped their gods.

Terraces

Temple of the Sun

RULE AND WORSHIP

The Inca king Pachacuti is believed to have built Machu Picchu. Kings were called Sapa Incas (supreme rulers). The Incas studied the stars and planets and worshipped the sun. The most important buildings in Machu Picchu were the Temple of the Sun and the Intihuatana Stone. At these sites, the Incas carried out elaborate ceremonies to worship the sun.

Can you spot...

- The Sapa Inca being carried to the temple
- Farmers working on the terraces
- The mummies of sacred Inca ancestors in the Temple of the Sun?

ANIMAL RESCUE

The endangered spectacled (or Andean) bear lives in the area around Machu Picchu. Can you find one in the picture?

BUILDING THE CITY

The Incas built Machu Picchu around the side of a mountain. Many earthquakes occur around Machu Picchu, so buildings were made of large stones that locked tightly together to stop them falling down. The town was carefully designed. There were areas for ordinary houses as well as places to worship the gods. The Incas also cut and carved flat terraces into the mountainside so they could create farmland and grow crops.

Intihuatana Stone

SEE MACHU PICCHU TODAY ON GOOGLE EARTH

Take a tour of Machu Picchu with Google Earth and click on 3D Buildings to explore a model of the ancient city. Then type in the co-ordinates **13 31 14.43 S 71 58 31.67 W** to visit the Incas' capital city, Cuzco. You can see what it looks like today on Google Earth. Much of the Inca city was destroyed when the Spanish arrived in South America in the sixteenth century. They took over the Inca people and demolished many of Inca buildings and built their own, such as the Cathedral of Santo Domingo, built in the seventeenth century.

Have you spotted the historical and geographical misfits?

LOST TREASURE

During the time of the Incas, South America was rich in natural materials, such as gold, silver and precious stones. The Incas made beautiful objects from these materials. The Spanish took much of this treasure back to Spain, but people believe that some still lies hidden. Look for the gold Inca masks in the picture. The total number of masks you find is the sixth co-ordinate you will need.

GOOGLE EARTH CO-ORDINATES: 55 45 03 N 37 37 02 E

THE RUSSIAN EMPIRE

Moscow, Russia, AD 1724

We are now heading to the Kremlin, in Russia, at the time of Peter the Great. Peter was the tsar (king) of Russia during the eighteenth century. Before his rule, Russia was poorly run and troubled. When Peter became the tsar he had great plans for the country. He went to Europe to learn about the latest engineering and architecture. When he returned he began to change Russia from an old-fashioned country into a great empire.

Cathedral of the Assumption

THE KREMLIN

Peter was born in the Terem palace within the Kremlin. This is an area of important buildings in Russia's capital city, Moscow. However, Peter came to hate the place. It was here that terrible fighting took place to make Peter's half-sister, Sophia, ruler of Russia. Sophia forced 10-year-old Peter and his mother to leave the Kremlin. As tsar, Peter refused to live in the Kremlin. Instead, he built a new capital called St Petersburg. However, Peter did return to the Kremlin in 1724 to crown his second wife, Catherine, empress of Russia. Here, Peter and Catherine are shown leaving the cathedral after the coronation.

Can you spot....

- Peter the Great with his empress
- The Tsar Cannon, the world's largest cannon
- A soldier handing out gold coins to the people?

ANIMAL RESCUE

Russia is still home to brown bears. Can you find one being forced to dance in the celebration?

SEE THE KREMLIN TODAY ON GOOGLE EARTH

If you visit the Kremlin on Google Earth, make sure you have 3D buildings ticked so you can see the cathedral and the other Kremlin buildings. You can visit the Armoury, the long building with a green roof to the southwest of the cathedral. Can you also see the Grand Kremlin Palace with the Russian flag flying on top? Then look out for the Tsar Bell just to the east of the Ivan the Great Bell Tower.

Ivan the Great Bell Tower

PETER THE GREAT

At over 2 m (6 ft 7 in) tall Peter the Great was a powerful-looking man. He had lots of modern ideas and was determined to make Russia great. He created the Russian navy and improved the army. In Russia, he made lots of changes and got rid of old-fashioned ideas. He even made noblemen shave off their beards to make them look more up to date! Peter's changes made Russia modern, but his ideas were not always popular. When he died in 1725, only a few Russians were sad about his death.

Have you spotted the historical and geographical misfits?

35

32   36   15   25

GOOGLE TOUR

Continue your tour in Google Earth by typing in the co-ordinates **55 45 09.45 N 37 37 23.08 E**. Head east out of the Kremlin to Moscow's Red Square. Here you'll find St Basil's Cathedral, one of the most important landmarks in Moscow. It is famous for its patterned domes. Which of these numbered dome patterns (left) is not on the actual cathedral? The number next to it is the second co-ordinate you'll need for your final destination.

BEFORE THE REVOLUTION

Versailles, France, AD 1783

Hold on to your heads! We are off to a royal palace in France, home to King Louis XVI and his wife Marie-Antoinette. In the eighteenth century, kings like Louis ruled with complete power over their people. Kings and queens had lots of food, money and fun, but ordinary people were left poor and hungry. It was time for a change, and the king and queen of France were about to lose their heads.

Palace of Versailles

THE ROYAL PALACE

The Palace of Versailles was built by Louis' ancestor King Louis XIV. The palace and its gardens were famous for their beauty. Louis was not a good ruler, but he enjoyed learning about science. When the world's first hot-air balloon was made by the Montgolfier brothers in 1783, he invited them to Versailles to demonstrate their invention. Louis then watched in wonder as the balloon rose into the air and disappeared over the rooftops.

Can you spot...
· The Montgolfier brothers
· The king and queen on the balcony
· A platoon of soldiers standing guard?

Have you spotted the historical and geographical misfits?

ANIMAL RESCUE

Can you find a chicken, a duck and a sheep? Let's hope they have a head for heights!

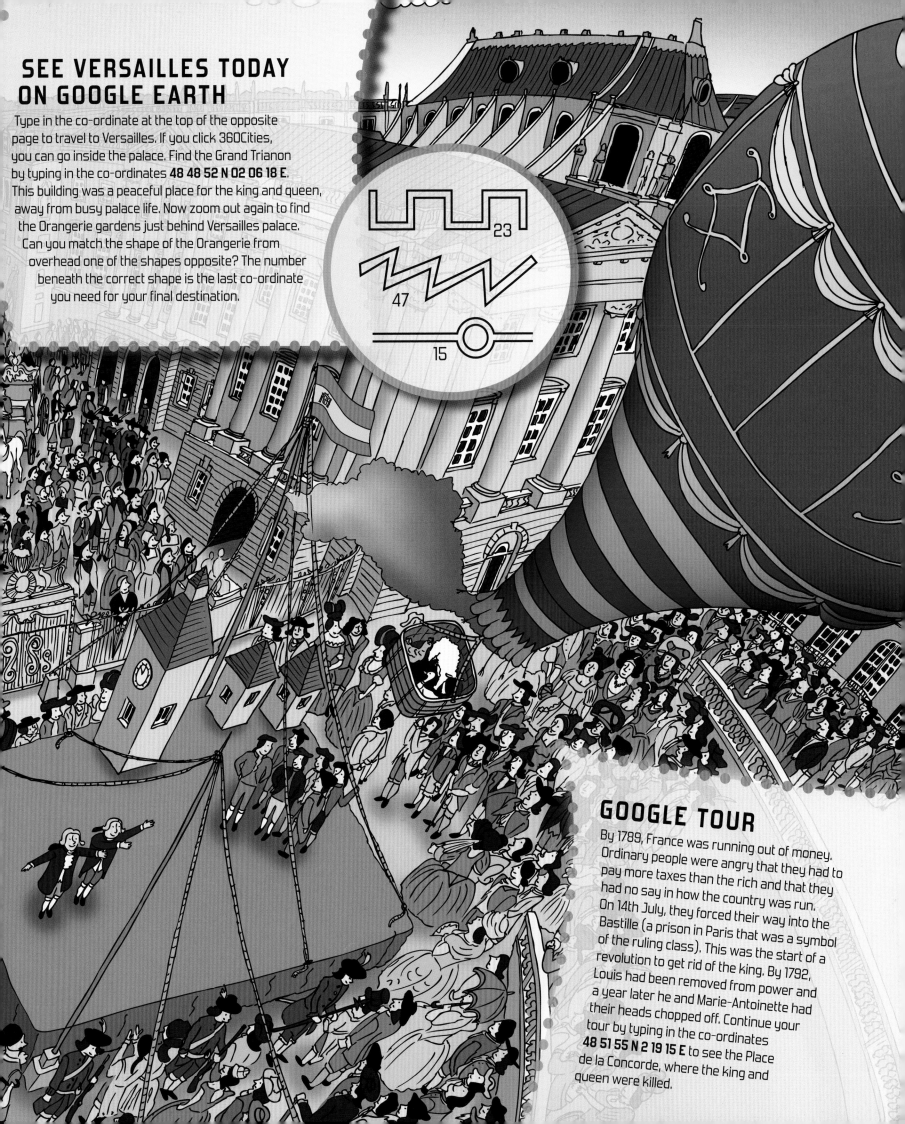

SEE VERSAILLES TODAY ON GOOGLE EARTH

Type in the co-ordinate at the top of the opposite page to travel to Versailles. If you click 360Cities, you can go inside the palace. Find the Grand Trianon by typing in the co-ordinates **48 48 52 N 02 06 18 E**. This building was a peaceful place for the king and queen, away from busy palace life. Now zoom out again to find the Orangerie gardens just behind Versailles palace. Can you match the shape of the Orangerie from overhead one of the shapes opposite? The number beneath the correct shape is the last co-ordinate you need for your final destination.

GOOGLE TOUR

By 1789, France was running out of money. Ordinary people were angry that they had to pay more taxes than the rich and that they had no say in how the country was run. On 14th July, they forced their way into the Bastille (a prison in Paris that was a symbol of the ruling class). This was the start of a revolution to get rid of the king. By 1792, Louis had been removed from power and a year later he and Marie-Antoinette had their heads chopped off. Continue your tour by typing in the co-ordinates **48 51 55 N 2 19 15 E** to see the Place de la Concorde, where the king and queen were killed.

THE INDUSTRIAL AGE

Detroit, USA, 1924

From the eighteenth century onwards, times were changing. New machines were invented which could make goods, such as cloth, using steam power. This lead to a big demand for metals to build the machines, and coal to power them. New factory towns were built, which gave people jobs and goods for them to buy. New railways took people and their goods to other parts of the country. All this work (or 'industry') was called the Industrial Revolution.

INTERNET CAFE

THE FORD FACTORY

In the late nineteenth century, a man called Henry Ford lived in Detroit, USA. He worked as an engineer, designing and making machines. In 1896, Henry decided to build and sell his own cars. When he started the Ford Motor Company in 1903, his factory was well organized. Henry Ford could make a lot of cars cheaply, which made him rich. By 1918, half of the people in America who owned a car had bought a 'Model T', built by the Ford Motor Company. In 1924, the company celebrated their 10 millionth car.

Can you spot...

- Henry Ford cutting the tape in front of the 10 millionth car produced
- A Model T police van
- A Model T farmer's truck carrying sheep?

ANIMAL RESCUE

Can you find the poor old horse struggling to pull a delivery truck? It's time for him to stop working!

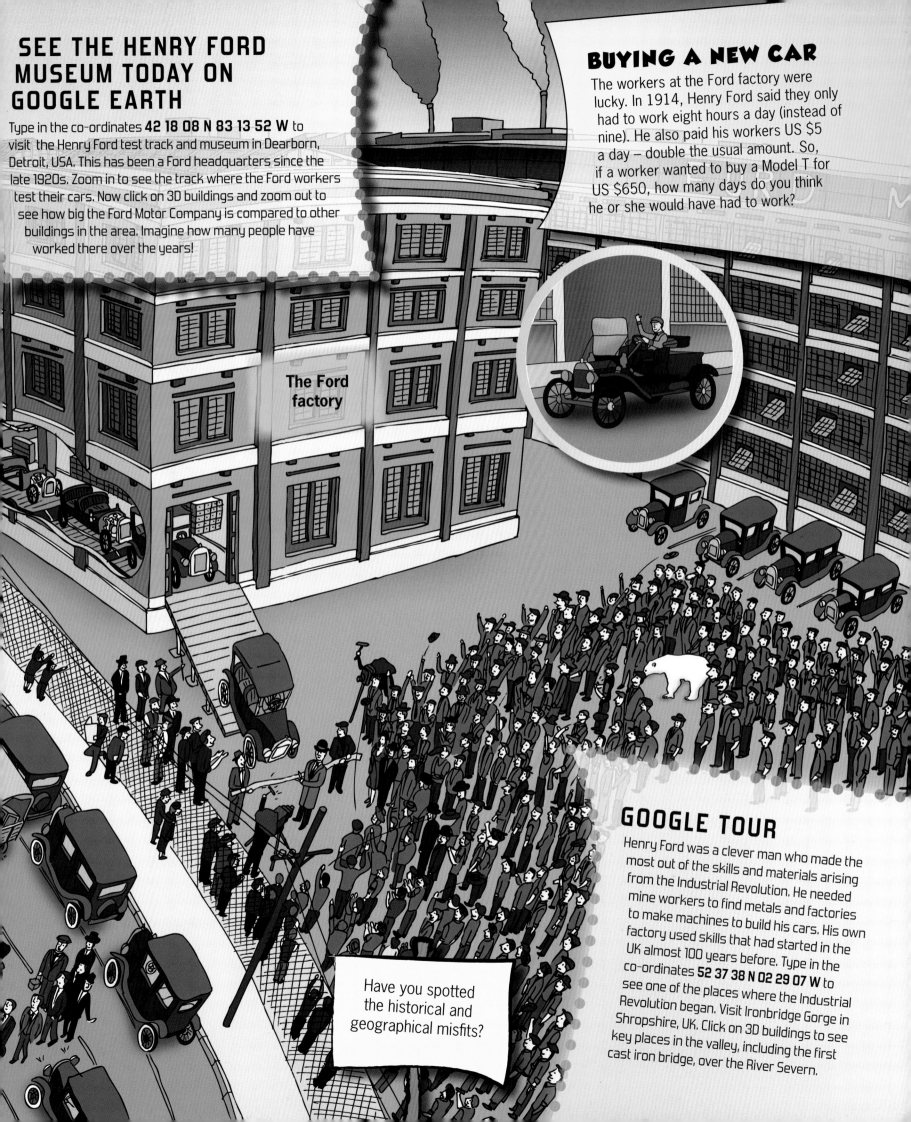

SEE THE HENRY FORD MUSEUM TODAY ON GOOGLE EARTH

Type in the co-ordinates **42 18 08 N 83 13 52 W** to visit the Henry Ford test track and museum in Dearborn, Detroit, USA. This has been a Ford headquarters since the late 1920s. Zoom in to see the track where the Ford workers test their cars. Now click on 3D buildings and zoom out to see how big the Ford Motor Company is compared to other buildings in the area. Imagine how many people have worked there over the years!

The Ford factory

BUYING A NEW CAR

The workers at the Ford factory were lucky. In 1914, Henry Ford said they only had to work eight hours a day (instead of nine). He also paid his workers US $5 a day – double the usual amount. So, if a worker wanted to buy a Model T for US $650, how many days do you think he or she would have had to work?

Have you spotted the historical and geographical misfits?

GOOGLE TOUR

Henry Ford was a clever man who made the most out of the skills and materials arising from the Industrial Revolution. He needed mine workers to find metals and factories to make machines to build his cars. His own factory used skills that had started in the UK almost 100 years before. Type in the co-ordinates **52 37 38 N 02 29 07 W** to see one of the places where the Industrial Revolution began. Visit Ironbridge Gorge in Shropshire, UK. Click on 3D buildings to see key places in the valley, including the first cast iron bridge, over the River Severn.

WORLD WAR II

Normandy, France, 1944

Our next destination is a French beach during World War II. This terrible war began in 1939. It was fought between Germany, Italy and Japan on one side, and 'Allied' countries including Russia, the USA, Canada, France and the UK on the other. In 1944, soldiers from America, Canada and the UK attacked the German army on the beaches of Normandy with the aim of freeing France from the Germans. This famous event became known as the 'D-Day Landings'.

OMAHA BEACH

The American soldiers landed on Omaha Beach. They wanted to get their men, tanks and equipment to the French shore in the early morning, but the sea current took them further along the coast. The Germans were good at defending the beaches, but the Americans eventually took control. Of the 34,000 Americans who landed that morning, about 3,000 were killed or wounded in the battle. The Germans lost 1,200 men.

Can you spot...

• A soldier throwing a grenade
• A tank about to sink into the sea
• A Nazi flag and an American flag?

ANIMAL RESCUE

Pigeons were used in World War II to carry messages. Can you find Paddy who flew from Normandy on D-Day with news of the attacks? He was given a medal for his flight.

SEE THE SITE OF THE D-DAY LANDINGS TODAY ON GOOGLE EARTH

Now check out Omaha Beach in Normandy on Google Earth. Can you find the cemetery just behind the beach? Zoom in to see the graves of American soldiers who died that day. Each grave is marked with a white cross. Zoom out to see how far the men had travelled from the UK. Can you find any of the other beaches used in the landings? They were given the names Gold, Utah, Juno and Sword.

Omaha Beach

Have you spotted the historical and geographical misfits?

25   37   68

GOOGLE TOUR

Eleven weeks after the D-Day landings, the Germans were forced out of France. Germany was losing the war in other parts of the world, too. A year earlier, in Stalingrad, Russia, a battle between the Germans and Russians saw over 1.5 million men killed. You can visit the memorial gardens of this battle in what is now called Volgograd in Russia. Type in co-ordinates **48 44 32 N 44 32 13 E**. Can you see a large statue, called 'Mother Russia' in the gardens? What is she holding in her hand? Beneath the right answer is the first co-ordinate you need for your final destination.

WHERE IN THE WORLD?

In this book, you have travelled through 3,000 years of history and visited some of the greatest civilizations on Earth. But this is only the start of your amazing journey. There are many other exciting places to visit on Google Earth that hold secrets to our past. But what about your final destination? Which exciting place will you be heading to next?

LIFE LESSONS

Your final, secret destination is somewhere that shows the way we live our lives today. The one thing that has changed our lives more than anything since ancient times is a better understanding of the world. We have learnt such a lot from the people who lived before us – people who built magnificent civilizations, men who found new countries, rulers who made new machines and weapons, and scientists who discovered how our world works.

INFORMATION AGE

Before things were written down, or printed in books and papers, people shared their knowledge by talking about it. Parents told children, teachers told pupils, rulers told their subjects and priests told the people who had come to pray. When books were made, this information travelled further than ever before. Today, we are very lucky. We have the biggest 'library' the world has ever seen. It is called the 'Internet' and its information can be shared all around the world. To use it, all you need is a computer.

So, gather all the co-ordinates you need for your final destination and put them into the box opposite to see where they take you!

Ancient Egypt
1250 BC

Roman Empire
AD 79

Byzantine Empire
AD 532

Medieval Europe
AD 1206

Ming Dynasty
AD 1420

New World
AD 1492

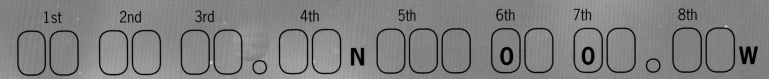
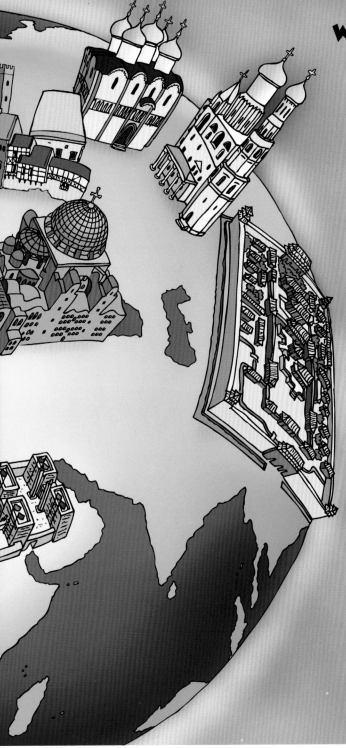

WELCOME!

Where have you landed? Look closely and you will see you have arrived in a place called Silicone Valley in California, USA. This is an important area for the Internet and computer science. Men and women who work in Silicone Valley help to make, design and run computer software for all the world to use. Their skills are helping to shape our future.

LOOK BEHIND YOU!

But beware! Just where you land, there is something from ancient times hiding in the trees – and it looks hungry! This creature comes from a time in history before humans even existed. Can you find it? You may need to use the Zoom! and Joystick tools to rotate the view to see it clearly.

Remember, whenever we look towards the future, we should never forget our past. It might come back to bite us!

Inca Empire
AD 1500

Russian Empire
AD 1724

Before the Revolution
AD 1783

Industrial Age
AD 1924

World War II
AD 1944

Ancient Egypt

The Hypostyle Hall had 122 smaller columns, so the fifth co-ordinate is **122**

Historical misfit – *A cameraman filming the procession*

Geographical misfit – *A snow-capped mountain*

The Roman Empire

Historical misfit – *A red Ferrari, made in Italy but nearly 2,000 years later!*

Geographical misfit – *A tall Chinese pagoda (a type of building)*

The time on the sundial is 9am, the time when the Forum and market would have been busiest.

The Byzantine Empire

The smugglers are carrying five mulberry bushes, so the seventh co-ordinate is **05.**

Historical misfit - *A mechanical digger*

Geographical misfit - *An igloo*

Medieval Europe

The number of serfs able to grow their own food on Count Hermann's lands is 7 x 11 = 77. So the fourth co-ordinate is **77**

Historical misfit – *An electric keyboard player*

Geographical misfit – *A Native American warrior*

The Ming Dynasty

There are 18 water vats scattered around the city, so the third co-ordinate is **18**

Historical misfit – *A fireman with a fire extinguisher*

Geographical misfit – *A penguin*

Spot the Fake – *The second vase is a fake (did you spot the dragon's glasses?)*

The New World

Historical misfit – *The hotel on the beach*

Geographical misfit – *A Japanese emperor*

Word search - names of the ships –

```
F  I  T  X  A  O  P  L  D  S  D
C  G  M  V  E  X  I  A  L  E  B
H  L  N  X  S  F  N  U  Z  R  X
B  O  I  L  E  B  T  W  A  F  G
S  A  N  T  A  M  A  R  I  A  W
K  O  A  B  P  X  T  Y  C  F  J
E  L  N  S  W  F  N  H  R  S  Q
```

The Inca Empire

There are five hidden gold masks in the picture, so the sixth co-ordinate is **05**

Historical misfit – *The cable car*

Geographical misfit – *A camel*

The Russian Empire

Pattern puzzle – The pattern that cannot be found on St Basil's cathedral is labelled '25', so the second co-ordinate is **25**

Historical misfit – *A Soviet tank*

Geographical misfit – *A llama among the horses*

Before the Revolution

You can find the Orangerie at **48 48 09.30 N 2 07 07.03 E**

The correct shape is labelled '15', so the eighth co-ordinate is **15**

Historical misfit – *A jet aircraft in the sky*

Geographical misfit – *The Spanish flag*

The Industrial Age

Historical misfit – *An Internet cafe*

Geograpical misfit – *A polar bear*

Earnings puzzle – If you thought it would take a Ford worker 130 days to earn enough money to buy a Model T in 1914, you are good at maths! Luckily for them, it took less than that because Ford also gave them a discount (money off the price of the car).

World War II

Mother Russia is holding a sword in her hand, so the first co-ordinate is **37**

Historical misfit – *A soldier firing a bow and arrow*

Geographical misfit – *Some skier troops*

Final destination

The final destination is the Googleplex, Google's headquarters in San Jose, co-ordinates:
37 25 18.77 N 122 05 05.15 W.
The thing lurking in the trees is a *Tyrannosaurus Rex* skeleton, nicknamed Stan after the real dinosaur fossil found in South Dakota, USA, and now in the Natural History Museum in London.

Minimum computer requirements for running Google Earth:

PC systems

Operating System: Windows XP, Windows Vista, or Windows 7

CPU: Pentium 3, 500Mhz

System Memory (RAM): 256MB

Hard Disk: 400MB free space

Network Speed: 128 Kbits/sec

Graphics Card: DirectX9 and 3D capable with 64MB of VRAM

Screen: 1024x768, "16-bit High Color" - DirectX 9 (to run in Direct X mode)

Mac systems

Operating System: Mac OS X 10.5.0 or later

CPU: Any Intel Mac

System Memory (RAM): 256MB

Hard Disk: 400MB free space

Network Speed: 128 Kbits/sec

Graphics Card: DirectX9 and 3D capable with 64MB of VRAM

Screen: 1024x768, "Thousands of Colors"

DAUGHTER
OF DUSK

Also by Livia Blackburne
Midnight Thief

DAUGHTER OF DUSK

LIVIA BLACKBURNE

HYPERION
LOS ANGELES NEW YORK

Printed in the United States of America

First Hardcover Edition, August 2015
First Paperback Edition, August 2016
10 9 8 7 6 5 4 3 2 1
FAC-025438-16169
Library of Congress Control Number for Hardcover: 2015006755
ISBN 978-1-4847-2366-1

Visit www.hyperionteens.com

SUSTAINABLE FORESTRY INITIATIVE

Certified Chain of Custody
Promoting Sustainable Forestry
www.sfiprogram.org
SFI-01054

The SFI label applies to the text stock

To my favorite astronomer and literary snob

ONE

The snow was a problem, the way it crunched beneath Kyra's shoes and bore marks of her passing. Though her Makvani blood made her light-footed, it wasn't enough to keep her from leaving a trail of footprints between the trees. The previous four times Kyra had come into the forest, she'd told herself it would be her last. If she were wise, she'd stay away. But apparently, she wasn't wise, not where her past was concerned.

The moon was almost full tonight. Its light passed through the leafless canopy, making the ground shine silver. Though the snow muffled the forest's sounds, there was still plenty to be heard. Wind blew through the trees. Occasionally an owl hooted. A shadow moved nearby, and Kyra trained her eyes on it, focusing on the shades of darkness that teased themselves apart if she looked hard enough. She sampled the odors of bark, new snow, and frozen leaves, and she listened. There was the snuffling of a raccoon, a scratching of tiny paws. Her Makvani blood sharpened her senses, and her brief time with the clan had taught her to use them to their fullest. It had been exhilarating to see the world like this, and Kyra had reveled in these new discoveries.

But they were no longer enough.

Even now, as she stood awash in the forest's sights, sounds, and smells, Kyra was thinking about something else. *A crisp fall morning. A circle of witnesses. Her life hanging in the balance.* She'd been a captive of the Makvani, fighting the assassin James in Challenge, and he'd beaten her. He'd had her at his mercy, and she'd been sure she was going to die.

But then she'd changed. Kyra could feel it still, the warmth that started in her core and expanded out until her body melted and her bones stretched into the frame of a giant wildcat. The world had come to her in stark clarity—sights, sounds, and smells overwhelming her with their strength.

And with it had come the bloodlust. Kyra shrank back from that detail, but it was there, as clear in her mind as the taste of the forest on her tongue. She'd wanted nothing more than to tear James limb from limb, to savage his body beyond recognition. Though Kyra had resisted the urge, the memory stayed with her, as did her horror at what she might have done. She'd sworn she would never take her cat form again.

And yet, here she was, back in the forest. Still in her skin but teetering on the edge, far too tempted for her own good.

Kyra placed her hand on a nearby tree. Its rough bark felt solid enough to keep her from being swept away. Kyra closed her eyes and sent her senses inward, daring herself to find the spark that would bring out her other form. But what would happen afterward? How long would she remain in her fur? What atrocities would she commit before she turned back?

She opened her eyes and stopped reaching. Maybe someday she would go through with it, but not tonight. Kyra glanced up at the constellations and noted the time, a habit formed years ago from her early days as a thief. She suspected she'd be checking the sky for the rest of her life.

That was when she heard something move, something that didn't have the small scurrying steps of prey. Though the footsteps weren't loud, she could sense a bulk to them—a difference in the feel of the ground and the way the air moved. A bear would have that kind of weight, but it would be louder. That left one other possibility....

Kyra backed against a tree, her heartbeat suddenly twice as fast as before. If it really was a demon cat coming toward her, climbing the tree would do her no good. She balanced her weight on the balls of her feet, muscles taut, as the beast came into view. Sleek muscle, long tail, pointed ears—a wildcat the size of a horse. Kyra didn't recognize this particular demon cat. Its eyes fixed on her, and its tail swished dangerously. There was no friendliness in its gaze. Kyra hadn't exactly left the Makvani on good terms.

"I mean no harm," Kyra said. "I don't come on Palace business." Her voice quavered. As if the beast would believe her. As if the beast would care.

It continued advancing, and though it would do no good, Kyra turned to run. The forest had gone silent around her, and all she could hear were her own quick breaths and the crunch of snow underfoot. She managed a few steps before powerful paws knocked her down. Kyra skidded along the ground. Icy snow spilled into her sleeves and melted against her skin. Kyra rolled onto her side and scrambled for the knife in her boot, only to drop it as the beast knocked her again to the ground. Hot breath bore down on her, and Kyra crossed her arms in front of her face to ward off teeth and claws. Could she change now? The beast gave her no quarter, not even a chance to breathe.

There was a roar. A creature—another demon cat—collided with the beast on top of her. The two cats tumbled along the ground, growling and snapping, a blur that was impossible to follow. Kyra had only just made sense of the scene when the two cats broke apart and faced each other. The second cat let out a low growl. After a long moment, the first beast turned and retreated into the forest, leaving Kyra alone with her rescuer.

Kyra's heart still beat wildly in her chest, and she couldn't quite believe that the threat was gone. She didn't recognize this new beast. She'd hoped it was Pashla, the clanswoman who had been her advocate during her time with the Makvani, but this tawny-yellow creature was much bigger, with muscular shoulders and haunches that were formidable even for a demon cat. As Kyra climbed to her feet, the beast's shape began to blur. A moment later, Leyus stood before her. Leyus, the leader of the Makvani, who had only grudgingly spared her life the last time she'd seen him. In his human form, Leyus was tall with long hair that matched the tawny yellow of his fur, and the same muscular shoulders he carried as a beast. Kyra kept her eyes on his face because, like all Makvani who had just changed into his skin, he was naked.

"You tread a dangerous line, coming back to this forest," said Leyus. He turned to leave without waiting for a response.

Kyra stood dumbfounded. "Thank you," she called.

Leyus looked over his shoulder. "You have chosen your loyalties," he said without stopping. "Do not expect to be safe out here. If you come into our territory, you alone bear the risks and the consequences."

And then he was gone.

TWO

Kyra's younger friends Idalee and Lettie were sound asleep by the time she returned to the small room the three of them rented from a wealthy jeweler's widow. The two sisters lay curled together on the straw pallet they all shared. Idalee's dark hair was spread wild around her on the pillow, while Lettie had burrowed completely under the covers and was only visible as a small mound at her sister's back. They didn't stir when Kyra climbed in next to them.

Though the bedding was blissfully warm compared to the icy forest, Kyra stayed awake long after she lay down, staring into the darkness as the attack and rescue played in her mind. It was a foolish thing, going back into the forest time after time with no reason. The Demon Riders had made it very clear that she was no longer welcome in their midst, and Leyus could very well have let her die. Kyra didn't know if it was residual gratitude for saving his clan, a desire to avoid trouble with the Palace, or Kyra's own mixed blood that had led Leyus to intervene, but she wasn't naïve enough to expect her good fortune to hold if she continued going. Trouble was, she couldn't seem to stay away.

She'd spent her entire life wondering who her parents were and where she'd come from. Just as she'd learned more about her history, however horrifying it was, it had been taken away from her. The draw of her past was strong, as was that tantalizing memory of those few moments she'd had in her second form.

But maybe there was a better way to go after her past—one that wouldn't get her killed. Pashla had once mentioned that Far Ranger trade caravans had long memories and might be able to give Kyra clues about her origins. Perhaps it was time to seek them out.

She was running through the forest on four legs, dodging trees and leap-ing over rocks. It was a joy to use her limbs this way, to stretch her back legs behind her and reach with her front paws for the next push. The trees were a blur around her, and she ran until she arrived, breathless, in front of Forge's walls. Kyra sat back on her haunches, tongue lolling, but something wasn't right. The walls were lined with Red Shields, and even as she climbed back to her feet, they streamed down from the walls and surrounded her. The last man to close the circle was Malikel, stern in his official's robes and looking much taller than Kyra remembered.

"It brings me no joy to do this," he said, "but you're a threat to the city. We can't let you live."

Kyra's fur stood on end, and she arched her back as the Red Shields raised sharp spears and pointed them toward her in silent unison. A growl stirred in her throat. If this was how it would be, then she would go down fighting....

"Kyra, wake up."

Kyra's eyes flew open and she reached under her pillow for

her dagger. She'd drawn the blade and was pushing herself to her feet when she finally regained her bearings. It was morning. She'd been dreaming.

The single room she shared with Idalee and Lettie was still. The muted noises of the street one story below filtered in through the window. The girls were nowhere to be seen, but her good friend Flick sat at the table across the room, looking as carefree as ever with his feet propped up on the table and his brown curls slightly mussed atop his head.

Kyra sank back into the bedding. "Fiery cities, Flick. Are you trying to scare me to death?" Flick lived with friends several streets away, but he spent so much time here that he might as well have been a fourth resident, especially since he'd stopped courting the wool merchant's daughter.

"What was it this time? Assassins? Demon cats? Old ladies wielding poisoned knitting needles?"

She sheathed her dagger and threw it at her pillow. "Red Shields. Malikel."

"Ah." Flick dipped a chunk of bread into a tumbler of watered wine and stared at it pensively before popping it into his mouth. "Hunting you down because they learned what you were?"

"Aye."

"At this rate, you're likely to worry yourself to death before they find out."

Given the way her heart was beating wild rhythms in her rib cage, Kyra couldn't argue with his reasoning. But neither could she stop worrying.

When the Demon Riders first started raiding farms around

Forge, everyone had assumed that the enormous wildcats they rode were simply well-trained pets. It was only after the barbarians captured Kyra that she learned they were shape-shifters, the mythical felbeasts of legend. Kyra told the Palace upon her return, but she'd kept one detail to herself: that she shared their shape-shifter blood.

Only five humans knew Kyra's secret. Tristam and James had seen her change shape in the forest, and Kyra had told her adopted family—Flick, Idalee, and Lettie—after she returned to Forge. While Tristam and her family could be counted on to keep her secret, James most definitely could not. After Kyra captured James and turned him over to the Palace, she'd gone to sleep every night expecting to be woken by soldiers at her door. But it hadn't yet happened, and though it was the best possible outcome, Kyra couldn't shake the feeling that something wasn't right.

"If you want, we could still go to Edlan. Play it safe," said Flick.

She rubbed the back of her neck. Flick's offer was generous, but he didn't really want to leave Forge. None of them did—Forge was all they'd ever known. "I don't know. Mayhap if I can earn Malikel's trust, he won't think me a threat to the city when he finally finds out."

Flick gave a noncommittal shrug. "I didn't wake you up just to get you out of that nightmare. Tristam's waiting for you outside."

"Tristam?" It was only then that Kyra noticed the angle of light coming in the room's small window. She'd slept past noon. "We're to report to duty today. I've found a member of the Assassins Guild." She threw a tunic over the shift and trousers she'd slept in, splashed her face at the washbasin by the door, then grabbed a hairbrush and tugged at her hair until she could tie it back with a leather thong. She tried a few times to smooth down the wrinkles in her tunic, but they just popped back up.

Flick tipped backward in his chair, eyeing her with amusement. "Why don't you go to such efforts to look presentable for *us*?"

Kyra gave up on the wrinkles. "All right if I let him in?"

"Fine by me. *My* hair's been combed all morning."

The door to their quarters opened into a plain wooden corridor that ended in a narrow staircase. When Kyra came out, she found Tristam at the top of the stairs, his tall form bent slightly as he peered over the low railing. She walked quietly up behind him and placed a hand on his back.

"Looking at anything interesting?"

His muscles tensed under her hand, and he whipped around, reaching for the dagger at his waist. But then his eyes landed on her, and his face relaxed into an embarrassed smile.

A warmth spread around her ribs as she looked up at him and returned his grin. He must have just washed this morning, because she could smell the soap on him, layered over the familiar scent of his skin.

"Latrine duty for you," she admonished. It was an old joke between them, a remark he'd made the first time she'd snuck up on him. "I'm sorry to keep you waiting."

"Late night?" asked Tristam. He straightened to his full height, and Kyra craned her neck to keep eye contact.

"Aye." She was thankful when Tristam didn't ask where she'd been. He was dressed in Palace livery—not that of a knight, Kyra noticed again with a pang, but the plainer tunic of a Red Shield, with an embroidered *F* on the left breast, over plain black breeches. He'd been stripped of his knighthood for a year because he'd rescued Kyra from the Demon Riders against direct orders from the Council. While Tristam had never complained about his punishment, Kyra couldn't help wondering if he regretted his decision. Though she noticed he wore this livery well. He held himself like a soldier, and his movements were precise and confident.

They returned to the room. Flick gave Tristam a sideways glance then and grunted a half greeting, not bothering to take his feet off the table. Flick was the illegitimate son of a minor nobleman and had decided long ago that wallhuggers could not be trusted. Kyra glared at him, but he'd already turned his attention back to his breakfast.

"Let me fetch my daggers," said Kyra. "And then I'll be ready to go."

She'd picked up the one on her bed and was rummaging through her chest for others when the door opened and Lettie stepped in, followed by Idalee carrying a basket of bread. The two sisters were bundled against the cold with matching wool dresses, scarves wrapped around their hair, and warm boots. Months of shelter and good food seemed to be paying off. Lettie now stood as high as Kyra's waist, and Idalee's dress was stretching tight around her chest and hips. The girl hadn't even started her monthly blood and she already had more curves than Kyra. They'd have to get her cloth to make a new dress soon.

Both girls stopped short when they saw Tristam.

"Ho, Tristam," said Lettie, breaking into a dimpled grin.

Tristam bowed. "Hello, Lady Lettie."

Lettie giggled, her dark brown curls bouncing beneath her headscarf.

Idalee gave Tristam a halfhearted curtsy and took her basket to the hearth without saying a word. Then she turned her back to the room, removed a loaf from the basket, and started vigorously brushing it off.

Kyra frowned and walked closer. "What are you doing?" She'd always had problems with Flick and Tristam getting along, but this was the first time she'd seen rudeness from Idalee.

"Nothing," Idalee said. A strand of black hair stuck to her forehead as she bent protectively over the bread. The girl was standing so close to the fireplace that her skirt almost brushed the embers.

Kyra saw now that Idalee's bread was covered with dirt. "What happened?" She put her hand on Idalee's shoulder, but the girl shook it off.

"I dropped the basket," said Idalee.

Kyra and Flick exchanged a worried glance over Idalee's head. Flick turned to Lettie. "Is that what truly happened?" he asked.

Lettie had climbed up onto one of the chairs. "A fatpurse pushed me in the market," she said, cringing at Idalee's warning glance. "Idalee yelled at him, and he knocked the basket out of her hand."

Kyra looked to Flick in alarm. His mouth tightened in a grim line, and he shook his head. Idalee had always been fiercely protective of her sister.

"Lettie, did the fatpurse hurt you?" said Flick. He used the low, steady tone he always did when trying to stay calm.

Lettie shook her head, and Flick looked her up and down, silently verifying her answer. Then he leaned against the fireplace mantel so Idalee would have to look at him, even if it was only out of the corner of her eye. "You're lucky it was only the bread that came to harm," he said.

Idalee put down one clean loaf and picked up the next. "It in't fair," she said to the bread.

Of course it wasn't fair. Kyra's own pulse was rising at the thought of any wallhuggers laying hands on either Idalee or Lettie. But acknowledging the injustice wouldn't keep Idalee safe the next time some nobleman offended her. "Idalee, you can't go testing your luck with the wallhuggers," she said. "If they do something you don't like, you walk away. They're dangerous and unpredictable."

The words had barely left her mouth when Kyra remembered that Tristam was standing quietly at the edge of the room. She shot a mortified glance in his direction. "I mean, not all—"

"No offense taken," Tristam said before she could finish. He pushed away from the wall, his gaze keen. "Idalee, do you know the name of the man who pushed Lettie?"

Idalee finally stopped attacking the bread, and her eyes were slightly hopeful when she raised them to Tristam. "No. Could you do something, if I did?"

"There are no laws against pushing, I'm afraid," he said gently. "But I would have liked to know." He glanced out the window. "It's about time we go. Kyra, are you ready?"

"Almost." Kyra ran back to her trunk and finally fished out her daggers. "Everything all right over here?" she asked as she tucked them into her boots.

"We'll be fine," said Flick.

She supposed they would have to be. "Take care, then," she said, and followed Tristam out the door.

Forge was laid out in rough concentric circles with the Palace at its center. The nobility lived in the ring just outside the Palace wall, hence their nickname "wallhuggers." Wealthy merchants, including Kyra's new landlady, lived in the ring outside that. As Kyra and Tristam set out from her quarters, they headed farther away from the Palace, toward the beggars' circle.

Kyra tried again to apologize for her comment about dangerous wallhuggers, but Tristam waved her words aside.

"It just means that you're comfortable enough around me to speak freely. I'm glad of it."

He'd thrown a cloak over his livery to disguise his affiliation with the Palace, and the two of them strolled down the street like any other couple. A silk vendor waved a gold scarf to get Kyra's attention. "It will bring out the warm tones of your skin, lovely lady." When she ignored him, the silk vendor turned his efforts to Tristam. "Young Lord, get your lady a scarf to match her beauty."

Kyra chuckled. The merchant's honeyed words would have

been more convincing if he hadn't said the same thing to every other person walking down the street.

The silk merchant's voice echoed after them. "You're a feisty pair of young lovers. I can tell that you adore each other."

Kyra's laugh trailed off, and she took an involuntary glance at Tristam. The street vendor's words rattled in her mind. Feisty? She supposed she'd been called that before. Young? That was certainly true. But lovers?

Six weeks ago, after they'd been released by the Makvani, the two of them had shared a kiss. It didn't take much effort at all to conjure the memory of his arms around her that night, or the tingle on her skin as they'd leaned their faces close. But that had been one moment in the forest, when they didn't know what the future held. Now they were back in the city, and things felt less clear. Tristam was the son of a noble house, and she was a pardoned criminal. How could a stolen kiss in the forest stand against that? After weeks of working together under Malikel, they were comfortable with each other, even flirted on occasion. But things remained . . . uncertain.

As they continued walking, the lively trappings of the merchant circle gave way to the blackened walls of the fire-burned district, the part of the city that had been destroyed in the Demon Rider raid orchestrated by James. The streets were lined with charred frames. A few of the ruins had been torn down, and some of the poor had set up tents and lean-tos in the burnt-out buildings. The air still smelled faintly of charcoal, and though the ash was gone, Kyra couldn't shake the impression that breathing too deeply would clog her nose with blackened dust.

"It doesn't look much different from before, does it?" said Kyra. "There's been some rebuilding near the merchant sector, but not down here."

"The landlords are likely waiting for the city to clean it up," said Tristam. "The first person to rebuild has to also clean the wells and unclog the gutters. Nobody wants to do that."

"It would only take a crew of Red Shields a couple weeks to clean everything," said Kyra.

"That sounds about right," said Tristam. Neither mentioned the obvious, that the Council hadn't seen fit to use its soldiers this way.

Their path didn't take them directly by the ruins of The Drunken Dog, for which Kyra was grateful. Her friend Bella, who had been like a mother to her, had died after the fire overtook the tavern, and Kyra didn't want to dwell on the loss today. She sped up her steps as they neared the vicinity of her old home and didn't stop until it was far behind her. Tristam kept pace with her and didn't comment.

Finally, they came to a place where the houses stood intact, though they were still marked by smoke. The beggars along the street became more numerous, and soon Kyra and Tristam neared a corner where she recognized other Palace men. All of them, like Tristam, wore plain cloaks to hide their Palace livery. In addition to Kyra and Tristam, there were three Red Shields and Sir Rollan, a knight new to Malikel's command. He'd been transferred after Malikel dismissed another knight for taking bribes while on gate duty. The Defense Minister was one of the few who actually enforced honesty in his men—most other commanders simply overlooked such infractions.

Rollan nodded a greeting as they approached. He was a big man with messy yellow hair, about ten years older than Tristam. "That's all of us. Kyra, give us an update."

The men gathered around. "Ashley's a low-ranking member of the Guild," said Kyra. "If he keeps his patterns from earlier this week, he should be home. He's a good fighter, so be careful."

It had taken Kyra considerable time to track him down. After the Palace pardoned Kyra's crimes, she'd agreed to help Malikel track down the rest of the Guild and bring them to justice. The first assassin, a taciturn man named Jason, had been easy to capture. But as word of Jason's imprisonment had spread, the rest of the Guild went underground. Kyra found nothing for weeks, until finally she'd run across rumors of Ashley hiding in an old house in the beggars' sector.

"Kyra, scout the house," said Rollan. "Brancel, go help her."

Kyra kept her head low as she and Tristam set off down the street. The streets here were narrow and dirty, with the upper stories hanging over the lower ones and blocking the light. She could sense the handful of loiterers and beggars on the street giving them suspicious looks. The Palace folk stood out here despite their efforts to blend in. Their clothes were too nice, and they carried themselves too straight. Well, it was too late to do anything about that. She quickened her steps and turned into an empty alleyway.

"You'll be climbing up here?" Tristam asked quietly.

Kyra nodded, pleased that Tristam knew her habits well enough to anticipate her movements. "Give me a boost?"

He checked over his shoulder to make sure no one was watching, then joined his hands to form a step for her.

She pushed off him and pulled herself over the edge of the roof. The old wooden shingles felt as if they'd come apart if she bent them hard enough, and she was glad she had gloves to protect her from splinters. "Thank you. You're a decent stepladder."

"You know," came his voice from below, "in some circles I'm known for my combat skills and quick strategic mind."

"And here I thought it was your pretty face," she said under her breath.

Kyra looked down from the roof to find Tristam's mouth quirked in a mischievous smile. "You think so?"

Their gazes met for a moment, and the flutter in Kyra's stomach was not at all convenient for running a mission. She scowled and traced the line of the rooftop with her gaze. "I'm off, then."

This entire street was lined with cheaply constructed boardinghouses, favored by landlords who often rented out each room to a different family. Kyra had to use a soft step and watch her way carefully so she wouldn't tread on any rotten tiles. There was far more creaking and shifting underneath her feet than she would have liked.

The assassin, Ashley, lived in an attic apartment. These rooms had windows that protruded out of the roof under slanted eaves, and Kyra counted them as she climbed over each one, finally stopping at the fifth. Though the shutters were closed, there was a thin gap where they met. When Kyra put her eye to the crack, she could make out a man sitting on the floor, doing some work with his hands. She had only seen Ashley once or twice during her time at the Guild, but it was definitely him.

Her target found, Kyra crept to the very edge of the roof. About ten people walked the streets below. Though they all could have seen Kyra easily in the afternoon sun, Tristam was the only one looking up. His eyes met hers, and then he walked casually away.

Her message delivered, Kyra went back to the window and waited, straining her ears for any sound from within—hard to do because the street noise below was louder. She thought she heard a faint knock—not loud enough to be someone at Ashley's door, though it could have been Rollan's men knocking on the building's main entrance. She risked another peek inside and saw Ashley pause in his work and inch his way toward the door. He held a dagger in his hand. Kyra drew her own blade but stayed put. Her orders were to wait by this window in case he tried to escape.

The door to Ashley's room crashed open and Rollan's men rushed in. The clashing of blades scraped Kyra's ears. A man screamed in pain, and Ashley pushed past the Red Shields out the door as Rollan yelled a command to follow him. Kyra squinted through the crack, trying to see who'd been hurt, but there was too much going on. She jostled the latch. When it wouldn't budge, she stepped back and aimed a kick at the window. The flimsy shutters gave way, and she swung herself into the room.

It was empty. The door was flung open. A Red Shield named Daly sat in the corridor outside while his comrade, a skinny young Red Shield named Fitz, bound a bandage around his thigh. Judging from the amount of blood, the wound looked deep.

"He needs a healer," said Fitz as Kyra came closer. Kyra crouched next to them, relieved that the injured man hadn't been Tristam, then feeling guilty for thinking it. Together, she and Fitz helped Daly to his feet. They had just started hobbling toward the staircase when Tristam and Rollan came running back up.

Rollan shook his head when Kyra caught his eye. "Gone. He went out a trapdoor."

Kyra sagged under Daly's weight. All that time tracking the assassin down, and he was out of reach again.

Rollan's brows knitted together as he took in Daly's condition, and he motioned for Tristam to take Kyra's place. "Back to the Palace. Everyone."

Rollan made the decision to continue hiding their livery as they helped Daly back to the Palace. There was no need to broadcast weakness on the Palace's part. The party did get its share of curious looks as it marched, but nobody stopped the group, and nobody asked any questions. Rollan dismissed Kyra when they reached the Palace gate.

"We'll have to consult with Malikel about the next step," the knight said. "But he'll be busy entertaining the Edlan and Parna delegations for the next week. He may not be ready to deal with the Guild until after they're gone."

As the others entered the Palace, Kyra gratefully headed back home. Idalee was probably cooking dinner by now, and

Kyra wanted to be in a place where she didn't have to hide her frustration. The merchant sector was starting to empty out for the evening. A wide avenue lined with shops had only a handful of people walking through. Kyra had just turned down a smaller street toward home when a wire looped around her neck.

A garrote.

Kyra almost didn't react in time. Another moment of hesitation, and the noose would have closed. As it was, she fell back into her attacker and managed to snake her arm between the wire and her neck so the metal dug into the wool of her tunic instead of the exposed skin of her throat. She ducked and grabbed the knife from her boot with her free hand, twisting around so her blade touched her opponent's stomach just as his grazed her throat.

Bacchus, James's second in command, wore a frightening grin as their eyes met. His wire was still tight around her arm, and his knife held steady at her neck. But he didn't press his attack.

"You've gotten quicker," he said. There was no trace of fear in his expression. Now that James was imprisoned, he was probably the highest-ranking man in the Assassins Guild. Kyra wondered what the Guild had been doing under his leadership.

"Put your blade away, Bacchus. It'd be a pity if we both died tonight," said Kyra. While Bacchus looked calm enough to have been taking an evening walk, every muscle in Kyra's body was taut. Her arm was going numb.

He snorted. "Why don't you withdraw yours?"

"Because my word means something, and yours doesn't," she said through gritted teeth. What would happen if she changed shape now? It had worked with James, but Bacchus could just as easily stab her while she was distracted.

To her surprise, Bacchus laughed and stepped back. He loosened his grip on her arm, and she flung the garrote to the ground. Kyra kept a firm grip on her blade and scanned the street around her. The few people who had been around before had all fled.

"If you're trying to scare me into stopping my work with the Palace, it won't work."

Bacchus spat on the ground. "You snagged one of our lowest-ranking men and failed at snagging another. I in't losing any sleep." Kyra couldn't tell if he was bluffing. "I didn't come to kill you," he added. "I bring a message." Kyra eyed the garrote on the ground, and he shrugged. "James said to leave you alive. He didn't say how alive."

James? Kyra couldn't help looking around. "Where is he?"

"Where you left him," he said. "But he's got a message for you."

"How did he get word to you if he's still in the dungeon?"

The assassin gave Kyra a look that conveyed just how stupid it was for Kyra to expect an answer to that question.

"He tells you to think carefully about what you're doing against the Guild. You think you're helping the city by cooperating with the Palace, but the wallhuggers aren't your friends. They never will be."

The last time Kyra and James had talked at length, he'd warned her that the Palace would betray her. Was he still trying to sway her to his side? Was he confident enough of her capitulation that he would show his hand like this?

"And James claims to be my friend?" she asked.

Bacchus's eyes glittered over his ebony beard. "Trust me, lass. He doesn't want you for a friend. But he wants you to go talk to him when you finally see clearly."

"I've no interest in seeing him," said Kyra. "He's in the dungeon, where he belongs. I won't fall prey to his schemes again."

Bacchus didn't seem surprised by her answer. He spun his blade in his hand and contemplated her thoughtfully. "You still living with the two girls?"

Idalee and Lettie. If he wasn't threatening them outright, he was smugly reminding her of the time James had blackmailed Kyra by threatening her friends. Hot rage ran through her. "I swear, Bacchus," she said. "If you ever so much as hint a threat toward my family again, I will kill James and track you down. You can't keep me out of your hideaways if I want to get to you." It was surprising how easily those words came out.

He laughed at that. "You've changed, lass, and I see I touched a sore spot. Don't worry. Your friends are safe for now. James's message is simply a request. The rest is up to you." He looked her over. "You don't look like one of them demon beasts."

Kyra went cold. James had told Bacchus. Why hadn't he told the Palace?

"Get away from me," Kyra said.

Bacchus gave a mocking bow and walked away.

THREE

Tristam let out a groan as he eased the helmet off his head. At least it wasn't summer, when the leather trapped the sun's heat in a miasma of oil and sweat. But even in the winter, he hated how the helmet pinched his temples. The icy breeze blew through his damp hair as he stood outside the guard armory after his morning shift, standing in line behind his fellow Red Shields to hang up his gear. Each Red Shield had his own armor and basic uniform, but the overcoat that marked on-duty guards was shared, as were the ceremonial shields and helmet covers.

"I could use a flagon right now," said a man from inside.

"Aye, me too," said another. "Though I've a craving for a good fine wine. My cousin gifted me a bottle last fall, and I still taste it in my dreams."

"You're turning into a right proper fatpurse." The man raised his voice in a snooty imitation of the other. "'I'd prefer me a fine wine.'" He cut off abruptly amidst muttered warnings to hush, and a few men in front of Tristam looked nervously in his direction. He ignored their stares and entered to put away his own equipment.

"Good day, all," he said after he finished, and left. The room remained silent behind him as he walked out the door.

A month in the Red Shield ranks hadn't yet inured him to the scrutiny of his comrades. His fellow Red Shields were too intimidated by his bloodlines to give him trouble outright, but there were constant whispers about "the disgraced knight," and nervous glances when someone forgot his presence and spoke too freely about the Palace's noblemen. Every morning, Tristam breathed a sigh of relief when his daily rounds ended. He rubbed heat into his arms as he made his way back to his quarters.

He'd gone about halfway when someone called his name.

"Brancel!" Tristam turned at the voice. Sir Rollan was coming toward him with long, rolling strides. "Malikel requires everyone's presence in his study."

"Do I have time to get changed?"

"No. He wants everyone now."

Whatever had happened must have been urgent, if everyone was being summoned on such short notice. "What is it?" Tristam asked.

"James managed to send a message out of the dungeon. To Kyra."

"*What?*"

Rollan smiled fiercely. "You're not the first to react this way."

Malikel's study was already filled with people when they

arrived. Tristam spotted Kyra right away, standing next to Malikel's desk and looking unusually subdued. He caught her eye, and she managed a wan smile in greeting. Was she all right? Had James threatened her? The room was too crowded and too quiet for Tristam to get a word with her. In addition to Kyra, there were the twenty knights and Red Shields under Malikel's direct command. The Defense Minister himself paced in front of his desk, his dark eyes cutting through anyone who matched gazes with him. They waited in tense silence for a few more people to arrive. Then Malikel spoke.

"This is unacceptable," he said, his voice hard as granite. "Our holding cells are not summer homes for criminals to lounge in and send missives from at their pleasure. I want the names of every man, woman, child, and dog who has come within a stone's throw of the prison building. And I want them all questioned today."

No one in the study dared respond or even move. After sweeping his gaze one more time around the room, Malikel started dividing the men into groups. "Tristam," he said. "Take Fitz and Cecil, and round up the guards who were on duty two nights ago."

Sir Rollan and another knight exchanged a glance at Malikel's words. Tristam noticed, and stared straight ahead to disguise his annoyance. The other knights under Malikel's command were still trying to figure out what Tristam's demotion really meant. Here, he'd been given command of Red Shields again, a role that should not have fallen to him.

"Is there a problem, gentlemen?" Malikel asked.

"No, sir," said Rollan.

"At your tasks, then," Malikel said. "Make this quick."

Tristam caught Fitz's and Cecil's eyes and led them out the door. He recognized Fitz as the wiry blond Red Shield who had helped the wounded Daly back to the Palace yesterday. Cecil, he didn't know as well.

"Are the two of you willing to take orders from me?" he asked as they left the building.

"Aye," said Cecil. "If Martin thought you were worth following, that's good enough for me." The look Tristam turned on Cecil must have been intimidating because the Red Shield immediately added, "I hope I've not spoken out of turn."

"No...no...of course not," Tristam said, pausing midstride to clear his head. "I just didn't expect you to bring him up." Martin had been a Red Shield and a subordinate, but he and Tristam had genuinely liked each other. He'd gone with Tristam in search of Kyra after she was captured by the Makvani, and he'd died at their hands. Tristam still couldn't quite forgive himself.

"I'm glad you feel that way," said Tristam. "Many think I led him to his death."

"You forget we actually knew Martin," said Fitz. "He wouldn't blindly follow anyone without good reason."

"Thank you." That, at least, was a weight off his chest.

Tristam took a wagon from the Palace stables so they could move about the city faster, and they started down the list of guards. Most of the guards they fetched were alarmed by the summons but came into the cart willingly. When Tristam arrived at the boardinghouse where the fourth guard lived, however, no one answered the door.

Tristam tried knocking again. "Open up. This is official Palace business."

Still silence. Fitz, waiting next to him, gave a nervous shrug. Tristam circled to a side window and peered through a gap in the shutters. It was hard to see much of anything, but something seemed off. He looked around the boardinghouse again. The landlord likely lived in another part of the city entirely, and it would take hours to track him down. Kyra would have been really useful right about now. He made a mental note to ask her to teach him lock picking next time he saw her.

Tristam picked up a large stone and returned to the front door. "Give me a hand, will you?" he asked Fitz.

Fitz's eyes widened, but he helped Tristam support the weight of the stone.

"On the count of three," said Tristam. "One, two..."

They swung the rock, and the latch gave way with a crash. The door opened, and Fitz whistled.

The living quarters were empty. The bed was in disarray, and several chests along the walls looked like they had been hurriedly emptied. Their lids had been left open, and discarded objects were strewn all around the floor.

"Looks like whoever was here made a quick escape," said Fitz.

The missing guard and his family could not be found anywhere in the city. Based on the testimonies of those who'd last seen them, the entire family had probably fled the night before. Had it been bribery? Blackmail? There was no way to know.

The rest of the guard force made it through questioning without raising suspicions. Though it seemed this man had worked alone, Malikel personally reviewed the prison guard roster to narrow the list to the most loyal and least vulnerable to persuasion.

Much later that day, Malikel summoned Tristam to his study. The Defense Minister's door was closed when Tristam arrived, so he waited in the corridor. After a while, Kyra stepped out, her jaw set and her eyes flinty. Tristam stepped back, surprised at her demeanor, and she walked past him without a word.

"Tristam, come in," came Malikel's voice.

Tristam threw one last concerned glance in Kyra's direction before stepping inside. The Defense Minister was seated at his desk. Now that the mystery of James's message had been partially solved, Malikel's gaze no longer carried the same murderous intensity. Tristam sat cautiously in a chair opposite him.

"I just informed Kyra that the Council has forbidden her from entering the prison or having any contact with James," said Malikel.

That would explain her ire. A command like this from the Council was an empty one and only served to underscore their mistrust. If Kyra wanted to see James, she'd find a way. Did the Council really think they could control her like this, or did they simply feel better having delivered a command?

"I tell you this because you wouldn't otherwise be able to concentrate on anything I say. But I didn't summon you to discuss Kyra," said Malikel. Tristam shifted in his chair, chagrined at being so transparent. "I realized today that it's time I speak with you about your future. I'm afraid I've not been the best mentor to you in the time you've spent under my command."

Tristam started to object, but Malikel raised his hand to stop him.

"I come from a different background than the rest of the Council members, and I sometimes make decisions that make me unpopular amongst certain of my colleagues."

That was an understatement. Malikel's rise to power was the stuff of legend. The idea of a mercenary from the southern kingdom of Minadel becoming Defense Minister of Forge would have been unthinkable thirty years ago. But a series of heroic acts—most notably, saving the life of the former Defense Minister in a skirmish—had moved him into positions of command. And from there, Malikel had flouted tradition and followed his own judgment on everything from the way he trained his troops to the way he structured their hierarchy underneath him. There had been disapproving glances and clucking of tongues for the entirety of his career, but no one could deny that Malikel was very, very good at what he did. And eventually, that had been enough. Tristam knew all this by heart, but what did it have to do with him?

Malikel's eyes crinkled, as if he could read the thoughts going through Tristam's mind. "Going against convention, disapproval from the court—these are waves I'm willing to make. But in a sense, the consequences for me are not severe. When I made my entry into court, I had very little social capital to risk. Being from Minadel, I had no family to which I was responsible." Malikel spoke matter-of-factly, and nothing in his manner invited pity. "That's not the case, however, with you."

"Sir?"

"I worry I've been a bad influence on you. You've already been demoted once. And though it's a temporary censure, that kind of mark will affect both your future and that of your family's."

"I don't regret any of the decisions I've made," said Tristam. Actually, it was more complicated than that. His entire attempt to rescue Kyra had been a disaster. Martin had died, and it turned out that Kyra hadn't actually needed rescuing. So in that sense, he had many regrets. But given what he'd known at the time, going after Kyra had been the right thing to do. The disgrace that he suffered now at the hands of his peers was a small price to pay.

"And that's admirable," said Malikel. "Just be aware of the choices you make, and make your decisions with your eyes open. It would be remiss of me as your commander not to mention it."

"Thank you, sir." Tristam didn't quite know what else to say.

"You will be at the diplomatic ball tomorrow night, correct?" said Malikel.

"Yes, sir." Every three years, the leaders of the three cities gathered for a summit that started with a diplomatic ball. All under Malikel's direct command were required to attend.

"Good. Take some time with Kyra there. She'll need some help learning the protocols of court. And think on what I've said. It's a lot to process but ultimately not something you can afford to ignore."

Tristam struggled to unravel his thoughts as he made his way out the door. Malikel's advice unsettled him. He might have expected such words from Willem or one of the more active members of court, but Malikel, he couldn't dismiss so readily. He looked down at his livery, contemplating the *F* that marked his rank. Somehow, he had the feeling that things weren't going to get any simpler.

FOUR

Flick had an excruciatingly loud wolf whistle. Kyra heard it often enough when he flirted with his favorite serving girls, but until this evening, she had never appreciated just how obnoxious it could be. That was probably because, until tonight, he had never directed it at her.

She scowled again, squinting at her reflection as she angled the bottom of a polished copper pot to see her entire body. She wore a gown that Malikel commanded she have made for diplomatic occasions. It was made of soft emerald silk and gathered with a velvet ribbon just below her bust. The same ribbon, a darker shade of green than the fabric, trimmed her sleeves, neckline, and hem. The cost of the dress would have covered her lodging for a month, but it was hard to maintain a proper sense of guilt at the extravagance when the silk fell so lightly around her feet.

Idalee, who had tied Kyra's hair into a simple twist, stood to the side with her arms crossed and a smug grin on her face. She'd recently started washing dishes at a nearby tavern and

33

had clearly picked up some tricks from the more fashionable serving girls. Lettie sat at the table, legs dangling and mouth open in a small O as she stared at Kyra.

And Flick, of course, was whistling.

"Will you stop that?" Kyra said. "You'll annoy the landlady."

"And besides," said Idalee, "Kyra looks too fine tonight to be whistled at."

"That's right," Kyra said. "Another whistle from you and I'll have one of my manservants toss you in the gutter."

Flick snorted. "Watch yourself, lass. I can still hang you upside down by your ankles."

Kyra stifled a giggle. It had been a while since Flick had tried that particular trick, but she imagined he'd be able to if he put his mind to it.

"You do look very pretty, Kyra," piped up Lettie. "I wish I could see the ball."

"Me too," said Flick. "Seems it'd be quite the spectacle."

"You, Flick?" said Idalee. "I thought you wanted nothing to do with the wallhuggers."

Flick shrugged. "Just because I don't like shoveling peacock manure doesn't mean I don't appreciate their plumage."

Her friends might have been intrigued by the ball, but Kyra herself was terrified. Perhaps her friends thought her glamorous, but she knew she wouldn't be able to keep up the act once she went into the ballroom. What did she know about nobles and foreign visitors? The night would end in humiliation. She'd bet money on it.

She slipped on her shoes, velvet as well, and wiggled her toes at their softness. "I just hope I don't get kicked out of the

Palace for some breach of manners," she said, heading out the door.

Kyra dodged the usual assortment of street vendors, servants, and beggars on her way to the Palace. She got a few curious looks, but nobody gave her any trouble.

The Palace gate was ornamented with winterberries and candles for the occasion. When the guard challenged her, Kyra reached inside her collar and brought out a medallion that bore Malikel's emblem.

"Malikel's command?" He waved her in.

Kyra fingered the medallion, running her fingers over the coat of arms before letting it drop. She respected Malikel and believed he respected her in return. The rest of the Council though, was another matter altogether. That was clear enough in their hurry to ban her from seeing James or even entering the Palace prison. The Council wanted her as a trained dog, a thief on a leash. They wouldn't say no to her skills, but they were quick to cut her off if they sensed her becoming a threat.

The outer compound looked finer tonight than Kyra had ever seen it. Extra torches and lamps had been brought out to light the pathway, and the gray-white granite walls of the buildings had been scrubbed until they shone. Even the snow, which had started to turn into muddy slush the past few days, had been cleared out and the ground underneath covered with fine rugs. Fire pits had been set up at regular distances so that guests could move about comfortably without heavy cloaks or furs.

A whole host of horses and carriages filled the main courtyard. Porters and servants took bags and led horses away, while foreign dignitaries stood mingling with Forge's nobility. Kyra recognized the Edlan dignitaries by their waxed beards and mustaches. Delicately waxed facial hair was the current fashion in Edlan and the butt of many a joke in Forge and Parna. Many of the Edlan men had women with them, some wearing sturdy travel gowns, others in their evening finery. The Parnans were harder to recognize, but Kyra suspected that many of the unfamiliar wallhugger faces belonged to that contingent.

The entire scene was intimidating. Kyra walked the perimeter of the courtyard, scanning the crowd for people she knew. She saw Malikel, his black, curly hair and beard freshly cropped against his dark brown skin, wearing a maroon tunic and breeches instead of his usual official's robes. The Defense Minister stood talking to a tall, stout man with a well-curled auburn mustache. Close by, Forge's Head Councilman, Willem, held court amongst a whole circle of nobles.

Kyra finally caught sight of Tristam next to one of the carriages, looking very handsome in a midnight-blue tunic and black breeches. He was talking to an older gentleman from Edlan, and his eyes swept over Kyra without seeing her at first. But a moment later, he snapped his gaze abruptly back toward her, a startled expression on his face. She waved a few fingers in greeting. To her surprise, Tristam immediately bowed to his conversational companion and took his leave. Kyra's arms felt awkward at her sides as he crossed the courtyard toward her. Her fingers itched to start fidgeting with her dress, but she forced them still.

When he came close, Tristam reached his arm toward her, palm up. After a moment's confusion, Kyra gave him her hand, and he bowed low, pressing his lips to her skin. It was hard not to shiver at the tingle that went up her arm. Tristam straightened, and his eyes swept over her. "You look beautiful."

She smiled, a pleasant warmth spreading through her chest. Until she'd seen Tristam's reaction, she hadn't admitted to herself that she'd been hoping for one. "You look very nice yourself," she said. "Care to introduce me to all this court fanciness?"

"My pleasure." He offered her an arm. "The crowd is moving to the ballroom. Shall we follow?"

Uniformed servants directed the guests through a massive set of double doors into the Palace's main ballroom. The sparkle of countless candle flames greeted them as they drifted in with the crowd, and Kyra couldn't help but gasp at the sight. The walls and ceilings were lined with mirrors, and they caught the light from crystal chandeliers overhead. The glass also reflected swirls of color from the hall—silk finery, feathered headdresses, rouged lips, and kohl-rimmed eyes. A group of ten musicians played at one end of the dance floor, while tables at the other end of the hall bore mouthwatering displays of delicacies, desserts, and wine. Servants weaved through the crowd, carrying platters that left tantalizing scent trails behind them. Uniformed guards in both Forge red, Edlan blue, and Parnan silver stood at attention along the walls, their stillness even more apparent against the constantly shuffling crowd.

"There's more soldiers here than I expected," said Kyra.

Tristam chuckled. "Well, yes. That's the uncomfortable truth about the three cities. We're not at war, but we're never completely at peace either. Don't let the pomp and ceremony fool you. We come together to 'enhance cooperation between our three peoples.' We'll smile at each other, even help one another as a gesture of goodwill. But behind the honeyed words, we're still trying to get an advantage on the others."

Kyra thought she could sense some of this tension in the careful smiles and polite conversations around her. "What do I need to know about Edlan and Parna?"

Tristam led her to a table, where a bowing servant handed him two glasses of sparkling wine. "Think of our three city-states as three brothers," he said, passing her a glass and lowering his voice. "Forge is the eldest, with a respectable inheritance of rich farmland and plentiful forests. We have the most people, the most fealty from families who live outside the city proper, and access to the best trade routes. Edlan is the second brother, living at the base of the Aerins in a harsher clime. They're a hearty city and a tough people, but they're always feeling second-best."

Kyra wondered if the Edlanese folk would agree with that assessment. "And Parna?"

"Parna is the young upstart who, while the two elder siblings were squabbling, stumbled upon a fortune of his own."

Kyra sipped her wine, savoring the feel of the bubbles against her tongue. "Your comparisons are getting unwieldy, Tristam."

His eyes twinkled. "Fair enough. Parna lies at the fork of the Vera River. She's the smallest and youngest city-state out of the three, but she's also extremely fortunate in her location and resources. The Parnans discovered some lucrative mines about two hundred years ago that have served them well. The river also provides an excellent defense for them, so the Parnan government spends its money on arts and learning instead of large armies. I visited their Palace once. They have poets and bards in residence, philosophers holding court every evening. It's really quite impressive."

"Are the Councils of Edlan and Parna similar to ours?"

"Edlan doesn't have a Council, actually. It's ruled by Duke Symon. He has his advisers, but they have very little power to overrule his decisions, whereas every decision made in Forge has to pass a majority vote. Parna has two Councils: one like ours and another that's chosen by the people every—"

Tristam stopped short as someone clapped him on the shoulder. Kyra turned to see a young nobleman even taller than Tristam, looking them over with a broad smile on his face.

"Enjoying the festivities?" said the newcomer.

Tristam leaned back, eyes wide, before his face also split into a grin. "Henril! I didn't know you would be here." He clasped Henril's arm with his free hand and turned to Kyra. "This is my eldest brother. I've not seen him in two years. Henril, this is Kyra, also under Malikel's command."

Brother. Henril had wider shoulders than Tristam, a heavier frame, and lighter hair, but the two men shared the same long face and tall nose. Henril took Kyra's hand and bowed low over it. "A pleasure to meet you, Kyra. Word of your deeds reaches even into the countryside."

Kyra wondered briefly just exactly what those deeds entailed. "Are you the brother who stole sweets from the kitchen and blamed it on Tristam?"

Henril laughed. "I'm wounded you would think such a thing, Lady Kyra. I would never betray my sibling for something as trivial as sweets."

"It's true," said Tristam. "He preferred to steal meat pies."

The two brothers were still grinning at each other, clearly looking forward to catching up. Henril looked friendly enough, but Kyra didn't want to be the one holding back the conversation. "I'm sure you have much to talk about," she said. "I should go check if Malikel needs me for anything."

"Are you sure?" asked Tristam, looking hesitantly between her and Henril.

She gave what she hoped was a reassuring smile. "If I can survive in a forest of demon cats, I'll survive some time by myself in the ballroom. I'll be back soon."

Tristam gazed after Kyra's retreating form. He couldn't seem to stop looking at her tonight, and he wondered if she'd noticed him gawking earlier. Compared with the fashionable noble-women around them, Kyra was underadorned. Her dress had no embroidery, and she wore no jewelry or face paint. But she had a way of bringing elegance to anything she wore. The silk of her dress skimmed her subtle curves and swirled in response to her movements in a way that was simply captivating.

But Henril was here, and Tristam had already let the conversation lag too long. He turned back to his brother. "She's not usually quite so scared. Diplomatic balls aren't exactly her element."

Henril crossed muscled arms over his broad chest. "I can imagine, if all I've heard is true. Did she really try to assassinate Malikel?"

"That she did. I found her on the ledge outside his bedroom

wall. She almost got away." He saw her as she'd been that night, how well she'd faded into the shadows, how impossibly fleet she'd been once she started running.

"I hear you tackled her. Kind of an unfair advantage, I'd say," Henril said.

Tristam laughed at that one. "Don't judge her by her size. She's better with a dagger than I, and I was fighting for my life. I'm glad she's on our side now."

"Is there anything more to that?" asked Henril, his expression carefully neutral. "Other than being on the same side?"

"No. We're comrades-in-arms. Nothing more." Tristam wasn't sure why he'd told that lie, and he despised himself as soon as it came out. Tonight, of all nights, it was clear to him that they were not simply "comrades-in-arms." But he found that he couldn't take the words back either. To answer any other way would have raised questions that Tristam didn't yet know how to answer. Especially since nothing between him and Kyra had actually been said.

Henril tilted his head in a gesture that didn't convey much confidence at all in Tristam's words, and Tristam decided to change the subject. "How have things been at home?"

At this, Henril's expression darkened and he hunched his shoulders as if huddling against a cold wind. "Not good. Demon Rider attacks have been increasing these past few weeks. Father and I have been riding the grounds every day, and we sent for Lorne to return as well."

Lorne was Tristam's second brother. "That bad?" said Tristam.

Henril lifted the sleeve of his tunic to reveal a bandage

around his forearm. "Got that from a demon cat two weeks ago."

Tristam's chest tightened at the sight. Demon Rider attacks on Forge itself had all but stopped since James's capture, but they still happened in the countryside. He'd known this, but it was a very different thing to see his wounded brother in front of him. And here he'd been, enjoying the respite. "It's strange the attacks have increased so much in the countryside, even taking into account that the barbarians avoid the city proper. If things are this bad, perhaps I should return home too."

His brother shook his head. "No, it's good to have someone within earshot of the Council. Father, Lorne, and I can handle the manor for now. Just keep an eye out for messages from us. We might need your help on short notice."

⊗ ⊗ ⊗

Kyra had no sooner stepped into Malikel's field of vision than the Defense Minister waved her over. "Kyra, we've need of you."

She hesitated. Though she'd told Tristam she was going to see Malikel, Kyra realized now that she hadn't actually meant to follow through. Well, Malikel had seen her. She steeled herself and approached.

Kyra didn't recognize the majority of officials standing around Malikel, and the one face she did recognize, Kyra was not at all happy to see. Head Councilman Willem had no special love for Kyra, and he made no secret of it.

"You already know Councilman Willem," said Malikel.

"This is Duke Symon of Edlan and Lord Alvred, the Edlan defense minister."

Perhaps this was the day for noticing family resemblances, because Kyra was struck by the similarity between Duke Symon's and Willem's features—something about the thin line of their lips and the way their well-trimmed eyebrows angled in on their foreheads. Kyra seemed to remember hearing that the two were distant cousins and that this relation was why Forge had been able to maintain peace with Edlan in recent years. She shifted her gaze to Lord Alvred, whom she now recognized as the large man she'd seen with Malikel earlier. He towered over her, and Kyra imagined that his hefty limbs might have been solid with muscle in his youth. Even now that he had a softer physique, Kyra got the impression he could crush her with very little effort. This was the man who would be Malikel's archenemy should war arise. Kyra wondered how they got along in times of peace.

"Lord Alvred had some questions about the Demon Riders," said Malikel. "They've had a few attacks in Edlan as well."

Alvred leaned over Kyra, absently smoothing down his mustache. "Is it true that they and their cats are the same type of creature?"

That was an easy enough question. "It's true," she said. "I saw them change shape many times."

He raised his eyebrows in keen interest. "And what have you found to be the best way of fighting them?"

"Spears, sir." Military strategy was Tristam's domain, but Kyra had been around long enough to answer at the simplest level. "That and telling folk to stay out of their way. They're usually going for livestock, though they're ruthless if you attack them."

Alvred had a few follow-up questions, and Kyra found she could answer them to his satisfaction. Other officials came to their circle as she spoke, and the air around her grew warmer with the crowd. Apparently, the Demon Riders were high in everybody's interest. As she spoke, Kyra became self-conscious about her lowborn speech. She was tempted to try to match the wallhuggers' smoother consonants and intonation, but she suspected she'd only come across as foolish.

Alvred downed his wine in one swig. "This is all very interesting," he said. "We've not found the Demon Riders to be much of a threat in Edlan. We did have a few attacks, which we fought off. After that, the barbarians have left us alone. Perhaps they've found easier marks elsewhere."

The insult didn't go unnoticed. All eyes went to Malikel, who looked to be suppressing a smile. "I congratulate you, Alvred, on the success of your excellent army."

"It's colder and rockier near Edlan, in't it?" said Kyra. "Mayhap the Demon Riders just prefer warmer weather."

Alvred peered down his nose at her. "And you would presume to know the minds of the barbarians? What kind of training does a girl like you have in warfare?"

Kyra flushed and squared her stance. "No formal learning, sir, but you'll remember I was their prisoner for a month."

Head Councilman Willem cleared his throat. His presence was commanding enough that everyone looked to him, though he didn't start talking until the pretty serving girl attending him had finished refilling his glass. "You raise a good question, Alvred, and one that we at Forge might do well to remember. Kyra *of Forge*"—he emphasized the city name, subtly underscoring Kyra's lack of affiliation with a noble house—"is a former assassin who was convicted of high treason, a member of the very group who first brought the Demon Riders against Forge. Certainly an unconventional choice to ask for counsel when the city's safety is at stake. But Malikel's choice in subordinates has always been unique."

Kyra choked at Willem's words. *Willem* had been the one to recruit Kyra into the Palace service after the pardon. How dare he reframe things now to cast suspicion on Malikel?

She might eventually have found her voice, but Malikel spoke first. "Thank you, Willem," he said mildly. "Kyra is valuable to us precisely because of her history with the Assassins Guild. Her experience with them and as a prisoner of the Demon Riders gives her a perspective that we lack. Any tome on strategy will fall short upon meeting an unfamiliar enemy. Sometimes firsthand experience is the best." He turned to Kyra. "I believe we've heard all we need from you. You are dismissed."

Tristam intercepted her before she could go very far, looping his arm into hers as if they were any one of the elegant couples in the ballroom.

"Don't leave." He spoke conversationally and looked out over the crowd, though there was a layer of compassion in his tone. "If you let him know he's upset you, then he's won. It's all part of the game."

Kyra let him guide her through the revelers, frustrated that he'd read her intentions so easily and wondering how much he'd overheard. "Can we go somewhere quieter at least? I can't stomach much more of this."

"How about here, by the wall?" He guided her to a space far enough from any posted guards to give them a semblance of privacy. "We can watch the dancing."

She nodded gratefully. Kyra started to lean against the mirrored walls but stopped when she saw Tristam standing straight. He gave her a faint smile. "Lean against me. I'm plenty sturdy, and the servants don't have to polish me at the end of the evening."

Kyra had to laugh at that, and she took his offered arm. They made quite a pair, the two of them in their finery, behaving in what must have been an incredibly unsociable way.

"Are you all right?" Tristam asked after a while.

Kyra nodded and found that she was indeed feeling better. "I'm used to Willem's barbs by now."

"Willem shouldn't have spoken like that, undermining our own people to Edlan officials. It's not even a matter of decorum. As Head Councilman, what he did was unacceptable."

"I suppose he just really dislikes me." Kyra tried to make her voice light, but Tristam just shook his head.

"No. Willem is too much of a politician to let his own feuds leak through to his official duties. He had a reason for saying what he did."

"And what was that?"

"I can't know for sure," said Tristam. "But Malikel's been gaining favor in the Council. He's been pushing an initiative against corruption in the Palace, and he's been convincing the other Council members. Perhaps Willem is trying to push back."

Across the room, Willem was enjoying a brief moment of solitude, attended by the same unusually pretty serving girl who'd refilled his cup before. The girl smiled at Willem, tilting her head as she refilled his glass, though it was clear to anyone with eyes in his head that her true function involved more than simply pouring wine. She wore the usual undyed linen dress of Palace serving women, but she'd cut it to a tighter fit, and the collar was much lower than the usual modest cut. The girl had accentuated her already striking features with a hint of kohl and berry stain, and she had the kind of figure that made men stop in the streets. Willem didn't even try to hide his glances at her cleavage as he leaned over to speak in her ear.

"Doesn't he care about word getting back to his wife?" Kyra snapped. She scanned the ballroom. Kyra didn't know what Willem's wife looked like, but she must have been present at such an important event.

It took Tristam a moment to discern whom she was talking about. "From what I hear, his wife has her own line of companions. Theirs was an arranged marriage."

"Is that how it's done with nobles? A marriage for politics' sake and a plaything on the side?" Kyra didn't bother to remove the distaste from her voice. Flick had come from such a union. His father had enjoyed his mistress's company and then abandoned her when illness took her beauty.

Tristam's gaze went to her face and lingered there a moment before he carefully replied, "It's commonly done but it's ... frowned upon. Many couples do try to make it work. My parents had a political marriage, but they now love and respect each other deeply."

Willem's serving girl sidled up closer to him, and the Head Councilman put a possessive arm around her waist. Kyra turned away. "I can't watch them carrying on like this. How can any serving girl stand to be that close to him? It turns my stomach."

Tristam looked at her in bemusement. "I've never seen you react this strongly to Willem, and he's done some pretty despicable things."

Kyra didn't want to think about why the sight of Willem with his mistress upset her so much. The answer was there. She just didn't like it. "Why's Malikel unmarried?" she asked. "All the other Council members have wives, don't they?"

"You know, I've never considered that. I suppose I always saw Malikel as a solitary entity." Tristam tilted his head thoughtfully. "To be honest, I think it would be difficult for him to find a family open to an alliance with him."

"Because he's Minadan? Even though he's a Council member?"

Tristam hesitated, then gave an uncomfortable nod. "Allowing a foreigner into the workings of one's city is hard enough. Allowing him into one's family...I can't see it happening."

Kyra chewed on his words. She supposed she wasn't all that surprised. Though Malikel had power and influence, he'd never completely lost the aura of an outsider. The children of Forge stared openly at Malikel when he toured the city, and Kyra remembered at least one serving girl new to the Palace who had been afraid to wait on the Defense Minister. In a sense, Malikel's situation was the opposite of hers. He was a good man and dedicated to the city, yet people feared him because of his dark skin and foreign ways. Whereas people who saw Kyra tended to underestimate her, seeing only a young girl of low birth.

"To be honest, Willem had a good point," she said. "I still wonder why Malikel trusts me. I did try to kill him."

"You were ordered to assassinate him," Tristam corrected. "And you didn't carry out that order. Furthermore, you captured James and turned him over to the Palace. That, if anything, should prove you're no longer loyal to him."

James. Kyra shivered as the assassin's face appeared in her mind. He'd changed her life the day he'd walked into The Drunken Dog to hire her. "There was a time when I believed in his cause. He really did think he was fighting for justice."

The problem was, he'd taken the fight further than Kyra had been willing to go. Things had gone sour when Kyra refused to kill innocent bystanders. And though she'd once been his most promising recruit, he'd eventually counted her his enemy.

Tristam spoke again. "And now you're working for the very people you once thought to bring down."

Kyra glanced sideways at him. "Are *you* doubting my loyalties now?"

He gave a faint smile. "Do I think you'll do anything to harm the city? No. Nor would I hesitate to entrust you with my life. But I do wonder sometimes if you regret joining the Palace."

Tristam owed her his life several times over, and she him. So she believed Tristam when he said he trusted her, and she took her time thinking his question over. When Kyra had been in the Assassins Guild, she'd feared that she was slowly becoming something she hated, that the horror of taking someone's life would fade into normalcy. What about now? She was glad she no longer had to follow James's orders, but was the Palace changing her in subtle ways as well?

"You do look lovely, you know." Tristam's words startled her out of her reverie. "I'm so used to seeing you in trousers."

She knew instinctively that he'd changed the subject on purpose, to give her permission not to answer right away. Kyra was grateful. "I prefer trousers. Certainly can't run anywhere in this dress," she said. "But you don't have to stand by the wall with me all night. Feel free to go charm the Edlan ladies."

Tristam pantomimed taking a lady's hand. "Good evening, fair lady. I'm Tristam, recently stripped of my rank. Would you like to dance?"

"They might find the idea of a disgraced knight romantic, if you frame it right."

Tristam nodded slowly in mock consideration. "You might have a point. But I'm too tired for courtly conversation." He paused. "Actually, the reaction to my disgrace has been much more complex than I expected. The richer and more influential families, the ones that used to view me as a promising match— they stay far away from me. But the slightly less respectable houses, their daughters seem to be paying me *more* attention. It's as if they think an alliance with Brancel is now within reach."

An alliance with Brancel. Kyra hadn't meant to steer the conversation to Tristam's marital prospects, and she regretted it now. Thankfully, a servant came by just then to offer them some lamb meatballs. Tristam took one, but Kyra declined.

"They'll be at this all night," said Tristam after the servants bore the tray away.

"What?"

He gestured toward the ballroom. Dancers twirled in pairs in front of the musicians, weaving patterns between and around each other that were hypnotizing to watch. "The dancers. It's amazing how they can keep it up for so long. Hours and hours of this, with only champagne and delicately frosted cakes to fuel their exertions."

"It all looks unnecessarily complicated," said Kyra. "How does anyone remember all the steps?"

"I would have thought you'd like dancing."

"Why's that?"

"You're not exactly someone who trips over her feet."

She turned her head to hide a smile. "I do like some dancing." There had been a few dancing girls at The Drunken Dog. Kyra had never bothered to learn what they did, mostly because she hated how the tavern's men leered at them. But once in a while on a festival day, someone would start up a circle dance in the dining room. Kyra had loved those. The steps were simple, and there was plenty of laughing and clapping and cheering. This Palace dancing was completely different though. The elegance of it intimidated Kyra, the feeling that everything had to be done exactly right.

"It looks complicated," said Tristam. "But really, the patterns make sense after a while." He nodded toward the dance floor. "This one, the valsa, you don't even have to learn any patterns—the gentleman chooses the steps and guides the lady through it. They say a good leader should be able to teach his partner to dance without speaking."

"Are you a good leader?" Kyra supposed Tristam must have been trained in these social graces at some point in his upbringing.

A smile touched his lips. "I'm decent."

Before Kyra could react, Tristam moved toward her, ringing her waist with one hand and taking her hand in the other. Without warning, he lifted her onto her toes and pivoted them both around until they stood at the edge of the dance floor. Kyra was speechless for a moment, then, seeing the sparkle in his eye, punched him in the chest.

"I could have stabbed you for that."

"Words, words, words. Don't worry. I'll be sure to catch you if you trip."

Maybe it was the pure absurdity of the situation, but the misgivings that had been weighing Kyra down all night dissipated. Kyra laughed and let him guide her through the steps. He kept them on the edge of the ballroom, out of the crowds. This was a stately dance, with tambour and bells keeping the rhythm as a trio of cornets trumpeted a dignified melody. Though Tristam had downplayed the dance's complexity, Kyra still found it a great challenge to keep up. It was only after the first few repetitions, after she started getting the hang of when she was to twirl and when she was to curtsy, that Kyra became more aware of his hand on her waist, the confident strength with which he led her. The frame of the dance was firm, and their bodies were separated by a good distance. But there was an energy between them, and Kyra wasn't sure whether she wanted to be farther from him or closer.

"I must be making a mess of things," she said.

"Not at all. You're doing great." He spoke calmly, his eyes intent on her face. In the strict confines of the dance, Kyra had no choice but to look back at him. Kyra found her mouth suddenly dry. It was hard sometimes to tell the difference between happiness and dread.

The dance floor was getting more crowded, and though Tristam kept them to the edges, more couples twirled around them. The occasional whiff of perfume wafted by, layered over the mustier backdrop of bodies in motion. Kyra stumbled just slightly when she noticed Tristam's brother Henril looking at them, his brow furrowed. But it was the sight of Willem dancing nearby that brought her to a complete stop. He was partnered with an older Edlan noblewoman, well coiffed and tastefully adorned with a headdress of three peacock feathers, and he paused as well to address them.

"By all means, keep dancing," said Willem. "It's not often done to bring one's mistress onto the dance floor, but given your situation, I'll let it pass." With that, Willem led his partner away.

Kyra stood rooted to the floor. She knew that the Councilman's words shouldn't bother her. Her opinion of him was as low as his opinion of her, but she still found herself flushing hot with shame.

"Kyra," Tristam began.

She shouldn't react to this. It was exactly what would bring Willem satisfaction. But then she noticed Willem's mistress standing on the side, one delicate hand to her throat as she watched them with interest. And Kyra finally admitted to herself why the girl upset her so much. She was a living reminder of a future that could very well be Kyra's, if she allowed things to continue with Tristam.

"I think that's enough for tonight," Kyra said. "This was a mistake." She didn't just mean the dance, and she could see that Tristam understood.

She ran for the ballroom door, and Tristam chased after her. "Kyra, wait. Talk to me, at least."

Perhaps that was one thing to be thankful for. Now that Willem had laid it on the table, Kyra was finally able to say the words. She ducked into a side corridor, where the ballroom's music faded enough to ease her frazzled mind. "Willem is right. I could never be more than a mistress to you."

He drew back as if she'd slapped him. "Is that what you think I'm doing? Using you as a diversion to throw away?"

Kyra started to speak and then stopped. "No. I mean, I don't think you're like—" She'd almost mentioned Flick's father, but that secret wasn't Kyra's to share. "But I know how things work. You're the son of a noble house. You have your duties to your family, and they don't involve anyone like me. Thing is, Willem doesn't even know the whole truth. He thinks I'm just a commoner and a pardoned criminal. He doesn't even know"—she looked around, then lowered her voice—"the rest." That she was a monster, bound by blood to the barbarians who were terrorizing their city.

Tristam opened his mouth again, and she knew from the set of his shoulders that he was going to argue.

"Please, Tristam," she interrupted. "Just be honest with me. You were just talking about the lesser noble houses of Forge as if they were a step down from Brancel. I come from the *gutter*, Tristam. If an alliance with Brancel is a reach for them, how could you think anything possible between you and me?"

His shoulders fell at her words, and regret washed over his features. "I'm sorry. I shouldn't have spoken so flippantly," he said.

Kyra gave a sad smile. "Whether or not you spoke flippantly, you spoke the truth. We both know that."

He fell silent. A few times, his mouth worked as if he were going to say something but decided against it. From the ballroom, a flute started trilling a quick tune over an accompaniment of viols. "So is this it, then? We're just going to be comrades-in-arms?"

Kyra swallowed hard. Part of her had still hoped he would disagree. "It's better to stop this now before anyone gets hurt, in't it?"

He chuckled wryly and looked to the mirrored ceiling. "Of course. Before anyone gets hurt. Shall I escort you back to the ballroom?"

Kyra backed away. "No, I'll leave now. Malikel's got no more need for me this evening."

Tristam studied her expression, his eyes scanning over her

features like so many times before, but this time without his usual warmth. He bowed, his face the perfect mask of courtly politeness. "Have a pleasant evening."

Kyra watched him return to the ballroom. Then she fled, walking as quickly as her dress would allow as the viols and flutes slowly faded into the distance.

FIVE

It took Idalee and Lettie about five seconds to realize that things at the Palace had gone poorly, and only a few more to understand that Kyra wouldn't be talking about it. They asked questions, and when Kyra refused to answer, the questions changed into significant glances behind her back. This continued for a few days, but after a while, even Kyra had to admit she was being difficult. She couldn't mope over Tristam forever.

She needed a distraction, and once again, the question of her origins came to mind. Now would be a good time to track down her past. Malikel was busy entertaining the foreign guests, and she had the leisure time to find Far Rangers who might know more about the Demon Riders.

Kyra had seen traders around before, though they were an insular bunch. There was a large market not far from the beggars' sector, and it seemed as good a place as any to find one. So when Flick suggested the four of them visit the city's gutter rats with a trip to the market afterward, Kyra agreed.

She should have suspected something when Idalee made a vague exclamation about a street juggler and pulled Lettie to walk ahead. But Kyra was too distracted by her own thoughts and thus was caught unawares when Flick cleared his throat.

"So," he said. "We couldn't help but notice you've been a mite morose lately."

Kyra almost laughed at how easily they'd maneuvered her in. "They decided you're the best person to get me talking?"

Flick flashed his most disarming smile. "I'm the most persuasive."

Kyra kicked a pebble. It rolled forward a few paces and bounced off the skirts of a serving woman in front of her. "Sorry," she mumbled when the woman shot a glare over her shoulder.

Flick tried again. "I've not seen Tristam around since the ball."

Actually, Tristam's absence was nothing out of the ordinary. It wasn't as if the nobleman came by all that often. But as much as she hated to admit it, Flick was right that this *was* about Tristam. She really was predictable. But then, so was Flick.

"It in't what you think, Flick."

"And what's it that I think?"

She threw up her hands. "Tristam's not thrown me aside. I'm not quietly mourning my broken heart."

Both Flick and Kyra stopped to make way for a passing cart. He had the grace to look slightly sheepish as they continued. "You know me well, I'll give you that. But I refuse to believe that there's nothing wrong. You've been acting strange for days."

Kyra glanced in the direction of the Palace. From this distance, she could see the Forge flag, a rearing horse on a red background. Flick was going to keep badgering her until she told him.

"I cut things off with Tristam. Or rather, I stopped anything before it started." It was easiest to get the words out quickly.

"That's . . . a surprise," said Flick after a moment.

"So you've no need to worry," said Kyra. "I know how the world works. I'm not a fool."

"Are you all right?" asked Flick.

"I'll be fine." And she would be. After a few more days.

Flick stuffed his hands into his pockets and cleared his throat, choosing his words carefully. "I've nothing to say against Tristam as far as wallhuggers go. It's just that—"

"I know, Flick," said Kyra. "Can we talk about something else?"

They were getting close to the beggars' sector, and Flick fell silent. Much of this neighborhood had burned down in the recent fire, though some of Kyra's old haunts had survived. The courtyard where Kyra had met Idalee and Lettie was untouched, the same dusty dirt square surrounded by run-down buildings, though it was crowded with more beggars since residents of the burned-out southwest quadrant had moved in. The entire area felt more dangerous these days, but Kyra still spied children climbing out of makeshift lean-tos, preparing themselves for a day of wandering the market. Idalee and Lettie were already talking with a street girl who'd been a friend of theirs.

It was a strange feeling, coming back these days. Kyra used to fret constantly over food and money—those worries had made up the bulk of her early existence. Now her material needs were no issue at all, thanks to the Palace. And though she had no desire to go back to the way things were, she couldn't help feeling a bit of guilt.

One of the boys spotted Kyra and ran to her.

"Ho, Kyra. Ho, Flick." Ollie was a few years older than Idalee and growing a little taller each time Kyra saw him. He'd been on the streets for years now, ever since his parents were thrown in prison for unpaid debts.

"Ollie, where'd you get that hat?" asked Kyra. It was a floppy, round style that Kyra often saw at the Palace, bright blue silk with a tassel hanging off the edge.

The boy grinned. "I found it."

"Found it?" asked Flick, one eyebrow raised.

Ollie's smile faded slightly.

"Nipped it off a fatpurse, did you?" Kyra asked.

Ollie shifted uncomfortably. "It was just in fun," he said.

Kyra couldn't believe the boy's stupidity. "You know better than that," she said. The lecture would have been more impressive if she'd been able to talk down at him, but Ollie was as tall as she was these days. "You want to nip something, you go for coin, food, or something you can sell. Fetching a useless trinket like that and parading it around will get you nothing but a beating."

The boy avoided her eyes. A crowd of children had gathered to watch, and he glared at them, daring anyone to make a comment.

Ollie straightened. "I see your clothes are mighty nice these days, Kyra. How do *you* get them? By kissing the wallhuggers' feet?"

There were a couple of gasps from around the circle, and Kyra herself drew back. She hadn't expected that. Out of the corner of her eye, Kyra saw Idalee stop talking and glance in her direction.

"What did you say?" Kyra said.

"It's what you're good at now, in't it?" said the boy. "Must be nice to eat off the Palace tables."

She had an urge to box the boy's ears. Except, again, he weighed more than she did, and his words rang a little too close to the truth. Flick squeezed her shoulder, the usual voice of restraint. She took a deep breath and told herself that the boy was just trying to salvage his pride. She stepped back from him and addressed the crowd.

"I brought coin this morning for folk who need it. If any of you want my help, you look me in the eye and you take the coin from my hand. If you don't like what I do with the Palace, you're free to stay back." She opened her bag. "Anyone?"

It didn't take them long to start coming. One by one, the children stepped around Ollie and took a copper from her. When almost all the children had received a coin, Kyra looked at Ollie again. He approached her grudgingly—not too proud to refuse money, though he'd stubbornly refused to take off his hat.

"Just be careful," she said as she pressed a coin into his hand. He mumbled something and left.

Kyra rubbed the bridge of her nose as Idalee and Lettie rejoined them. Idalee folded her coin pouch with studied care, and Lettie looked back and forth at everyone's faces, eyes wide.

"He didn't mean what he said," said Flick as they made their way to the market.

"Aye, he did," said Kyra. To be honest, she should have expected it sooner. Kyra had noticed a change in the children the past few times she'd come. The newer ones especially, the ones who didn't know her as well, looked upon her with suspicion. They took her money, but they kept their distance. It couldn't be helped, she supposed. She was there passing out bags of Palace coin. And as far as they knew, everything from the Palace was suspect.

"Do they say the same things to you, Idalee?" she asked.

"A few, but it in't so bad," said Idalee. "I'm not always spending time with the wallhuggers like—" She stopped.

"It's fine. You can say it. I'm the only one who spends all my time with wallhuggers," said Kyra. Ollie's comment still rankled. "Everybody thinks that's a problem. Either I've sold my self-respect for money, or I'm a love-struck victim waiting to be chewed up and spat out. Does everyone really think that badly of my judgment?"

Flick winced at her words. "It's not a matter of judgment, Kyra," he said. "My ma was a woman of good judgment." He broke off abruptly. "Sorry. We're done with that topic now. I promise." Flick squeezed her shoulder apologetically. "I'm going to go track down a locksmith for some tools. Good luck with your traders." He disappeared into the crowd.

"You should marry Flick, Kyra," Lettie said as they looked after him.

Coming from anyone else, that comment would have rubbed Kyra's already raw nerves, but Lettie looked so earnest that Kyra had to chuckle. She and Flick had been getting those types of comments since before he could grow a full beard, but Flick was too much like a brother to her. It would have been strange.

She bent down to Lettie's level. "He's far too good-looking for me, Lettie," she said, her face a mask of perfect seriousness. "Everyone would stare at us and say, 'What's that handsome lad doing with a girl in trousers?'"

Lettie's face scrunched up. "But you're pretty, Kyra, even if your bosom in't very big."

Idalee had a sudden and very violent coughing fit.

"Thanks, Lettie," Kyra said drily. Maybe next time she should just say that Flick belched too loudly. "Idalee, do you two have somewhere to be?"

"We need more wool for our dresses," said Idalee.

"Off you go, then. I'll see you back home."

The marketplace was still getting set up. Vendors pushed their carts into place and raised awnings to block the sun. None of the actual sellers at the stalls were traders, but they were the first step to finding the caravans that supplied them.

Kyra sweetened a fishmonger's opinion of her by buying a bag of smoked mussels, then asked if he knew where the caravanners stayed. He pocketed her coin and pointed her toward a large, boxlike storehouse a few streets away. It was not unlike the building that the Assassins Guild had once used for its headquarters. There were a few wagons hitched out front with rough-looking, travel-worn men and women walking amongst them. Kyra approached cautiously.

A tall man stood near the front gate, directing wagons in and out. He looked at her. "You with a caravan?"

Kyra shook her head. "No. But I've need of a Far Ranger to talk to. Are there any here?"

"Depends on what you mean by Far Ranger."

"Someone who's crossed the Aerins."

The man squinted at her. "You looking to cause trouble?"

Kyra pressed a coin into his hand. "I'm just looking to chat. The Far Rangers have got their ear to the ground more than most."

He fingered her coin and looked her over. Then he jerked his head at a wagon toward the back. "Jacobo's caravan travels the Aerins."

There were wagons of all types in this courtyard, ranging from flat carts for hauling lumber to covered wagons that could serve as semi-permanent homes. The people who came out of them were equally eclectic in their look and dress. There were brown-skinned Minadans who wore heavy furs over their native tunics and tucked their bright pantaloons into winter-friendly northern boots. Plenty of traders from the three cities were here too, clad in sturdy neutral-colored clothing. The trader women wore trousers like Kyra, so she actually looked less out of place here than she did in the rest of Forge.

Jacobo's wagon had seen its share of repairs. The awning was patched in several places, and not all the wood of the wagon's body matched the rest. Kyra slowed as she came closer, unsure what to expect. A trader stepped out from behind the wagon and fixated on her immediately. His skin was tanned, tough, and wrinkled, and there was more than one scar across his face. He looked like someone who had weathered storms, ice, and hunger, and thought little enough of it that he did it over and over again.

"Are you Jacobo?" said Kyra.

He gave a careful nod. "I'm Jacobo. And you are?"

Kyra extended her hand. "My name is Kyra. Of Forge."

The trader glanced at the tall man at the gate. "Gregor let you in here?"

"I made a convincing case," Kyra said, indicating her coin purse. She wasn't quite sure if admitting to a bribe was the best idea, but this trader didn't seem the type who appreciated being lied to.

Jacobo chuckled. "I reckon he wasn't too hard to convince. Well, maidy, why take the trouble of searching out my company?"

"I'm looking for a Far Ranger," said Kyra, hoping she was projecting at least some confidence. "Your people have a reputation for a long memory."

"Depends on what you mean by long."

"Have you heard any stories of Demon Riders crossing the mountains before this year? Mayhap in the past twenty years?"

Jacobo gave her a curious look. "That's an odd question. Why do you want to know?"

"I work under the Palace defense minister. We're trying to learn more about the barbarians." All true, except that Malikel had no idea she was here.

"The Palace has never come to us for information before. And you don't look like the usual fatpurse's crony." Kyra was wondering how to persuade Jacobo to talk when he continued.

"About fifteen years ago, a trade caravan was attacked near Forge, in the forest right above the upper waterfall. The wagons were destroyed and the crew was scattered, some killed. One survivor said they were attacked by felbeasts—that's what they're called across the mountains."

Fifteen years? Kyra didn't know her exact age, but she'd guessed she was about seventeen or eighteen years old. If there had been a clan around the three cities about that long ago . . . She tried not to let her excitement show. "You said there were survivors?"

"You say you're from Forge?" asked Jacobo abruptly. "You don't look it. Your skin's a shade darker than most, and the slant of your cheekbones . . ."

"Not everyone from Forge looks the same," said Kyra, scrambling to make sense of his words. Did he know something?

"How old are you?"

"I don't know."

Jacobo kept studying her. "I've met one of the survivors from that caravan," he said. "I could send word to him, see if he has anything to add, if that suits you."

Kyra rummaged around in her belt pouch and pulled out a piece of parchment. She scribbled Flick's address, thinking it better not to leave anything that would lead directly back to her. "You can find me here if you learn of any news. I'd be grateful."

Jacobo tucked the parchment away. "I'm in Forge for the winter. We're camped a quarter day's walk to the west, along the main road. If I hear from the survivor, I'll find you."

She thanked him and went on her way. The market was filling with people, but Kyra barely saw them as she mulled over

Jacobo's words. A clan had come to Forge over a decade ago. Could she be descended from them? It was still morning, and Kyra had no plans for the rest of the day. The upper waterfall where the attack had happened wasn't far. Everything would be gone after so long, but she was still tempted to take a look. Kyra turned toward the city outskirts. She could probably get there in an hour.

She was just making her way out of the market when she heard a scream.

The cry came from someone young, and it came from close by. Now that Kyra was listening for it, she heard other shouts as well. She sped up toward the commotion.

A courtyard next to the market was crowded with people, all watching something in the center. There was a sickness to the air. As Kyra came closer, several people broke away from the crowd and hurried away.

"You'll learn to respect your betters," came a man's voice. "Tell me why we shouldn't cut that tongue of yours clean out."

Kyra thought she heard a whimper in response. She nudged a beggar woman next to her. "What happened?" she whispered.

"Some kind of row between fatpurses and a gutter rat. Gutter rat's getting the worst of it now."

Kyra redoubled her efforts to break through the crowd, her thoughts immediately going to Ollie. Had a nobleman taken exception to his hat? A few people protested when she pushed past them, but most were too distracted by the spectacle in the square.

There was a sickening thud and a low moan as Kyra pushed

in front of the people blocking her view. Now that she was through, she saw that the crowd pressed against the outer perimeter of the courtyard, leaving the middle empty. Folk were afraid to get too close to the scene in the center, and Kyra couldn't blame them.

Three young noblemen, peacocks in their colorful silk tunics, stood over a muddied body in the courtyard. The victim wore a dress—it wasn't Ollie, then, though the girl looked to be in bad shape. Then the victim rolled over, and Kyra's heart stopped beating.

It wasn't Ollie. It was Idalee.

The girl was hunched over in the mud, her face twisted in pain as a nobleman waved a dagger in front of her eyes. Even as Kyra watched, the wallhugger, a skinny young man in a purple tunic, grabbed Idalee's hair and pushed her face into the mud. His friend pulled his leg back for another kick. Kyra drew her dagger and made a mad rush into the circle. "Stop!"

Her momentum was enough that the noblemen jumped back, and Kyra threw herself in front of Idalee. The wallhuggers stared. If a squirrel had jumped off a roof and started talking to them, they couldn't have been more surprised.

"Kyra?" Idalee seemed to have trouble focusing her eyes on her.

Kyra crouched and placed her hand on Idalee's shoulder. The girl's nose was bleeding, and her lip was torn. "I don't know what imaginary offense this girl committed," said Kyra. "But this is far beyond anything she could possibly deserve. Leave her be."

The one in the purple tunic looked her over, still more confused than angry. "Who *are* you?"

He took a step toward her. Kyra raised her dagger.

"You'll answer to the magistrate," said Kyra. "There's a courtyard full of witnesses."

That was apparently the wrong thing to say. Purple Tunic's expression changed from confusion to annoyance, and he advanced on her.

"The lesson we were teaching the girl could just as easily be extended to you," the nobleman said, drawing his sword. All three of the wallhuggers had swords, she saw now. They were probably good with them too, and there was no way she could fight them all with a dagger. Kyra scanned the crowd, looking for anyone who might help her. Faces stared back at her, but no one stepped forward. There were even two Red Shields in the crowd, simply watching. Lettie was nowhere in sight, though Kyra supposed that was a good thing at the moment.

Well, there was one way she could defeat three swordsmen. Kyra felt inward for the sense of her fur. But she was surrounded by people. What would she do to them if she changed? She snuck another glance at Idalee behind her. The girl lay with her temple against the ground, too tired even to lift her head.

There was a flash of motion in her periphery as Purple Tunic chose that moment to attack. Kyra jumped to the side to dodge his blade, remembering at the last moment not to impale herself on her dagger. The slick mud cushioned her fall, but it was also ice-cold and sucked at her clothes when she tried to stand. The nobleman advanced on her. As Kyra regained her feet, he stopped and stared at her neck. Kyra looked down to see that Malikel's medallion had come out of her tunic.

"Where did you get that? Did you steal it?"

Kyra gripped the medallion in her hand. "My name is Kyra of Forge. I'm under the Defense Minister's direct command."

"Liar."

But then one of Purple Tunic's companions stepped forward. "Santon, Malikel did take on the girl criminal recently."

Santon looked at Kyra again, his eyes narrowing. Kyra dropped into a defensive crouch, but the nobleman spat on the ground and backed away. "I don't know who you are, wench, but be careful. Not even Malikel's protection goes very far."

The three wallhuggers turned, and the crowd parted for them as they left.

Kyra rushed to Idalee's side, choking back a sob as she tried to discern the extent of Idalee's injuries. There were cuts and bruises on the girl's face, and the way she lay there without propping herself up made Kyra wonder about her arm. Idalee's breathing was pained and shallow, and her skin was deathly pale.

"I'm sorry," Idalee whispered. Her voice was devoid of emotion.

"Shush." Kyra wiped the blood from Idalee's nose. "It wasn't your fault." Then Kyra sat up in panic. "Where's Lettie?"

"She's here." The crowd parted to reveal Ollie holding Lettie's hand, and Kyra squeezed the girl to her chest. "Are you all right?"

"Aye." The child was trembling, but she was otherwise composed. It wasn't the first beating she'd witnessed.

The gutter rats crowded around now, a tangle of rags and bony limbs. A girl with mousy features wiped the mud off Idalee's face, while a pale boy poured water over her cuts. It suddenly struck Kyra how efficiently they went about their tasks, how everybody seemed to already know what to do when one of their own was gravely hurt.

"Tell me what happened," Kyra said to Lettie.

Lettie wiped her nose with the back of her hand. "It was the same wallhuggers who overturned her bread basket. Idalee called him a sniveling purple-headed worm."

Oh, Idalee.

"We need to get her to a healer," said Kyra. She looked down at Idalee. "Can you walk?"

Idalee nodded, her face lined with pain, and Kyra took her good arm to help her up. But after a few steps, Idalee started to whimper and her legs folded underneath her. There was a layer of sweat on the girl's brow as Kyra eased her back to the ground, and she was so very pale.

"Stay with her," Kyra said to the children. "I'll be back."

Kyra wasn't aware of much as she sprinted to the Palace, just the next corner to turn and the next person or obstacle to dodge. If anyone complained about her passing so carelessly, she didn't hear it. After the Red Shield at the Palace gate waved her in, she made straight for the Palace healer named Ilona, who had tended to Kyra's wounds before. Though she was in the Palace's employ, she wouldn't hesitate to help an injured child of low birth.

Ilona was a slender woman with ebony hair and a heart-shaped, freckled face. She took a half step back when she saw

Kyra's wild expression, and listened intently as Kyra related her story. Once Kyra finished, Ilona gathered two apprentices and took a wagon down to the beggars' sector. Her lips pressed into a thin line when she saw Idalee. In a commanding voice that belied her small frame, Ilona ordered the gutter rats away and commanded her apprentices to help Idalee up.

As the wagon rolled out of the courtyard, the beggar woman Kyra spoke to earlier called after them.

"The noblemen who beat your friend were the three sons of Lord Agan," the woman said. "If anyone at the Palace cares to know who did this, or cares at all."

Or cares at all. That was the question.

Idalee was listless by the time they arrived at the Palace, her head lolling side to side whenever the wagon hit a bump in the road. They brought the girl into Ilona's patient room, and the healer set to work right away. She wasted no breath in explaining anything, and Kyra relegated herself and Lettie to the corner of the room, huddling next to shelves of dried spices and staying as much out of her way as possible. Lettie's eyes never left her sister. The girl stared at Idalee as if she couldn't see the healer or apprentices circling her bed at all. It broke Kyra's heart, and she wrapped her arms around Lettie, wishing she could tell her that Idalee would be just fine. But she couldn't bring herself to lie.

Footsteps sounded in the hall, and Malikel swept through the door. "Kyra, what is this?"

Kyra hadn't expected to see Malikel so soon. Ilona must have dispatched some servants. "Sir, my sister was beaten by Lord Agan's three sons."

Malikel came to a stop at the head of Idalee's bed, looking far too much like Death's messenger looming over Idalee in his flowing red robes. "How is she, Ilona?"

"Not good, sir," Ilona answered quietly.

Malikel turned to Kyra again. "Tell me what happened."

The Councilman didn't interrupt Kyra as she told him what she'd pieced together. "They could have killed her," she said. "The magistrate should know about this."

"You say there were witnesses?" Malikel asked.

"A crowd had gathered to watch, but nobody interfered. Two of them were Red Shields," Kyra said. *And they'd stood by while Idalee choked on mud.*

Idalee whimpered again, and Ilona apologized, though Kyra wasn't sure if Ilona was speaking to Idalee, Malikel, or Kyra.

Malikel took one last look at the girl. "I'll speak to the magistrate on her behalf. We'll see what we can do."

Kyra was afraid to hope for justice, not with everything she'd seen on the streets. But if Malikel were behind Idalee . . . "Thank you, sir."

"Don't thank me yet."

After Malikel left, Lettie started to nod with fatigue. Kyra took a blanket from a shelf next to Idalee's bed and coaxed Lettie to lie down. Lettie resisted at first, but she finally gave in, and Kyra rubbed her back. The floor was hard stone, and the blanket was a closely woven wool that didn't offer much padding, but the girl nonetheless fell quickly asleep. Kyra left her there and found a servant boy to carry a message to Flick. Then she sat in the corridor outside Ilona's door and sifted through the guilt-laden questions whirling through her head.

Should she have tried harder to get Idalee to listen to her warnings? Anger flared through her at the thought. A child shouldn't have to fear for her life every time she misspoke, no matter whom she was talking to.

She'd been there a while when Tristam came hurrying around the corner, still in uniform. Though their argument was still fresh in her mind, Kyra's spirits lifted to see him. She began to stand, but he motioned for her to sit back down.

"I heard," he said softly, those two words heavy with concern. He peered carefully into Ilona's room. "How is she?" Under these circumstances, their fight seemed sadly trivial.

"Ilona's been working on her a long time," said Kyra. Her voice sounded hollow.

Tristam's face grew shadowed as he watched Ilona's movements. Finally, he backed away and sank down onto the floor opposite her. "Is there anything I can do to help?"

"Malikel's reporting to the magistrate. Ilona's doing what she can."

"Ilona's one of our best," Tristam said.

Kyra nodded, staring at the empty space in front of her. The cold of the walls and floor seeped through her tunic, and she hugged her knees closer to keep warm.

"Lord Agan has three sons," said Tristam. "Santon's the oldest, then Douglass. Dalton, the youngest, was in my cohort when we were squires. They've always had a reputation for causing trouble, getting into fights when the commanders weren't looking."

"Ever been punished?" asked Kyra.

"A few times."

Not enough to dissuade them from beating a child to near death.
"I've been beaten before," said Kyra. "Once a couple Red Shields
wanted to take my coin for a fake bridge toll. I tried to run
away, but I wasn't fast enough. Things like that aren't uncom-
mon in the city."

Tristam shook his head in disgust. "Now that I spend more
time in the Red Shield ranks, I see things. Soldiers abusing
their power, extorting money from the citizens. There are a
few commanders who almost certainly take bribes to look the
other way. And the Council turns a blind eye. Rumors say that
Willem is one of the worst offenders."

"Must be nice to have the city's forces do your bidding."

Tristam didn't reply. Kyra could hear Ilona's soft footsteps
in the patient room, the clank of mortar and pestle, the swish
of pouring water.

"I'm sorry about the ball," Tristam suddenly said. "I reacted
badly to what you said."

It took a moment for Kyra to follow Tristam's words, but
once she did, she met his eyes gratefully. His apology released a
ball of tension inside her that she'd forgotten she was carrying.

"I didn't exactly bring it up in the best way," she said.

He met her gaze from across the hallway, eyes relaxing a
little. "You're just trying to think ahead, and really, it shouldn't
have fallen to you to bring it up. Though I hope you know that
I've never seen you as... I mean, I would never see you as just
a potential mistress."

"I know."

Ilona came out then, and both Kyra and Tristam stood to meet her. The healer moved as if her entire body were weighed down by stones.

"Two broken ribs, a broken arm, a knock on the head, and many bruises. She's bleeding in her abdomen as well," she said. "I've given her herbs to sleep, and that will be the best for her right now. You and the little one should go home and rest. I'll send word if anything changes."

Kyra rubbed her dry eyes and thanked Ilona. There was nothing more she could do.

Idalee seemed better early the next morning. She still slept, thanks to one of Ilona's concoctions, but Kyra imagined that some of her color had returned. The healer was already there when Kyra arrived, and Kyra wondered if Ilona had slept at all. Though perhaps Ilona was indeed tiring, because she finally allowed Kyra to help change the girl's bandages. They had just finished when Tristam came through the door.

"I thought I might find you here," he said. "Malikel says to go see him when Idalee no longer requires your attention." Tristam might have caught the hopeful cast of Kyra's face, because he spoke again. "Don't expect too much. I'm not sure how much even Malikel can do."

When Tristam and Kyra arrived at Malikel's study, the Defense Minister motioned for them to sit down in front of his desk. He wore an expression that Kyra had only seen on him after the most frustrating of Council meetings, and Kyra's heart sank.

"I spoke with the magistrate," he said. "He's adamant that the evidence does not warrant a trial."

"Evidence? There were well over fifty witnesses," said Kyra.

"I did inform him of that. Regardless, the magistrate is not convinced." Malikel's eyes conveyed far more meaning than his words.

"What can we do, then?" said Kyra. A knot of panic was forming in Kyra's stomach, a looming inevitability that she refused to accept.

"Willem is a powerful man. This particular magistrate is one of his favorites, as is Lord Agan. There may not be much we can do."

It was an expression of powerlessness that Kyra heard every day in the beggars' sector, but she had never expected to hear it in the Defense Minister's study. She glanced over at Tristam and, in growing disbelief, saw the resigned expression on his face as well.

"You're a member of the Council, Malikel," she said. "Idalee was beaten in broad daylight."

"By some very well-connected young men," said Tristam. He was speaking gently now, as if she were some madwoman who might go into fits. "It's crazy and wrong, Kyra, but there's a reason why they thought they could get away with it."

Kyra stared at Tristam, unable to wrap her mind around the fact that he agreed with Malikel. "There's a lass on the brink of death and more people who could testify to this than could fit in the magistrate's study. I don't understand the difficulty."

Malikel and Tristam exchanged a glance, and the look of

understanding that passed between them was the final straw. Kyra stood up so quickly that her chair toppled backward and clattered on the stone behind her. "Are we finished here?" She needed to leave before she did something she would regret. When Malikel didn't respond, she stormed out.

It was all she could do not to scream her frustration as she ran out into the courtyard below. She'd known it would be hard to get justice for Idalee, but somehow she'd allowed herself to hope that Malikel, at least, could help her. *Are you really so surprised? Did you really think you could go up against three noblemen and bring them down in the courts?* She'd been a fool to think anything would be different now that she was in the Palace. A gutter rat in fancy clothes was still a gutter rat. The sons of Lord Agan would go on with their lives as if this had never happened, while Idalee struggled to draw breath in Ilona's patient room.

Kyra headed for the Palace gate, unable even to look at the fatpurses she passed. Who were these people who lorded over the city and did what they wished? *The wallhuggers are not your friends, and they never will be.*

She'd walked only a short distance when she noticed Tristam trailing her. She didn't slow, but he caught up.

"Are you content to let this go too?" she snapped.

He took a while to answer. "I'm sorry," he said, his voice subdued. "I hate this as well. Malikel tried everything in his power."

"Tried what?" Kyra asked. "He's a member of the Council. He's not some beggar off the streets." A servant coming down the pathway toward them stopped short at Kyra's murderous gaze and stepped off the pathway to go around them.

"Malikel is bound by the law," said Tristam. "He cannot simply ignore the magistrate's ruling and do as he wishes. But he's been making changes. He's been gathering support from other Council members who also hate the corruption, and together they're starting to form a block of votes."

"I don't want a lesson in politics. I want the men who did this to hang from the city walls."

Kyra froze. Standing near the pathway were Willem, Lord Agan's three sons, and a man in black magistrate's robes. They looked to be finishing a conversation. The magistrate left in the opposite direction, but Willem came toward them.

"Kyra of Forge." Willem's voice was sharp as a raptor's, and there was a hardness in his gaze. "Be careful you do not overstep your bounds." He left without waiting for a reply. Kyra clenched her jaw until it hurt.

Tristam opened his mouth to say something but stopped as Lord Agan's sons approached. Santon's smile didn't reach his eyes, and Kyra's fingers curled for her knife. Next to her, Tristam moved his hand closer to his scabbard.

"Kyra of Forge, is it?" said Santon. "So you weren't lying about being in Malikel's service. Though I suppose it makes sense. More convenient for him than going to a brothel."

Kyra felt Tristam's hand clamp around her wrist, and none too quickly. "Watch your words, Santon," he said. "You're not untouchable."

"Perhaps you should follow your own advice, Red Shield." Santon's voice dripped with contempt. Tristam's grip on Kyra remained firm as Santon and his brothers walked away.

I could kill you in your sleep, Kyra thought to their retreating forms. *I could slip right past your bodyguards and have you begging for mercy. Let's see how cocky you can be when you don't have Willem's skirts to hide under.*

"Kyra." Tristam still hadn't let go of her. She tried to pull her arm away, but he didn't budge. "Kyra, it's not worth it."

"What's not worth it? Idalee's life?"

"Doing something stupid because you're angry," he said. "Promise me you won't go after them. Ending up under another death sentence will do you no good at all."

She stared at Santon and his brothers. They were still talking and laughing, their voices fading as they walked away. Kyra wrenched her arm from Tristam's grip. "Funny that you say Malikel can't walk in and do what he wishes," she said. "Seems to me that if you know the right people and have enough coin, you can do exactly as you wish."

SIX

Kyra lay awake that night and combed through her memories of James—not the most recent ones, where he'd betrayed her and tried to kill her, but their interactions from earlier. There had been a time when she and James had been in accord, surprisingly so. He'd been the one to show her that she could be more than a petty thief, that she could use her skills to correct wrongs done by the wallhuggers. Discovering her own power had been exhilarating, and James had shown real pride in her progress. They both took pleasure in bringing the fatpurses down a notch, in hitting the nobles where they thought themselves invulnerable. Kyra had admired James once, and—if she was honest with herself—had been attracted to him as well. Which had made it all the more devastating when he'd turned against her.

In the end, they'd disagreed not on their goals but the means by which to accomplish them. She'd refused to shed innocent blood, and he'd called her naïve. *We're dealing with the Palace and the Council, the most powerful men in the three cities, and the swords they control,* he'd told her. *You don't win this war with petty raids on their storehouses. You draw blood.* That had been his philosophy, that it simply wasn't possible to end the abuses by the wallhuggers without a costly fight. If someone had asked Kyra a week ago whether she agreed with James, she would have said no.

Kyra hadn't seen James since his capture. Even before the Council's explicit prohibition, she'd kept her distance. James knew too much about Kyra, and he still embodied too many painful memories. It had made sense to stay away. But now...

She started preparations the next day. When Flick took Lettie for a walk, Kyra locked the door behind them. She tore a few strips of cloth from an old tunic, placed them on the table, and drew her dagger. Then she hesitated. The Makvani thought nothing of spilling a few drops of their own blood, but Kyra still found it difficult. After a few false starts, she sliced a shallow cut across the top of her arm. It wasn't deep, but it stung, and Kyra drew a sharp breath through her teeth as the blood welled out. She sopped up her blood with the cloth strips, rolled them into balls, and tucked them into her belt pouch.

The next day, she dutifully reported to the Palace to discuss the rash of new Demon Rider attacks in the countryside. The Defense Minister had no further news on Lord Agan's sons, and Kyra didn't press him. Instead of leaving the Palace afterward, she took a back path that led to the prison building. She was somewhat familiar with the layout. The building itself was built solidly of stone, with barred windows in the aboveground floors. Since her series of break-ins to the Palace, Malikel had gone through and made sure that none of the windows were vulnerable. Not that it mattered much. The most dangerous and valuable criminals were imprisoned in holding cells two floors belowground.

The building was thoroughly guarded, with Red Shields patrolling the corridors at all hours. The locks were well crafted and impossible to pick—she'd tried a few times out of curiosity. The only keys were kept by the head warden in the guardhouse in front of the building. He knew Kyra—had guarded her when she was a prisoner there—and probably wasn't keen to trust her. The warden was supposed to keep his keys on his person at all times, but Kyra, who still paid attention to things like guards and keys, knew that he often removed his key ring from his belt and placed it on his desk while he worked.

Now she approached the guardhouse from the back, out of view from passersby. The window was open. The warden was at his desk, and his keys were next to him. *Perfect.*

The holding cells also had dog patrols—usually a deterrent to intruders, but in this case, Kyra would make them work for her. She pulled out the strips of cloth, stiff with her blood. Looking around one more time to make sure nobody was watching, she tied the cloth pieces to some bushes in front of the guardhouse, low enough so they wouldn't be easily seen. Then she backed some distance away and waited.

The dog patrol came by half an hour later, a Red Shield with a mean-looking wolfhound on a leash. Kyra watched the dog carefully as its handler brought him closer. A low growl came from its throat as he neared the place where Kyra had secured the cloth strips. The Red Shield pulled on the dog's leash and looked around, but urged the animal forward when he found nothing awry. The dog's growling continued, and as it came closer to Kyra's dried blood, the growls turned into full-on panic. The Red Shield cursed and struggled to get the animal under control as it tried to bolt.

"What's going on?" The prison warden came out of the guardhouse, voice sharp.

Kyra made her move, creeping closer to the guardhouse as quickly as she could. There was a slight wind, and she could hear the dog's panic increase as it caught a whiff of Kyra herself. She needed to be fast. The back window to the guardhouse was open, thankfully, and she lifted herself easily through it. She could still hear the warden yelling at the Red Shield outside as the dog continued to bark and growl. His keys were still on the table.

She made a mental note of the key ring's position before she lifted it up, holding it carefully to keep the keys from clanging. They were arranged by floor, and she wanted the farthest cell in the lowest level. When she found it, she took a piece of clay from her belt and pressed the key into it—once on each side. She also copied the key to the main prison itself. The dog was still barking madly when she climbed back out.

It took her four nights to file keys that would work, using one of Flick's files that she'd borrowed and neglected to return. Kyra might have finished sooner, but these keys were complicated, and she wanted to be absolutely sure they were done right. Plus she had to do it when neither Flick nor Lettie was around. They wouldn't have understood.

On the fifth night, she dressed in dark clothes and snuck out of her quarters as Lettie slept. Kyra had an odd feeling of nostalgia as she crept back into the Palace. She hadn't scaled these walls since her capture. She supposed she could have come in through the gates, but she didn't want any record of her having entered the compound that night. Her muscles remembered the routine well—the angle at which to cast her grappling hook, the familiar scramble up the side of the wall, the slight slipperiness of the granite against her leather shoes. The guard schedules were different now, changed in part thanks to her, so she had to be careful not to let old routines lower her guard. She kept her eyes alert and her ears open. Her blood flowed faster as she sped up her pace. It was exhilarating.

Kyra made her way from building to building, finally slowing as the prison's shadow loomed above her. The entrance was lit by two torches, and two guards stood on either side of the arched entryway. They never left their post, and they kept their eyes sharply trained on the path in front of them. They were attentive guards, for sure. But they hardly ever glanced upward.

Kyra checked the sky, estimating that she had about a quarter hour before the Palace clock rang out the time. She skirted to the back of the building, keeping her steps soft. She didn't hear any guards coming, so she ran straight for the wall and clambered skyward, wrapping her fingers around bars, ledges, and outcroppings in the stonework. Four stories up, then she pulled herself onto the roof and crossed to the front.

The next step was more delicate. Carefully, Kyra worked her way back down. If she peered over her shoulder, she could see the guards standing sentry on either side of the entry archway below her. If she dislodged anything and it fell between the Red Shields, she'd have to run.

She crept her way down until she neared the circle of light created by the torches on the wall. Kyra wrapped her fingers around some solid outcroppings and thrust her toes into secure niches. Then she pressed herself flat and waited.

It wasn't fun. The wind was freezing, and Kyra wondered whether her muscles would cramp up before the turn of the hour. Three hundred and twenty breaths later, the clock finally chimed, and Kyra sprang into action, her limbs cold but thankfully functional. She checked quickly over her shoulder to see if there were any people around besides the guards, breathing a quick word of thanks for her halfblood vision. Then, she climbed down into the circle of torchlight. As the clock finished up its hourly melody, she lowered her legs into the entryway and swung her entire body into the archway behind the guards. The chimes masked the sound of her landing. The clock started to mark the time—it was three in the morning. Kyra slipped her key into the door.

First chime.

Kyra turned the key. It rotated halfway and then caught.

Second chime.

She jiggled the key. The tumblers gave way.

Third chime.

The lock clicked open. Kyra slipped in and closed the door behind her. As the clock's chimes faded from her ears, she let out a slow breath. She was in.

Kyra stood in a dark and mercifully empty entryway. A stone corridor stretched out ahead, with solid wooden doors lining each side. The first floor consisted of interrogation cells and a few holding cells. Though there were no guards in her immediate line of sight, she could hear boots echoing not far away. She hurried for the stairway down.

As Kyra moved into the lower levels, the smell of mold and human waste became stronger, and the silence was broken by the occasional shout or moan. Progress was slow. Several times, she had to dive into a niche or perch atop a doorframe to evade a passing Red Shield. But she did work her way little by little until she stood in front of James's cell. She doubted that he would be unbound, but she readied her dagger just in case. Her key worked on the first try.

Her first glimpse of James knocked her back several steps. Kyra had expected to hate him. She'd steeled herself for memories of Bella and of her own near death at his hands. Those images did come back, but she also saw James as he was now, and it left her speechless.

He was shackled to the wall by short chains that connected to rings around his wrists. He wore the same tunic and trousers that he had been captured in, though now they were soiled and torn. James's face was covered with bruises and cuts, as was what exposed skin Kyra could see. His white-blond hair was matted with what looked like blood.

He hung from his chains with his face cast down, and at first Kyra thought he was asleep. But then he slowly raised his head. His eyes were still the same cold, clear blue as they had always been.

"I wondered when you'd come," he said.

She had nothing to say. James watched her, and there was a hint of an amused smile on his lips. "Surprised at the sight of me? The Council spares no expense in welcoming its guests."

Kyra didn't know why the marks of torture on James affected her so much. She had certainly known what the Palace did to criminals, though her own treatment while imprisoned had been nothing compared to this. Was it because she had cooperated early on? Or was it because the knights of Forge still held too much to their chivalrous notions to torture a young woman?

Kyra took a few steps closer to James, though not within his reach. He was still a dangerous man, and she had the scars to prove it. But she wanted a better look at him. Now that she had gotten over the shock of his appearance, she could see that James's imprisonment hadn't taken the glint of intelligence out of his eyes—nor had it broken him, she suspected. Kyra felt her old wariness return.

"Did they torture you for information about the Guild?" she asked.

"Did you come down simply to check on my well-being?" he asked. His eyes flickered over her dark clothing. "Why do I get the feeling that Malikel doesn't know you came to see me?"

Yes, James was still definitely all there.

"I don't have to answer to you anymore," Kyra said.

James actually laughed, though the laugh ended in a cough. "And yet, you're here. No, Kyra. If you've gone to this much trouble to speak to me, you want something from me. And unless you plan to add your own cuts to those your masters have decorated me with, then I'll have something from you in return. Starting with the real reason why you came."

Funny. Kyra had planned this break-in perfectly, from fashioning the keys to getting past the door guards. But here in this cell, her plans came up short. As she'd lain awake plotting, she'd known that she wanted to talk to James. But now she didn't have the words.

"You've not given me away," she said.

"Of course." James's eyes refocused on her face. "Your... surprising identity. Did you know what you were before the Demon Riders took you?"

Kyra didn't answer.

"I'll wager you didn't. You didn't have their bloodlust. And you still don't."

"You tried once to tell Malikel about me." She had only barely convinced Malikel that James was lying.

"And you want to know why I didn't continue to try," he finished for her. "It was a mistake on my part even to attempt the first time, and I should thank you for not letting me succeed. It might have turned them against you, but it would have gained me nothing more than short-lived satisfaction. Information is power in my trade, Kyra. I hold on to it until it gains me something."

"If you think you can blackmail me into letting you go," said Kyra, "you're wrong. I knew when I turned you in that I'd risk getting found out."

"And I believe you," he said calmly. "Is that the only reason you're here? To satisfy your curiosity about your good luck?"

It wasn't. Yet Kyra was reluctant to give the reason James was waiting for, to admit that there might have been some truth to his words all along. *The wallhuggers aren't your friends.* James wasn't either, but she would hear him out.

She rubbed her forearms, trying to scrub the dungeon's stink from her skin. "A lass was beaten by three noblemen." She couldn't bring herself to say Idalee. "Lord Agan's sons."

James leaned his head against the wall and stretched his arms within the confines of his chains. "They've been a problem for a while now." Kyra supposed she shouldn't be surprised that he knew their reputation. James had long maintained informants in the Palace, and she suspected she only knew a tiny fraction of what he had done as leader of the Assassins Guild. "And then what happened?" he asked.

"The magistrate pardoned them," she said, her fury returning as she spoke. "There was a courtyard full of witnesses, yet the magistrate said there wasn't enough evidence for a trial." She paused. "It's wrong."

"Are you surprised?"

Kyra didn't answer, and there was clear understanding in James's eyes at her silence.

"You think I'm evil," James finally said. "You cringe at the fact that I'd spill the blood of innocents to take down my enemies. But what you've refused to understand, and what you're resisting even now, is that there's no other way. The powerful do not let go of their positions so easily. Change doesn't occur without blood."

Blood. James had made sure there was plenty of that. "I won't become like you," said Kyra. "Burning down half the city to save it marks you just as guilty as the wallhuggers."

"Then why are you still here?"

To that, she had no answer.

James shifted his position. Pain flashed across his face, and it was a few more moments before he could speak again. "I didn't start out trying to destroy the city," he said. "I don't take pleasure in the pain of others."

In that, at least, Kyra believed him. There were some in the Guild who enjoyed violence—Bacchus, for one. Kyra had seen it on the few jobs they'd taken together. He'd smiled as he beat his victims, and it had frightened Kyra to the core. James was different. He was ruthless, and he tolerated people like Bacchus, but everything he did, he did for a reason.

"After Thalia died," he said, "I took possession of the Guild. It took me a year to weed out those who weren't loyal to me. I solidified my control, and then I considered what I wanted to do. For a long time, the Guild had become another tool of the wallhuggers. I put an end to that and thought, *Why not go further?* Who was it, after all, who decreed that the fatpurses should keep their positions? Why should they dictate how we live and how we die?"

"And that was when you started infiltrating the Palace," said Kyra.

"The wallhuggers don't pay attention to their servants nearly as well as they should. I learned much about the upper levels of Forge simply with careful bribes."

He'd learned much, but there had still been things he couldn't get to, like secret documents, trade schedules, and guard assignments. For that, he'd needed a thief who could get deep into the compound. He'd needed Kyra.

James continued. "At first I thought I would only go after the bad ones. The first wallhugger I targeted was named Hamel. He was the lowest kind of worm, and few people considered his death a loss to Forge. Yet folk suffered nonetheless when I killed him. Those who'd been in his employ went hungry that winter, and the political gaps left by Hamel's death were soon filled by another."

"Willem," Kyra guessed.

"He was already Head Councilman at the time, but he gained allies as those who'd looked to Hamel were cast afloat." James's gaze swept across the cell, as if he were viewing the myriad connections that held Forge together. "My point is, corruption in the city's not like a scab to be torn away. It's a tumor, spread throughout the body, and it grows back when you excise it. You can't remove a cancer without digging out healthy flesh."

"But what's the cost?" said Kyra. "What's the point of destroying the cancer if the body dies as well?"

"What's the point of having a body if it's riddled with disease?"

Kyra shook her head to dispel the headache that was starting to take root. "You can't mean that. You don't really want to raze the city to the ground."

"And you don't really believe me capable of obliterating the city." He locked his eyes on hers. "It's pointless to talk in extremes, because none of it will actually happen. But no matter how far we range with our philosophical fancies, the hard truth remains. You hold a blade now, Kyra, as does everyone who possesses power in this city. And every time you wield this blade, you must decide how deeply you wish to cut."

SEVEN

Tristam was in his quarters, getting changed after his morning rounds when someone knocked on his door. A servant of Malikel's bowed when Tristam answered.

"Sir Willem has called an emergency Council meeting at the tenth hour to discuss several Demon Rider attacks that occurred this morning. Your presence is required."

Demon Rider attacks? He immediately feared the worst. "Were the attacks at Brancel?" *Henril. Lorne.*

"No, milord. Sir Malikel requires your presence because of your expertise with the Demon Riders, not because of any connection to Brancel. You are to observe the meeting and be prepared to answer questions if called on."

For a moment, he was selfishly relieved, though the attacks in question must have been bad if they warranted an emergency Council meeting. "I'll be there."

The clock had chimed half past nine a short while ago, so he didn't have long. Tristam changed out of his plain tunic into more appropriate court finery—an embroidered silk tunic with breeches and soft leather boots—and headed out the door.

The Council Room antechamber was a large room in its own right, lined with smooth black marble decorated with gold accents. A crowd had already gathered in anticipation of the meeting. Tristam saw no sign of Malikel, but Kyra came through the door soon after he arrived. She wore a gown of wine-colored linen to accommodate the Council's dress expectations, though she no doubt still had at least one dagger strapped to her leg underneath. He knew she chose her dresses based on their sturdiness and how easily she could climb in them if needed. Her gaze drifted around the room, not quite focusing on anything, and Tristam had to call her name twice to get her attention. That was almost unheard of. Kyra was nothing if not alert.

She raised tired eyes to him as he approached. "Ho, Tristam."

"Are you all right?"

There was the slightest pause before she answered. "I'm fine. Just didn't sleep well last night."

He might have questioned her further, but a herald announced the beginning of the meeting, and the crowd filed through the double doors. On the far side of the main room was a raised platform where the full Council sat in two semicircular rows of tables. Observing benches lined the floor between the door and the Council seats, and Kyra and Tristam settled near the back with other observers of low rank.

Willem called the meeting to order, and a scribe took the stage. "Two farms and the guesthouse of one manor were attacked in the predawn hours. Two deaths have been reported thus far, and several more were injured."

Concerned murmurs spread throughout the crowd. Three

attacks in one morning was alarming indeed. Tristam thought back to the day he and his friend Jack had stumbled upon a farm in the midst of a raid. He still remembered the chaos, the fleeing people, the panicked bleats and bays of livestock. Jack had died that day at the hands of the Demon Rider Pashla and her companion.

The scribe finished speaking, and Willem took the stage. "This is the biggest threat that has faced the city since our war with Edlan twenty years ago." Willem was a convincing speaker when he wanted to be. He spoke with authority, punctuating his points with bold sweeps of his hand. "And our Defense Minister does nothing. The Demon Riders sleep safely in our forest and pillage our fields at their pleasure. What can possibly be your justification for this, Malikel?"

"The Demon Rider threat must be met with caution," said Malikel from his seat. His voice was level, though Tristam could sense anger just beneath. "I've explained this to the Council many times. The Demon Riders are not a threat like Parna or Edlan that we should simply throw our soldiers at them. They refuse to face us in open battle. They know the forest better than we do, and they're better at disappearing into its depths. Without a sound strategy, sending our soldiers to meet them would result in far more casualties than we currently suffer."

"You argue for a good strategy," said Willem. "Let's hear it, then."

"Our best course of action is to focus on defending our vulnerable farms and manors while we prepare our soldiers with new weapons and tactics. The Palace smithies are forging new spears as we speak, and our soldiers are learning new formations for forest combat. We secure our farms first. Then we start driving the Demon Riders back and establishing larger and larger defensible boundaries."

"And how long before we'd be rid of the barbarians?"

"We're already training private guard forces around Forge. The majority of our farms could be much better defended within a year."

"The majority, you say. But the barbarians would still plague our people."

"If you have a counter proposal," said Malikel, his voice tight with impatience, "let's hear it."

Willem straightened and slowly swept his eyes across the Council. "As Head Councilman, I'm not usually involved in directly planning the city defense, but in trying times, when demands outweigh what our Defense Minister is able to handle, I'm forced to take a more direct approach. I propose a systematic sweep of the forest with our soldiers."

Tristam frowned. That was a horrible idea. Willem should have known better.

"That's preposterous," said Malikel, rising to his feet. "We do not have nearly enough men to do this. It would be sending them to their deaths, one battalion at a time."

"You're right, Malikel, that as it stands we do not have enough troops to mount such an attack. But the laws of Forge give the Council authority to expand our defense forces from within the city during times of need."

Tristam's head snapped up at these words. Willem couldn't possibly mean . . .

"Are you suggesting conscripting soldiers from the city population?" said Malikel.

"Indeed, I am," said Willem. "Circumstances are dire enough."

"Dire enough to send untrained citizens to their deaths? Willem, the current raids are alarming, but even with the uptick in attacks, we still count the weekly casualties with one hand. If we take your strategy and go on an offensive with untrained and underarmed peasants, we could lose hundreds, if not more."

"What kind of city are we?" Willem's voice rang through the hall. "Did Forge become the great city it is by shrinking into the corner at the first sign of an enemy? By hiding like a mouse? Last month, our Defense Minister assured us the Demon Riders were a diminishing threat. Last night, we were called out of our beds by reports of not one, not two, but three attacks. What will next month bring? The only way to protect ourselves is to remove the threat now. Our neighboring cities have already taken steps to fight the barbarians. Edlan's people do not suffer the shame of sitting by while their farms are ravaged. Do we of Forge continue to be meek, or do we step up and show our strength?"

Kyra shifted uncomfortably. Tristam gave her hand a quick squeeze and received a grateful smile in response. Kyra hated the farm raids as much as anyone, but it was hard for her to hear people talk of Demon Riders as monsters and barbarians, to be reminded what kind of reaction she'd get if her secret was revealed.

Back on the platform, Willem raised his voice. "Answer me one question, Malikel. If we sweep the forest with the numbers I propose, given what you know about these clans, will we succeed in driving them out?"

There was a long silence as all eyes settled on Malikel. The Defense Minister stood with one hand on his table, staring down at it as if he meant to crush it by thought alone. "We have a reasonable chance at success," he said slowly. "But our casualties will be many times theirs, and the citizens of Forge would be bearing a burden that should rightly fall to the military."

"Let the Council decide where the burden should fall," said Willem. "I call for a vote."

Tristam leaned forward, his eyes fixated on the Council as Willem called each Councilman in turn to speak his vote. As the numbers fell evenly on each side, the air in the room became increasingly tense. When the last Council member gave his choice, Willem nodded. "The final tally is eleven for, eight against, and one abstain," he said. "The measure is passed."

Tristam stayed motionless as the scope of what had just happened sank in. When Willem formally ended the meeting, the room filled with the sounds of a hundred different conversations. He glanced at the stage to see Malikel in forceful dialogue with one of the Councilmen who had voted in support of Willem.

The crowd filed out, and Tristam waited with Kyra in the courtyard for Malikel. Servants were already running from the Council building, foregoing the pathways and running directly over the snow in their haste to carry their masters' messages. Councilmen and courtiers split off into groups, some huddled in quiet conversation, others shouting. When Malikel finally appeared, he was angrier than Tristam had ever seen him. Tristam got the impression that anyone in his way would have simply been knocked down.

"Follow me," he said.

Once they were in Malikel's study with the door closed, the Councilman turned to address them.

"Were you able to hear the proceedings?" he asked. When Kyra and Tristam indicated that they had, he continued. "Willem knew I wouldn't support a conscription of the citizenry. A similar thing was done in Minadel. It's how I became a soldier, and I've seen what happens when you throw peasants into battle with no training," said Malikel. "But the Council is scared, as is the nobility, and I'm bound by the oaths I've taken to uphold the will of the Council."

"Is there any way to overturn this?" asked Kyra.

"A vote this close can be brought up before the Council for reconsideration. But it can only be done once, and we cannot count on any of the other members changing their vote."

"What now, then?" asked Tristam.

Malikel pushed back the sleeves of his official's robes, though they fell right back to his wrists. "I will continue trying to sway my colleagues who voted with Willem. In the meantime, we do our best to prepare those who will be sent in. I'll have the smithies work as fast as they can. Tristam, I want you to help me develop training drills and formations for unskilled soldiers against these beasts."

"Yes, sir." He was already sifting through the possibilities. Basic spear work was essential. Any complex maneuvers would be too difficult, but perhaps some simple formations . . .

"Kyra," said Malikel.

She straightened. "Aye?"

"I need your help with the Demon Riders. I realize they've warned you to stay away, but your history with them still makes you better suited to approach them than anyone else in the city." There was something unnerving about the way Malikel looked at Kyra, and Tristam wasn't sure if he detected another layer of meaning behind his words. He wondered again how much the Defense Minister knew and felt a stab of guilt at deceiving him.

Malikel continued. "I need to make one more effort to negotiate peace. They've not been willing to talk to us before, but perhaps, if we impress on them what lies ahead, we can avoid mutual destruction."

Slowly, it dawned on Tristam what Malikel was asking. "You want to send Kyra as an emissary for peace? Sir, if I may speak freely, we have no reason to think we can trust any promises made by the Demon Riders." If Malikel had seen firsthand how the Makvani looked at humans, he would understand how naïve it was to try for peace.

A flicker of something passed over Kyra's face, but Malikel spoke before Tristam could give it more thought.

"In affairs of the city," Malikel said, "I will decide who is trustworthy."

Tristam bowed his head, and the Defense Minister turned again to Kyra. "Kyra, you're not sworn to me as a soldier or an emissary. I can't command you into the forest, given the risks. But if you are willing to go back to the forest once more, the city would be grateful."

Kyra met Malikel's gaze for a moment before she looked down again. "I'll have to think about it."

The Defense Minister dismissed them after that. Kyra left the compound, and Tristam worked his way through the still-buzzing courtyards back to his own quarters. To his surprise, an old courier of his father's waited outside his building. The man bowed as Tristam approached, and Tristam's fear for his family returned.

"Stanley," said Tristam. "Is all well at Brancel?"

"Your father and brothers are well, milord, though they fight hard. I carry a message from your father." The servant bowed again as he handed a parchment to Tristam. It was addressed in his father's unmistakable bold script.

"Thank you," Tristam said, breaking the seal. The letter inside was long, and he began to read.

◈ ❈ ◈

Despite Kyra's show of reluctance, she knew she'd go back to the forest. She'd been feeling the need to return, the same itch that had driven her out there the night the demon cat attacked her. Malikel's request was just the excuse she needed.

The city was abuzz with activity when she left the next morning. Word of the Council's new measure had gone out. Heralds made rousing speeches against the Demon Riders in the city squares, and many citizens declared they would volunteer to fight the menace. Kyra wondered how long this excitement would last once folk started dying. Word was that a few units would be recruited and deployed immediately to test new strategies and start securing the forest, with the main offensive to happen in a month.

Once Kyra left the city, she wasn't quite sure what to do. There was no point in trying to find the Demon Riders herself. She couldn't sneak up on a full-blooded demon cat. But she *could* go into the forest and make herself available to be found, and there was that caravan attack Jacobo the trader had mentioned, the one that had happened just above the upper waterfall. Kyra had wanted to see the place for herself before Idalee's beating drove it from her mind.

It took her a few hours to walk to the waterfall, and the sound of crashing waters guided her the last few steps of the way. Big blocks of ice were piled at the bottom, though water still flowed underneath. Kyra scrambled up a boulder-strewn track. There was a clearing at the top scattered with young trees, as one would expect from a campsite that had been abandoned a few years ago. Kyra's imagination kept her jumping as she wandered. Perhaps this scrap of wood sticking out of the snow had been a wagon wheel. Or maybe that glint of metal came from a wheel sprocket. But whenever she looked closer, it turned out to be a trick of the eye.

There were wildflowers here, tall stalks that came up to her waist with cone-shaped clusters of blue, pink, and purple blossoms. They were called forever sprays because they bloomed all year round. Their perfume evoked a memory in which she stumbled through a field of these flowers. In her memory, the flowers grew as high as her head.

"What are you looking for?" a low woman's voice asked from behind her.

Kyra suppressed a shudder, and she slowly turned around.

A middle-aged Demon Rider woman stood ten paces away,

scrutinizing Kyra with a stare that could have sliced glass. She was beautiful, with large dark eyes and an arched nose, an angular face, and long black hair with the slightest hints of gray. She wore the familiar wraparound tunic and leggings of the Demon Riders, though the leather was tanned a darker color than the ones Kyra had seen. Behind her stood a Makvani man about Leyus's age. His features were milder and less stern compared with the woman's, and his gaze held more interest than suspicion.

"You're the halfblood, are you not?" demanded the woman in heavily accented speech. "The one who lets Leyus fight her battles."

Kyra backed away, unable to make sense of the woman's words. The Makvani man laid a hand on the woman's arm.

"She doesn't recognize you, Zora. You were in your fur."

The woman was the one who'd attacked her, then. The one Leyus had stopped from killing her. Kyra backed up, ready to reach for her dagger. If they tried to change, she would have an opening.

"Why are you here?" asked Zora.

Kyra did her best to stand tall. "I've got a message from the city for Leyus."

"I don't mean why you are in the forest. I want to know why you are in this clearing."

This clearing? Why would they care why she was in this clearing?

The man cut in. "We bear you no ill will." Given the glare Zora shot at him, Kyra thought he should amend that to "no ill will, for now."

Just then, a new voice spoke from behind her. Kyra couldn't understand the words, but she recognized the speaker, and she felt a sliver of cautious hope. She turned around.

Pashla looked exactly the same as Kyra remembered: tawny-yellow hair spilling over her shoulders, proud bearing, and a way of looking at Kyra that made her wonder, always, what the clanswoman was thinking. Their eyes met for a moment, and Kyra breathed easier when she saw no animosity in Pashla's gaze.

"Zora, Havel," Pashla said, nodding to each in turn. Then, to Kyra's surprise, Pashla ran one finger down the front of her neck in the Makvani bow of respect that Kyra had only ever seen Pashla give to Leyus. Zora asked Pashla a question in the Makvani tongue, which Pashla answered respectfully. Zora took another look at Kyra, then turned abruptly and left. Havel's gaze lingered on Kyra for a moment longer before he followed Zora.

Kyra stared after them, wondering what had happened. Pashla stood next to her, calmly watching the two Demon Riders disappear, and Kyra found she didn't know what to say. Pashla had nursed her back to health after James almost killed her, and she'd been deeply hurt when Kyra turned her back on the clan to return to Forge. Over the past weeks, Kyra had often wished to see Pashla again, to somehow make amends, but she didn't know where to begin.

"Be careful with Zora and Havel. They are new to this side of the Aerins, and they do not look as kindly on humans as Leyus does." She spoke with the same patient inflection she'd used when teaching Kyra the ways of the forest.

Kyra fought a perverse urge to laugh. If Leyus was a shining example of human–Makvani relations, then Forge was in deep trouble indeed. But Pashla's other words concerned her more. "What do you mean, they are new to this side of the mountains?"

"Have you not noticed? A second clan has crossed the mountains. Zora and Havel are their leaders."

Pashla was looking at her as if she had missed something patently obvious, and Kyra couldn't help but wonder if she had. Did Havel and Zora look any different from the others? Of course, a new clan would explain the recent increase in attacks. "They are in contact with your clan?"

"They used to be clan mates with Leyus. Leyus and Havel are like brothers."

Kyra took a moment to ponder Pashla's words. Things had been bad enough with one clan. With two... She had to try to make peace.

"Pashla, I'm here on behalf of the Palace," she said.

The effect on Pashla was immediate. Her expression closed off, and her voice when she spoke again was cool. "What errand do they send you on?"

Pashla's reaction stung, but there were more important things at stake. "I need to speak with Leyus. The clan is in danger. The city means to mount an attack, but our Defense Minister wishes to negotiate peace."

"Leyus will not speak with you. He has no desire to negotiate with humans."

"Even if they outnumber his people by a hundred-fold? It would cost the city greatly to destroy you, but they could do it."

"That's enough," said Pashla, a hint of anger in her voice. "I didn't think you'd be so foolish as to deliver threats while in our midst."

Kyra fell silent. She had gone about this all wrong. "I'm sorry. I don't mean to deliver threats. And I wish I wasn't here on Palace business. I wish we didn't have to be enemies." Truth was, Kyra had missed Pashla—the long walks they'd taken in the forest, the clanswoman's patience and gentle touch. Was it too much to hope for forgiveness? "You taught me so much, and I owe you more than I could ever repay." Immediately, she felt embarrassed and very small, but it was too late to unsay her words.

The clanswoman studied her again, her gaze gliding over Kyra with the serenity of falling snow. "Your wounds have healed well."

Kyra put a hand to her stomach. "I just have a light scar. I don't feel it at all."

Pashla motioned for Kyra to lift the edge of her tunic so she could see. The clanswoman ran a finger over the scar. It was an odd sensation, Pashla's touch on her toughened scar tissue.

"Time forms bonds," Pashla finally said. "Those we grow up with, those we live with, we become connected to them, even if they're different from us."

Pashla's words were an olive branch, the clanswoman's way of saying that she somewhat understood Kyra's choice to return to Forge, if not completely. "Thank you," Kyra said. When Pashla didn't respond right away, Kyra found her courage and kept going. "Does it have to be one or the other? Why must I choose a side? I've been coming back into the forest by myself. I know it's foolish, but I can't stay away."

"I know you've been coming," said Pashla.

Kyra stopped. "You know?"

"Of course we watch those who come from the city." The clanswoman broke a forever spray off its stalk and rolled it between her fingers. "Your blood calls to you, does it?"

Calls to her? She hadn't thought of it that way, but it seemed apt.

"I can't stop thinking about what it was like to change shape," said Kyra. "Though I've not been brave enough to do it."

The wind blew snow off the trees around them, and Pashla dusted off her sleeves. "I suppose it can't be avoided. The temptation is too great. You cannot silence something that is yours by right."

Was Pashla just expressing sympathy? Or was she actually . . . Kyra was afraid to breathe for fear that her hope would be extinguished. Just the thought that she might experience her other form again . . .

The clanswoman tossed the wildflower to the ground. "If you must change, then better to do it with my help."

Kyra's breath rushed out of her.

It was late enough in the morning that the sunlight shone straight into the clearing. Pashla turned her face to its rays for a moment, eyes closed, before turning again to Kyra. "The sun is warm today. Take off your tunic, your trousers, and anything else that will tear. You can keep your cloak to block the wind. Once you are in your fur, you won't feel the cold at all."

"Right now?" This was exactly what she'd been hoping for, but somehow she hadn't expected the lesson to start immediately.

"Do you have somewhere to be? I do not know when we will cross paths again."

She was right, of course. Kyra gathered her courage. "I don't have anywhere to be," she said. And she reached to untie her belt.

The first few tries, she couldn't go through with it. As she stood there, eyes closed with a cloak wrapped around her and the cold breeze whipping at her bare feet and ankles, Kyra concentrated and found the sense of her other form. She nudged it, coaxing it like a small flame, feeling it burn stronger. But when she sensed it reaching the point of overflow, Kyra drew back and opened her eyes again.

Pashla watched her. After the third time, she simply said, "Do not be afraid."

Kyra nodded and closed her eyes again. This time she didn't stop.

It was just as she remembered. The spreading warmth in her limbs, the sense of melting and growing, her fur forcing itself through her skin and making her arms tingle. She threw off her cloak as her limbs stretched and her muscles thickened. Her vision darkened for a moment, and when it returned, everything was clear. So very clear.

Pashla stood in front of her, still in her skin. The clanswoman held herself with her muscles relaxed and her hands down by her sides. While Kyra's previous transformation had been in the heat of battle, this time her feral instinct was muted. She could still feel its presence, a constant readiness for a fight that hovered in the back of her mind. But she was far more interested in the world around her. The wind, so bitingly cold a few moments before, now blew ripples in her fur and raised a tickling sensation along her back. She bent down to smell the wildflowers. The scents were heady, almost too strong. And such vivid colors. Kyra sneezed, then stepped around Pashla. The snow's coolness seeped through the tough pads of her feet.

Behind her, Pashla spoke. Kyra ignored her, but Pashla persisted, and Kyra finally took the effort to pay more attention. She found she could make sense of her words if she tried hard enough. Pashla was telling her that she'd done well.

A new scent reached her nostrils. Unlike Pashla's words, the meaning of this new smell was immediately clear. There was a deer upwind, just a short sprint away.

"Kyra, stay here."

Kyra shook off the command like water from her fur and started off toward the scent.

"No, Kyra." A hand on her flank, and a firmer command this time. Kyra spun around and slashed at Pashla, who jumped back, stumbling. As Pashla regained her balance, Kyra whipped around and sprinted toward her prey. She dove into the trees at the edge of the meadow, jumping over rocks and dodging branches. The scent was as clear to her as a path she could follow. Ahead of her, she caught a glimpse of the deer and smelled its alarm. Birds took flight at her approach, wing beats like drums against the air, their warning calls sharp and bold. Kyra ran faster.

Something heavy landed on her back and knocked her paws out from under her. The weight was so strong, so sudden, that Kyra realized it must have fallen from a tree. Kyra writhed and twisted to face this new attacker, striking out with her claws. Her opponent kept out of her way and opened cuts on Kyra's forelimbs with her teeth. It stung, and the pain infuriated her.

The deer was getting away. She could hear its light hoof-beats fading, and she roared with frustration. Her attacker—Pashla, it was Pashla, Kyra realized—was strong, and Kyra couldn't get the best of her. She tired, and it gradually became clear to Kyra that they shouldn't be fighting at all. She stopped moving and let Pashla pin her to the ground.

As Kyra's breath slowed and her blood cooled, she felt the sense of her fur waning. She let herself melt back into her skin.

Pashla, her own form still shifting, pulled Kyra to her feet. "Get dressed before you freeze."

It was a cold run back to her clothes. Kyra wrapped her cloak around herself to block the wind, then reached with stiff fingers for her trousers and tunic.

Pashla joined her. "You need control. But it was not too bad."

"I'm sorry I slashed at you."

"If I'm slow enough to let some young cub touch me, then I deserve it."

Kyra finished dressing and rubbed the heat back into her limbs.

"I almost envy you," said Pashla after a while.

"Me?"

"You know the ways of the humans, and now you're learning ours."

Her hands were starting to regain some warmth. "I'm surprised you'd want to learn about the humans."

"I've no interest in being human. But it would be useful to know how to move in their world. With your mixed blood, you're able to blend in anywhere."

Kyra remembered that Pashla had been the liaison between James and the Makvani, back when the clan had been allied with the Guild. It made sense that Pashla would value advantages like this. Though Kyra didn't exactly see herself as being able to blend in anywhere. On the contrary, half the Palace thought her a criminal, the Demon Riders didn't want her in the forest, and even the gutter rats didn't trust her anymore. It was a fine line, she thought, between being able to blend in everywhere and nowhere.

Kyra left the forest a short while later. And though she had failed in her mission, Kyra felt hopeful. She'd spoken to Pashla again, and the clanswoman had forgiven her. Perhaps it was selfish of her to be relieved when the city was still under threat, but Kyra couldn't help feeling that a weight had come off her shoulders.

There remained plenty of energy in the city when she returned. Kyra skirted past the busy streets and squares toward home, avoiding the crowds that still loitered in the public spaces.

Lettie was not home yet—Tristam had taken her to see Idalee that morning—but Flick sat waiting at their table. Kyra hadn't bothered to give him an extra key; he just picked the lock when he so desired. But it was rare to see him waiting at their place when no one was there.

"Flick," said Kyra. "You're here early."

He wasn't smiling as he tossed a sheet of parchment on the table. Kyra slid it closer and picked it up. Her stomach dropped.

"A notice of conscription already?" she asked.

"Looks like I'm a lucky member of the early units," said Flick.

Kyra took the parchment and turned it over, as if she could find something in the back that would mark it false. Her stomach churned. Suddenly, her inability to speak to Leyus today seemed a much graver failure. "Of all the folk in the city, what are the chances they would pick you?"

Flick's voice was humorless when he responded. "That's what I wondered myself. I don't suppose you've offended anyone in the Palace recently?"

Kyra was tempted to crumple the parchment in her hands. "I can't believe Willem would do this."

"You've got enemies in high places, Kyra."

Kyra had seen soldiers die at the hands of the Makvani before. The thought of Flick—jovial, charming Flick—facing off with the barbarians was unbearable. Kyra racked her mind for any way to change this. "Your father. Can he do anything?"

"He wouldn't even acknowledge my dying ma's existence, much less mine. He won't do anything on my behalf."

"I'm so sorry, Flick," Kyra said. She meant every word. "I'll speak with Malikel as soon as I can."

It was becoming an all-too-familiar routine, sitting in Malikel's study and filtering through the truth for what she could reveal. Kyra wasn't a natural liar. Flick could spin fifteen different tales to twenty different people and keep the details straight, all the while maintaining a face that convinced the most skeptical of listeners that he was the soul of earnestness. It was different for Kyra. She found it hard to keep track of the lies as they piled on top of each other. Plus Malikel wasn't exactly the best audience for someone engaging in selective truth-telling. The Defense Minister listened carefully—very carefully—to anyone who spoke to him, from fellow Councilmen to lowly serving maids.

"Pashla found me after I was in the forest awhile," she said. "She wouldn't let me speak to Leyus, but I did learn that a new clan's crossed the mountains and that the leaders of the clan are very close with Leyus."

Malikel leaned forward. "A new clan? Did you get any sense of their numbers?"

"I saw only the two leaders."

"Judging from the uptick in attacks though, we can assume they are numerous. Did you speak with Pashla about anything else?"

"No," she lied. Then Kyra gathered her courage. "Sir, there was one other thing I wanted to talk to you about. I understand that a few early units have been conscripted already for Willem's forest sweep."

Malikel indicated his desk. It was covered with maps and diagrams of Forge and its surrounding forest, some with symbols representing soldiers in battle formations. "I will be training the new units myself. Hopefully, these early groups will give us a better overall strategy when we bring in the rest of the new conscripts."

"Were the new units chosen at random?" Kyra asked.

"Yes. Why do you ask?"

"Flick, my good friend, was conscripted yesterday."

Malikel had reached out to take hold of a map, but upon hearing Kyra's words, he drew his hand back again and fixed a keen gaze on Kyra. "And you suspect that it wasn't an accident."

"Aye, sir."

Malikel folded his hands in front of him. He didn't speak for a while, and his face darkened with every passing moment of silence. Just when Kyra was wondering if he'd ever speak again, he did. "I'll be honest. There are many ways an official could influence who was chosen. And many ways an official could then cover his tracks."

"Is there anything that can be done? I'm not asking for special treatment for Flick," she hurriedly added. "It's just that, if someone had picked him on purpose to get at me..."

"Willem, you mean," said Malikel. "We can speak plainly in this study."

"After what happened with the Agan brothers, he warned me not to overstep my bounds. He might be sending me a warning."

The Defense Minister raised his hand. "Or it could be chance—I'm not saying it is, but you don't have any proof. If it was indeed Willem, it was a clever move on his part. I've built my entire career on fighting corruption. If I were to specially excuse one of the conscripted soldiers, it would undermine my entire position." He raised a hand again before Kyra could object. "That's not to say I cannot help you at all. But I would need proof that Willem had something to do with Faxon's original conscription." Malikel used Flick's real name, which he had learned when the Palace had sheltered him from the Assassins Guild.

"Proof?" Kyra echoed. How could she get proof?

"I'll have some of my men investigate," said Malikel. "And you would do well to avoid attracting any more of Willem's attention in the meantime. I know you might be tempted to take this matter into your own hands, but any misstep on your part could make things worse for your friend."

"Yes, sir," she said. She wasn't sure if Malikel really believed she'd sit back while Flick's life was at risk, but she saw no use in arguing.

It took her a moment to realize that Malikel was looking intently at her. "Kyra," he said, and there was something in his voice that demanded attention.

Kyra snapped to attention. Had her previous response been too flippant?

"There are several skills that a good Defense Minister needs on a regular basis. One is an ability to judge the truth and see through anything that obfuscates it. When facts have been kept from me, it's almost always better if the one who's been hiding these things reveals them first." Kyra had the distinct impression that they were no longer talking about Flick.

"I'm charged with upholding the law, but I also don't consider the law a rigid thing. Character comes into account, as do the specific circumstances. We can't always control our past."

"I don't understand, sir." Who knew what the expression on her face was right now?

"I cannot have someone under me who only entrusts me with partial information. I understand it is hard to throw your fate in with the Palace when there are so many people, like Willem, who may not look on you as their equal. But those people will always exist. In the end, you must make a decision. Either you decide that you can accomplish something for this city and you commit fully to the job. Or you leave."

"Leave the Palace?"

"Leave the city," Malikel said.

Her mouth had gone completely dry. He knew about her bloodlines, or at least suspected. Kyra licked her lips in a failed attempt to get some moisture on them. "Can I ask a question, sir?" she said.

"You may."

"Why don't you return to Minadel? You could be respected there, live a normal life without folk looking at you sideways because you're a foreigner."

Another man might have thought her question a deflection, but Malikel seemed to take it in stride.

"I was a common mercenary in Minadel. I would have amounted to nothing there. It was here in Forge where fate smiled on me. That was why I stayed at first, though you are correct that if I were to leave now, the Minadan court would welcome my expertise and experience." He turned to look at a map on the wall, his gaze lingering on his old homeland. "But I have unfinished work in Forge. There are times when I want to wring the necks of my colleagues at the Council, but minds are slowly changing."

"If I may speak plainly, sir, hundreds of folk might lose their lives in the forest before minds in the Palace are finished changing."

"If one wants to live under the rule of law, one must accept both the good and the bad. I don't pretend to have perfect solutions, but think on what I've said. About everything." Malikel turned his attention back to the parchment on his desk. "You may go."

It took a moment for Kyra to realize that she'd been dismissed. She managed a stately walk down the rest of the corridor, but once she got to the staircase, her nerves won out and she bolted down.

Outside, the Palace staff went about their business as usual. A contingent of Red Shields marched past on their way to replace the gate guards. A nobleman strolled behind them, dictating thoughts to a courtier who scribbled them down on a slate. Kyra slowed and pushed back a strand of hair that had fallen from her ponytail. Maybe she should tell Malikel the truth of what she was. He was a fair man, and she trusted him to look beyond her bloodlines to what she'd done for Forge. But the thing was, her actions hadn't exactly been impeccable. Would they be enough to deem her not a threat? And even if Malikel himself decided he trusted her, the Council was something different altogether. There was no way they would be able to look past what she was.

It was with immense relief that Kyra spotted Tristam crossing the courtyard. She ran to him, desperately needing to talk this over. Kyra started to say his name, but the expression on his face gave her pause. Tristam stopped in his tracks, and Kyra would have sworn that he looked guilty. Belatedly, Kyra noticed the strange path he took. He hadn't been heading to the building that housed Malikel's study. Instead, he'd been walking toward one of the smaller administrative structures. And he wasn't in uniform. Instead, he was once again in full court finery.

"I've not seen much of you these few days," Kyra said. "Have you been busy?"

He paused for just a moment, looking very tired. "I've been performing some duties for my father."

"Oh," Kyra said. "Everything is all right, I hope?"

"They're fine. I mean—" He wasn't exactly avoiding her eyes, but he wasn't looking straight at her either. "They're not fine, but that's to be expected. We've been having some troubles at our manor with Demon Riders. My father asked me to spend some time here negotiating on the family's behalf."

Tristam rarely mentioned his duties to his family. As far as Kyra knew, his older brothers bore the majority of the responsibility. "Do the negotiations have something to do with the Demon Rider attacks?"

"There's a family from Parna offering to help us with our defenses." He rubbed his temples. "How have you been? How is Idalee?"

"Idalee's doing much better. Ilona says she might be able

to come home in a few…" Kyra trailed off. Tristam's thoughts were clearly elsewhere. "Tristam?"

"I'm sorry, Kyra. I'm a bit distracted." He paused again. "I should go. There's a courtier expecting me."

He continued on his way before Kyra finished saying good-bye.

EIGHT

"How much do you hate me, James?" Kyra stood at the opposite side of his cell, shifting her weight from one foot to the other when she tired. She had no desire to lean against the damp moldy walls.

James looked slightly better this time. None of his wounds looked fresh. Perhaps everyone was too busy dealing with the Demon Rider threat to spend much time on him. "Were I free right now, I would slit your throat, though I'd regret having to do so."

"That's sentimental of you."

"You let your talents go to waste. I've always thought that, even before I found out what you really are."

She shifted uncomfortably. Insults and threats, she was prepared for. Praise, though, felt wrong. "There's to be a war," she said. "Willem wants to launch an all-out attack against the Demon Riders, and he's conscripting soldiers from the city to do it."

"Why tell me this?"

"It will be a bloodbath. Hundreds will die, most of them

from the poor. And meanwhile, Willem will be marked a hero." *More people will die than perished in James's Demon Rider raids.* That thought disturbed her in more ways than one.

A guard's footsteps came through the door of the cell. James looked on in amusement as Kyra froze, then relaxed as the guard walked away. "There's more," he said. "You'd not come to me again simply out of concern for your city. They've conscripted someone important to you, haven't they?"

She didn't answer, but Kyra guessed that her thoughts were plain on her face. James gave a satisfied nod. "It's always personal. You can handle the abuse when it happens to others, or at least you don't care enough to make an extra effort to stop it. But when they take someone you care about, that's when you're willing to put yourself on the line."

It was frightening sometimes how right he could be. First Idalee, then Flick. And each time, Kyra became willing to do just a little bit more. Was this what had happened with James? Kyra thought about Thalia, the mysterious girl whom James had fallen in love with, and who had died at a nobleman's hand. How much of what James had done was because of her?

"Do you still think about Thalia?" The anonymity of the dungeon made it easier to ask such questions.

For a long moment, he didn't respond, and Kyra wondered if she'd inadvertently ended the conversation. The only sound in the room was the occasional drip of water somewhere in the darkness.

"Every day," James finally said. As he spoke, Kyra caught a hint of fatigue in his voice, true exhaustion that for a moment was written all over the lines of his body.

"What would she think of everything you've done?"

James lifted his head, his eyes regaining their steely focus. "We'll never know, will we?"

That answer hung between them, heavy with its implications. There was an entire lost lifetime in those words. Decades in which a woman Kyra had never met might have loved, fought, and grown old. Kyra realized that this was one story she would never know.

Finally James shifted. "I tire of this conversation. Tell me what you came for."

"You've got spies in the Palace," said Kyra. "I know you do. If I knew more about what Willem was doing, if I could find something against him, I might stop this."

"If you wanted my help, mayhap you shouldn't have handed me over to the Palace."

"We're not allies, James, but we have a common enemy. I'm offering you another chance to bring Willem down. You said you didn't give me up to the Palace because you might still get something from me. This could be it. Mayhap I can do something with that information to serve both of us."

His eyes were shrewd as he considered her offer. "Everything about my spies stays with you. No word of this goes to Malikel or any wallhugger."

Kyra thought for a moment. "I can do that."

"Make no mistake, Kyra. You'll owe me for this. Someday I'll call in a favor from you, and I'll hold you to it."

Kyra stepped back, widening the space between them. "There are some things I won't do. You know that."

"I know your limits," said James. The way he said it made

it sound like a weakness. "I won't push you to break them. But you'll be indebted to me. I want your word."

Dealing with James was never straightforward. He was so quick, so deadly most of the time that it was easy to think violence his only weapon. But you couldn't discount his subtler skills. He understood people, knew how to assess their strengths and manipulate their motivations. On the surface, he was asking for a promise he couldn't enforce, but Kyra knew better than to make such a vow lightly. She didn't know his whole game. She never did, but that was a risk she would take.

"I won't help you escape," said Kyra. "But you have my word that I will repay you within the limits of my conscience."

James scrutinized Kyra, and she stared right back at him. Finally he nodded. "I've an informant in Willem's household. He's a servant named Orvin, and he's good at overhearing things. I pay in silver for each useful piece of information. He's a tall man with dark brown hair that's thinning at the front. About forty years of age, and he wears a tunic with Willem's family crest when he's on the Palace grounds. Go talk to him."

Kyra asked one of Malikel's servants about a man named Orvin in Willem's household. The man did, in fact, exist. After a couple of days discreetly watching the pathways leading to Willem's quarters, Kyra spotted him. When she tailed him home, she saw that he lived on the first floor of a boardinghouse in the merchant district. Kyra counted at least six children when she peeked in the windows.

Now that she had him, the question was when and how to approach him. The Palace was too dangerous, and surprising him in his house seemed too threatening. Kyra watched his door that night and followed him as he left the next morning. Luckily, he didn't head straight for the Palace but instead went to the markets. That would be as good a place as any. Kyra pulled her cloak over her head and sped up until she fell in step with him. The man was deep in thought, and it took a while for him to notice her. He stopped in his tracks.

"James told me he paid you in silver. That right?" Kyra said.

Stark fear crossed his face.

"I in't planning on turning you in," she said quickly, worried that she would have to grab him to keep him from bolting. "Otherwise you'd already be in the dungeons. But I'd like your help, and I can pay for it."

The man squinted at her, trying to see beneath her cloak. "Who are you?"

Kyra supposed she didn't look or sound like anyone from the Palace or the Guild. Marketplace shoppers brushed past them, and the shouts of vendors made it hard to hear. She jerked her head toward a nearby alleyway. "Best for both of us to be out of sight." He hesitated to follow her, and Kyra sighed. "You and I can have this chat out here or in the alley. Your choice." The look he gave her wasn't kind, but he followed her to the back street. It was empty and darker than the thoroughfare. The smell of rot that always plagued alleyways near the markets was dampened by the cold. Kyra glanced around, checking to make sure there were no windows. She dropped her hood.

Fear crossed Orvin's face again. "You're Malikel's woman."

It looked like her days of anonymity were over. "I've sworn no oaths to Malikel, and he doesn't know I'm here. I just want some information."

"And if you don't get it, will you turn me in?"

She had to think before she answered. Blackmail would have been easy, and certainly tempting, but she shook her head. "I won't betray a city man to the wallhuggers without good reason. But I'm guessing that you've no love for Willem, if you've sold information to James before."

His stance lost a bit of its defensive tilt. "I'll have you know that I didn't choose this path lightly," he finally said. "I have seven mouths to feed, and His Grace is stingy with his wealth.

You're common-born like me. You know what it's like to be under them. If it comes out that I've betrayed the Palace, my family will starve."

"I know," said Kyra.

He let out a resigned breath. "What do you want to know?"

"Willem's pushing a strategy against the Demon Riders that's almost certain to end in many deaths. I'm looking for any weakness on his part that I might be able to use against him."

Orvin's eyes showed clear understanding as he took in her words. "Willem's ambitious, I'll give him that. He has a vision of Forge as a bastion of greatness—what Parna has done, but bolstered with our greater numbers." He indicated Kyra. "You yourself have benefited from Willem's ambition. The Palace healers are some of the best in this part of the world, and it was Willem who invested in their training. Of course, gains made by the more refined layers of society are paid for by the masses. This Demon Rider offensive is just the latest. Glory for the city, paid for by the blood of soldiers on the ground." He threw a quick glance over his shoulder and lowered his voice. "I can tell you this. Willem has been receiving private messengers late at night, about once a week. They come into the Palace past midnight, when the main gates are closed."

"What messages do they bear?" asked Kyra.

He shook his head. "The meetings are closed, with only Willem and the messengers. I wouldn't even have known about them had I not been paying extra attention to His Grace's movements. But he would not receive the messengers in such secrecy if he had nothing to hide."

She made note of his words. "One other thing. I suspect Willem might be making changes in the conscription lists. A good friend of mine was in the first conscripted unit, and it seems too much a coincidence. Do you know anything about that?"

"It wouldn't surprise me," said Orvin. "But I've heard nothing of it, though that kind of evidence would be hard to find. You'd have to track down whichever scribe he persuaded to change the lists."

That was disappointing, but Kyra was marginally familiar with the Palace's roster of scribes from all the time she'd spent stealing Palace records. She could look into some of the more likely suspects. "And what about at court? Does Willem have any new allies or enemies?"

"He's never been a friend of the Defense Minister, as you surely know. The rivalry seems more pronounced lately after Malikel was voted Second to the Head Councilman last month."

"That's right," said Kyra. It had happened shortly after Kyra started working for Malikel, and it meant that Malikel would become Head Councilman if something were to happen to Willem. "But Willem couldn't possibly think that Malikel would consider foul play, would he?" said Kyra.

"No, I don't think Willem worries about assassination. But Malikel's been pushing a good number of controversial measures—a law was passed last week requiring landlords to wait two months before evicting a tenant. Changes like these tend to be unpopular amongst the nobility who form the core of Willem's support. So Willem's been attempting to undermine

Malikel's competence. He might hope, for example, that your friend's early conscription into the army would distract you from Malikel's assignments."

"By making me chase scribes instead of pursuing peace with the Demon Riders?" Kyra asked, chagrined.

"Aye. And the Brancel marriage negotiations are another example. Willem's voiced his support, and the only reason he'd do so would be to hinder Malikel."

Brancel marriage negotiations? Orvin had brought it up in such an offhand way, as if he expected her to already know about it. She grasped for something to say that would get more details out of him. "But would Willem really undermine Forge's war efforts just to hurt Malikel?"

Orvin shrugged. "It'll be a bloodbath either way. A few more deaths won't matter. And Malikel's plenty competent. If your friend Tristam were to marry, it would take him away from Forge for the duration of the nuptial preparations. Malikel would lose Tristam's help, but it probably wouldn't change the overall outcome."

Orvin kept talking, but his words became like buzzing in her ears. *Marriage negotiations. For Tristam.* Kyra was vaguely aware that she needed to say something, to pretend that what she'd heard was nothing new to her.

Orvin trailed off and squinted at her, and Kyra wondered if her attempt at a calm expression had worked at all. "That's useful information," she said. Before Orvin could speak again, she took out a bag of coins and pressed them into his hand. "I can't pay as well as James, but I hope this will help."

The pouch disappeared under his cloak with a smoothness

that spoke of experience. "I'll keep watching, and I'll send word if I learn anything else," he said.

"Thank you," said Kyra. Somehow, she maintained her composure until Orvin had disappeared from view.

It was ironic how the conversation with Orvin had turned out. Kyra had expected to surprise him, had in fact worried that the shock would scare him away. But instead, Orvin had quickly adjusted to his circumstances, and Kyra was the one left in the alleyway, reeling at his words.

It made sense now, when she thought back to her past few days with Tristam. The endless meetings, the courtiers, his evasiveness at her questions.

Why hadn't he told her? The reasonable part of her recognized that she had no right to be upset. She was the one who had cut things off in the first place. And yet . . .

Kyra dug her fingernails into her palm. Perhaps Orvin was wrong. How well could a turncoat servant be trusted? And regardless of whether the news was true or false, she couldn't stay here and flounder. Ilona had sent word this morning that Idalee was ready to return home, and Kyra had promised to come get her.

She saw no sign of Tristam on her way to Ilona's patient room, for which she was grateful. Idalee was already dressed and waiting for her, looking subdued but ready to go. The girl's arm was in a sling. She was thinner than she'd been before, and her coloring was still pale, but Idalee was in far better shape than she'd been when she came in. Kyra gave the girl a careful hug.

"I'm glad you're better," she whispered.

"Idalee should be fine to walk home," said Ilona. "Just make sure she doesn't push her body past her limits."

Idalee's grip on Kyra's hand tightened as they left the herb-scented safety of Ilona's room and made their way down the stairs. The girl faltered at the building's main entrance.

"Are they here?" Idalee asked.

It took Kyra a moment to realize whom Idalee was talking about, and when she did, she felt like the worst friend in the world. Here she'd been preoccupied about whether she'd run into Tristam, when she really should have been making sure that Santon and his brothers were nowhere in sight for Idalee's departure. "I didn't notice them on the way in," she said. "We'll go quickly."

The girl's features strengthened into resolve, but her eyes remained haunted, and it tugged at Kyra's heart. This was the girl who'd thought nothing of attacking boys twice her size in order to protect Lettie, and now she was frightened even to cross a Palace courtyard. Kyra did her best to dispel the hopeless anger building in her chest. It would do Idalee no good.

There was no sign of Lord Agan's sons as they stepped out onto the path. "All right so far?" Kyra asked.

Idalee nodded. Since they couldn't walk quickly, Kyra pulled Idalee to the side to let two noblewomen bundled in furs go past. When they stepped back onto the path, Idalee said, "Look there!"

Kyra's eyes snapped to follow Idalee's gaze, her nerves keying up as she scanned the grounds for Santon. She didn't know whether to laugh or cry when she saw that it was Tristam whom Idalee had seen, coming out of the same administrative structure he'd been hurrying to a few days before. By now, he'd turned to walk toward them, taking away Kyra's initial hope that they might have passed unseen. Funny how a simple piece of information could change everything. The fine tunic that Kyra had admired before now seemed ostentatious. And the hint of guilt she thought she'd detected a few days ago now permeated every single movement he made.

"Idalee," said Tristam. "I'm glad to see you on your feet."

Idalee curtsied. "Ilona says I'm out of danger's way now."

"Are the two of you going home?" he asked.

"Malikel gave me the day to see Idalee settled," Kyra said. "And how are you, Tristam? Still negotiating with the family in Parna?" *Who is she? How much money does her family have?* She wasn't sure how good a job she did of keeping her voice neutral, but Tristam seemed too distracted to notice.

"Yes, and it's taking a while. They're an old family. Old money, lots of influence. They control a large private guard force." He spoke the last part as if it pained him.

It was falling into place far more easily than Kyra wanted. The family from Parna had offered to help defend Brancel Manor. Of course they'd want something in return, like a permanent alliance with the family. Kyra felt a pang in her gut. If what Orvin said was true, then Tristam was lying to her, or at the very least deliberately hiding the truth.

She didn't know what to do. Kyra couldn't confront him with Idalee right there. Even if she and Tristam had been alone,

Kyra didn't know if she was ready. She gave Tristam her best attempt at a smile. "We should be getting home. I wish you progress on your negotiations."

Unexpectedly, Tristam took her hand. "It's good to see you, Kyra," he said, with more fervency than those words usually warranted. "Both of you."

Kyra stood stock-still, unable to react at first. Then she carefully extricated her hand from his. "Have a good day," she said, and left, pulling Idalee after her.

Kyra wondered if James ever got used to the dungeon's smell. The stink faded after the first few minutes, but it never quite disappeared. Though, as she looked at the fresh bruises on James's face, she realized that the smell would be the least of his worries.

"Did you make contact with Orvin?" he asked.

"He told me Willem's taking private messengers in the middle of the night. I'm going to try and find out what they're for." She deliberated a bit before asking her next question. "How reliable is Orvin? Had he ever jumped to false conclusions?"

"Everything from Orvin's always been accurate," said James. "He's very keen on the affairs of noblemen."

That was good for her mission, though not for the selfish part of her that still hoped Orvin was wrong about Tristam.

A guard's footfalls sounded in the corridor, and Kyra wondered if she should go. There was nothing more that she needed from James tonight. Actually, she hadn't needed to come see him at all, but she found herself reluctant to leave. Somehow, over the past weeks, the prison cell of her enemy had become the one place where she could speak freely. Kyra wouldn't say she enjoyed visiting James—he still set her off balance far too easily. But James had a keen mind and an incisive tongue, and she could discuss things with him that she couldn't discuss with anyone else.

"What do you think makes Willem the way he is?" she finally asked. "Or any of the wallhuggers who trample on the rest of the city. Are they really that different from us?"

"Power is seductive. Once you have a little, it's easy to go after more."

"To the point of sending hundreds of people to their deaths for political power?" *Or negotiating a loveless marriage.* She told herself that this wasn't about Tristam, but thoughts of him kept intruding into her mind.

"Is it really that hard to believe? Can you honestly say you've not used your new position at the Palace for personal gain?"

James always had a way of stripping away her excuses. She saw herself in Malikel's study just a few days prior, pleading with the Defense Minister to get Flick out of the early units. Of course, if Flick had been excused, someone else would have been conscripted in his stead, but that hadn't stopped Kyra.

"What's the point, then?" Kyra wasn't sure if the disgust in her voice was aimed more at the wallhuggers or at herself. "What's the point of fighting against the ones in power if others'll just take their place? Mayhap it's better just to live my own life and let things fall as they will."

"That was the life you were living before I took you into the Guild. But I don't believe you can just turn a blind eye, once you've seen what the world is like. I couldn't."

"What do you want for Forge?" Kyra asked. "Would you see the whole Palace razed to the ground?"

"Does the city truly need to make its decisions in marble-lined halls? Would we really forget how to live our lives if the Council were not there to dictate it?"

"You can't possibly want anarchy," said Kyra.

"There are ways to rule that don't require the rich to step on the weak. The city's trade guilds rule themselves adequately without wallhuggers. Parna's people elect representatives that rule in concert with the nobles."

"So my efforts to discredit Willem—is that goal too small for you?" she asked.

"It's a step. Willem must go, but he cannot simply be dispatched. He's a good enough politician that his death would make him a martyr and cement his cause. No. Willem must be disgraced before he's brought low."

Kyra wondered again about what kind of man James had been before. For a moment, she imagined what might have happened if she'd stayed in the Guild, if she hadn't killed that manservant so early on, or if she hadn't had Bella or Flick to keep her grounded. Would she have followed in James's footsteps, becoming just slightly more ruthless, year after year? Would she have become his lover and protégé, taken up his cause?

James looked at her again, perhaps sensing the direction of her thoughts. "You and I are not very different," he said. "Not very different at all."

"You keep saying that," she said. The dankness of the dungeon settled on her skin.

"I say it because it's true."

ELEVEN

If it hadn't been for the whole "being sent out to fight demon cats" thing, Flick might well have enjoyed being conscripted into the early patrol units. His fellow recruits were friendly folk—men ranging from Kyra's age to those with young grand-children. The Palace fed them well enough (some of the merchants complained about the food's quality, but Flick wasn't picky), and he learned quite a few new skills. And while Sir Malikel and his men exhibited some wallhugger snobbishness from time to time, Flick had encountered far worse.

Since his conscription, Flick reported to the Palace every day for training. Today, he and his unit congregated on the training fields. The large, flat fields were supposedly covered with grass during the summer, though the surface was now well-packed straw and dirt. While the grounds were large enough to run horses, the only people currently on it were on foot.

Malikel's crew took turns training the new recruits. This morning, Tristam arranged them in concentric circles: Flick stood with four men in the outer circle with their spears pointed diagonally up, while three more stood in the middle with spears angled closer to vertical. Sixteen men formed two of these formations, while the remaining four members of their unit stood to the side, holding sticks with bags of straw tied to the end—stand-ins for demon cat heads.

"This is a variation of the formation our infantrymen use against cavalry charges," Tristam said. It was interesting to finally see the wallhugger in his element. Tristam was comfortable here and competent (at least, to Flick's untrained eye), and he seemed to genuinely want this ragtag group of soldiers to do well. "The difference, of course, between cavalry and demon cats is that cavalry don't come at you from above. That's why we have three men in the middle whose job is to watch the trees. You'll have an easier time holding ranks if you brace your spears against the ground. Remember, these beasts pack a lot of force."

"So the demon cats will oblige us by attacking only while we're in this formation?" piped a young baker named Tommy.

Tristam ignored the sniggers that followed the question. "You take this formation when you are able, whether it's because you've had advance warning of an attack or because your enemy has given you enough quarter to re-form. If they give you no space, then you will have to use another strategy."

He gestured toward the four men of Flick's unit who held cat head targets. "All right, demon cats. See what you can do."

Shouts rose up from the trainees as they fell into mock battle. Funny enough, these exercises reminded Flick of the games he used to play as a street child. The level of chaos was certainly comparable, though the participants were a little less nimble. Flick raised his spear as a demon cat charged in, digging his feet into the mud to get a more stable stance. He got a good thrust into the center of the sack as it came at him, though he was momentarily distracted by an image of Kyra's face as he pulled his spear back out. It was an odd duality, the thought of Kyra as both the young street urchin he knew so well and a different sort of creature altogether. Over the last few months, she'd experienced things that were far beyond his ken. Flick couldn't keep up with her anymore, and he worried how she'd fare by herself in uncharted waters.

Loud guffaws came from the next circle over. Apparently, one of the target holders had tripped and fallen on his face. The fallen man regained his feet, covered in mud, and joined in the laughter. Tristam's lips tightened with impatience as the ranks dissolved, but Flick understood the compulsion to laugh. The wallhuggers might have been raised with the expectation of riding out to battle, but this type of danger was new to the men in this unit. They needed to laugh, if only to dispel their fear.

"Hold it together," said Tristam. "You could be facing live ones tomorrow."

That quieted them down. Orders had come in the morning that their unit was to start trial sweeps of the forest the next day. It was much earlier than anyone had anticipated. Even Malikel, usually so stoic, had failed to hide his surprise.

They drilled like this a while longer, then Tristam called out a break. "Get some water. Sir Rollan will take up your spear training in a quarter hour."

The recruits laid down their weapons and gratefully made their way to the edge of the field. Malikel was there, handing out ladles of water. Flick had to give the Defense Minister credit. Malikel had been at the training fields almost every day, and not just ordering his subordinates around. He'd been in the thick of things and had spoken to every man in the unit at least once.

There was a rustle behind Flick. He turned to see Tristam wipe his brow, pick up a demon cat head, and stuff the protruding straw back into the sack. He paid Flick no mind.

"They still get to you, don't they?" said Flick.

"They're not trained military. I need to remember that," said Tristam, his voice gruff. He moved on to the next target and retied the knot securing the bag to its stick.

"I don't mean the recruits. I mean the demon cats."

At that, Tristam stopped what he was doing.

"I see it in your eyes when you tell us about them," Flick said. "Sometimes your hands shake. What do they call it? Battle ghosts?" Flick didn't know much about it firsthand, but he'd heard enough stories from former soldiers. Sometimes a battle stayed with a soldier, haunting his dreams and never quite letting him move on.

Tristam's expression closed off. "I fight the battles my commander orders me to. Whatever ghosts they create are irrelevant." He put the target on the ground and turned toward the water barrels.

"What do you see when you're with Kyra?" Flick asked. "Given what she is, I'm surprised that the two of you, uh..." He stopped, remembering that Kyra had cut things off.

Tristam's jaw tightened. "Kyra's a fellow soldier. Nothing

more." He took a few steps toward the water barrels, then looked back again. "Her bloodlines do scare me, but they frighten her much more. That's the difference between her and the others."

As Tristam joined Malikel by the sidelines, Flick picked up the fake demon cat head and looked it in its nonexistent eyes. "I'm beginning to think I've been too hard on that wallhugger."

The hemp bag swayed back and forth on its stick. If it had any insights, it kept them to itself.

Kyra arrived at the training fields just in time to see Flick charge a straw demon cat with a spear. It went cleanly through, and he pulled it out again. He caught sight of Kyra watching from the sidelines and waved. A knight, Sir Rollan, barked an order, and Flick continued his exercises.

"How do they look?" Kyra asked Malikel. Tristam was also there, along with several knights. It was a slightly overcast day, and the sun blinked in and out of the clouds.

"Decently against straw," said Malikel. "Against live cats, on the other hand, there is more work to do."

She watched their progress for the next hour. Kyra was supposed to give suggestions based on what she knew of the cats, but military strategy was beyond her. While Tristam could comment on formations and tactics, Kyra could only think that these men needed to move much faster if they wanted to stay alive. It gave her a modicum of comfort that Flick seemed one of the more competent with a spear.

"When will they be sent out against live cats?" asked Kyra.

"They're to do a training round in the forest tomorrow."

"Tomorrow?" The knights standing around her turned at her exclamation, and Kyra lowered her voice. "You must see they're not ready."

"It is the wish of the Council," said Malikel. His tone warned her not to object again.

"The Council is—"

"That's enough, Kyra. You are dismissed."

Kyra stood immobile for a moment, wanting to argue more, but there was a dangerous set to Malikel's jaw, and she could see that it was hopeless. She turned and stormed from the practice fields. She'd gone maybe a hundred paces when Tristam called after her.

"Kyra, wait!"

"Don't you have some courtiers to talk to?" she snapped. Tristam flinched at her words, but Kyra wasn't feeling inclined to pity.

"You can't question a commander like that in front of his men. He won't have it."

Kyra wondered why Flick hadn't told her he was being sent into the forest the next day. Had he been trying not to worry her, or had he not known either? She'd spent several nights trying to track down the scribe responsible for Flick's conscription, but the search had proved difficult. That, along with Orvin's insight into Willem's true reasons for conscripting Flick, had forced her to halt her efforts. Though now she wondered if she should have tried harder.

"Do you have some time?" said Tristam. "I'm off for the afternoon, and I'd like to talk a bit."

Kyra lowered her head so he wouldn't see her irritation. Now he wanted to talk? After Malikel had proved himself impotent and Tristam had shown himself to be untrustworthy? "Where would you like to go?" she asked.

"To my quarters?"

She nodded and turned in that direction without making eye contact. Tristam's living quarters had been a subject of some controversy after he was demoted and could no longer stay in the officials' dormitories. He could have lodged in the barracks, but the thought of the son of a noble house, even a disgraced one, rubbing shoulders with common soldiers had been offensive enough to influential people at the Palace that the option was ruled out. Instead, he'd moved into a small but comfortable room in a building that housed visiting noblemen.

They walked there together now, and Tristam held the door open for her. His neatly made bed sat next to the window across from a writing desk and a dresser. His sword and armor hung on racks against the wall. Tristam also had a small table, where he pulled out a chair for Kyra before sitting down himself.

"Is there anything in particular you wanted to talk about?" she asked.

"Yes, there is." Tristam stared at his hands and appeared to collect himself. It suddenly occurred to Kyra that he might tell her about the marriage negotiations after all, and she had no idea how to respond. She wiped her palms on her trousers. *Don't say it, Tristam. I don't want to have that conversation right now.*

"I'm sorry about Flick," said Tristam. "I've been doing my very best to prepare them. We all have."

Kyra took a moment to swallow the ball of disappointment

and annoyance that was quickly replacing the panic in her chest. She was being silly, she knew, wanting one thing and then the other. "How long will the rounds in the forest be? How dangerous?" she asked.

"The first round will just be a few hours in the morning, basic maneuvers in more realistic terrain. It could very well be uneventful. But even if something does happen, the new recruits are already much better than they were when they started. I honestly think that many of them, Flick included, have a fair chance of killing a demon cat if they run across one."

Killing a demon cat. Of course, if Kyra had to choose between Flick and any one of the Makvani, she would pick Flick in a heartbeat. But Tristam's words still left a bad taste in her mouth.

"I wish there was some other way," she said.

"What do you mean?"

"Why does it have to be a slaughter? If only I'd convinced Pashla to take me to Leyus."

Tristam drummed his fingers on the table, his nostrils flaring slightly. "I hold Malikel in high esteem, but in this endeavor I think he's misguided. I don't trust the Makvani to keep any promises they make."

"I trust Pashla," Kyra said. "And there might be others like her."

"Pashla killed Jack. If she's the best of the lot, then I see no reason to trust them."

If Kyra had been in a better frame of mind, she might have acknowledged that he had a fair point. It was actually Pashla's companion who'd killed Jack, but Pashla had allowed it to happen. Though Kyra's own experiences with Pashla had been good, she wasn't naïve enough to forget the disdain with which the Makvani viewed humans.

But it had been a long week with many unwelcome revelations, and there was a layer of disgust in Tristam's voice that Kyra couldn't ignore.

"If you don't trust them, then why trust me?" she asked.

Tristam looked up at her, uncertain. "Kyra?"

"I share their blood. I could hunt someone down as easily as they. Why trust me if you can't trust them?" She didn't bother to hide the hardness in her voice.

He pushed off the table, backing away from the unexpected attack. "Kyra, I would think we know each other well enough now that—"

That was too much.

"Know each other?" she snapped. "How well do I actually know you? Do you want to tell me what you've actually been talking to those courtiers about all week? What that family from Parna really wants from you?" Her last word rang in the air, and then there was absolute silence in the room. The shock in Tristam's expression slowly turned to guilt, and any last hope of a misunderstanding slowly faded away.

"How did you find out?" Tristam had the look of a criminal who'd just been handed his judgment.

"When were you planning to tell me?"

He stared at her, and several times his jaw worked as if he were about to start speaking. "You may or may not believe me, but that was the real reason I wanted to talk to you today. I knew I couldn't keep putting it off, but I couldn't find the courage to actually say it."

Kyra stared at him without response.

Finally he sighed and collapsed back against his chair. "Everything I've told you about that family and Parna is true. They are rich and powerful, with a great deal of resources. Our manor at Brancel has been falling more often to Demon Rider attacks. In addition to our manor, we're responsible for the protection of a small hamlet nearby, and we take those duties seriously. With our resources stretched thin, we've not been able to protect them. The family from Parna could help us...if we were family as well."

"What's the lass's name?" Kyra asked. She wasn't quite sure why it was important, but she wanted to know.

"Cecile," he said reluctantly. "She's the fourth daughter of Lord Salis of Routhian. They don't live far from Brancel, actually, but they swear fealty to Parna. I've never met her, but everyone says she's pleasant."

The name had sharp edges that dug into her chest. "And you have to accept this alliance?" It occurred to her that maybe she shouldn't assume Tristam opposed the marriage.

Tristam stared at the table in front of him. "It's complicated. I've already brought disgrace on my family by losing my rank as a knight. I'm unlikely to gain any position of political influence because of that, at least in the near future. The only way I can serve my family now is through a marriage, and the Routhian household cares much less about my disgrace than any house of Forge would. And we do need help."

She thought she'd been upset when she first learned the news, but it was far worse to hear Tristam talk about it, to hear him actually considering it, when two months ago, they'd held each other in the forest and kissed. He was expecting her to say something, but she couldn't. Moment by moment, the silence between them stretched longer.

"Kyra, please say something. This is not . . . something that I would choose."

He wanted her to talk to him? What could he possibly expect her to say? Kyra finally managed to clear her throat. She tried for a smile, but it didn't quite work. "I shouldn't be surprised, I suppose. That's why I broke things off in the first place, wasn't it? I guess I'd not expected to be proved right so soon."

She saw in Tristam's face the precise moment her words sank in, and felt a perverse pleasure as her jab hit home. She wanted to be alone. Kyra pushed her chair back from the table. "I should go."

She left before he could stop her.

The sun had completely set now, and Kyra was glad for it. She didn't want anyone to see the expression on her face as she rushed through the courtyard, making for the Palace gates as quickly as she could. At least the grounds had calmed now from the midday frenzy, and there were fewer people walking the torch-lit pathways. Kyra kept her head down and her steps quick. She needed to get out.

She'd just left the inner compound when someone called her name. His voice was thick with disdain, and Kyra's stomach knotted in recognition even before her mind registered who it was. She turned to see Lord Agan's son Santon walking toward her, flanked by his two brothers.

"Where are you going, Kyra of Forge?" he said. There was an unnatural loudness to his voice and just the slightest hint of unsteadiness in his step. A wind blew from their direction, and Kyra smelled wine.

Kyra cursed under her breath. Of all the times to run into these wallhuggers. The pathways around her were empty of passersby. Just her luck. Or had they waited until no one was around? *Not tonight. I don't need this tonight.* The mere sight of them disgusted her. Kyra backed away, though she didn't want to move so quickly that she'd appear frightened. The wallhuggers drew closer.

"Off to interfere with someone else's business?" said Santon.

"Girl doesn't know her place," said his younger brother. Kyra thought he was the one named Douglass.

"Just like that gutter rat she played hero for," said the third brother, Dalton.

Her eyes flicked quickly to the swords they wore at their belts. It was too bad that the unevenness in their step wasn't more pronounced. They'd still be able to handle the swords well enough to give her trouble. The wise thing to do would be to run away. There were plenty of places she could escape to. At least she wasn't boxed in by crowds as she'd been the last time, but the thought of turning tail and fleeing the cowards left a bitter taste in her mouth.

"How's your gutter rat friend, Kyra?" Santon asked. "She healing up all right?"

Just ignore them. These noblemen weren't worth the trouble. The building next to her had a chimney she could scale. She could be out of their reach in a few moments. Kyra did her best to push images of Idalee out of her mind, the fearful way the girl had scanned the Palace grounds as they'd left Ilona's care.

"Too bad the magistrate never found the people who beat the wench," said Santon with a savage smile. Kyra gritted her teeth. She took a firm hold on the chimney and dug her fingers into depressions in the stone. It was icy cold, but she barely felt it.

"Gutter rat wasn't worth the magistrate's time," said Dalton. "Her type's only good for cleaning chamber pots and the occasional late-night sport."

She froze.

"Better flip the order of that, Dalton. Imagine the stink otherwise," said Santon.

Kyra lowered her hand and slowly turned back toward the wallhuggers. "Shut your mouths and go home," she said, her voice dangerously quiet.

It took the noblemen a few moments to process her words. They hadn't expected her to come back toward them. They hadn't expected her to give them a command. And they were far too arrogant to heed the threat that infused every one of her words. Santon stood for a moment, and then the smile slowly returned to his face. "Girl wants to play hero again."

"If you know what's good for you," said Kyra, "you'll leave right now." There was a spark of anger in her stomach, and she nurtured it. Even as she spoke, she was hoping they wouldn't listen to her. She saw Idalee's crumpled form on the ground as the wallhuggers kicked her, heard the girl's choked cries. No, Kyra most definitely did not want Santon and his brothers to do as they were told.

"Don't be giving threats to those above your station, Kyra," said Santon, closing the distance between them. "You think you're safe because you're on Palace grounds? You're nothing but a glorified gutter rat, and you'll end up just like your friend."

He struck her across the face then, his hand moving fast and sure. She put up an arm to block him, but Santon was strong enough that the blow still connected and knocked her halfway over. Kyra stayed bent over, one hand to her aching jaw, waiting for the tears to clear from her eyes. There was a coppery taste in her mouth where she'd bitten her cheek. Her dagger was in her boot, but she didn't reach for it.

Santon grabbed her arm and shoved her to the ground. Pain lanced through Kyra's shoulder as she hit the cobblestones, and she rolled away from him. Before he could come closer, she unfastened her cloak and pulled her tunic over her head, shivering as the icy wind blew through the thin shift she wore underneath. The small voice of restraint inside her whispered one more warning, and she thrust it savagely into a far corner of her mind.

Santon slowed, staring at Kyra as she stepped out of her boots and onto the frigid ground. For a moment, he was uncertain, his wine-addled mind trying to make sense of her actions. Then his smile took on a different tone. "Well, this is new. Is this how you actually managed to rise through the ranks? Maybe Sir Malikel has better judgment than we gave him credit for." Douglas and Dalton circled behind her. Kyra's skin crawled, but still, she didn't move.

Footsteps sounded from around the corner. A Red Shield, a guard on patrol, stopped dead in his tracks, his eyes going from Kyra, huddled on the ground in her shift, to the brothers surrounding her.

"Continue on your rounds," Santon ordered. "Stay clear of this space for a while."

In an all-too-familiar routine, the guard backed away and left. Kyra couldn't keep the fury from her face as she stared after him. *Coward.*

Santon's lips curled, and he bent down to her level. "Don't be so naïve," he said. "And try to smile a little. This is better than you deserve." He grabbed a fistful of her collar, pulling her face close to his.

And Kyra let her anger explode.

TWELVE

Santon didn't seem to realize what was happening at first. He was too close to see her clearly, and his mind was slow from drink. But soon enough the leer on his face turned to confusion, and Kyra could tell by the exclamations behind her that his brothers had noticed something wasn't right. Santon lost his hold on her as her bones lengthened and her limbs stretched. She pushed him away and kicked off her trousers as her shift began to tear and rip away. Santon hit the ground with a grunt. Kyra climbed to her feet and settled herself onto all fours.

In hindsight, it had been a mistake to wait until the wall-huggers were so close before changing. If they had been thinking clearly, they could have killed her right then and there. But thankfully the three of them stood paralyzed even as Kyra's vision took on that newly familiar clarity and her thoughts faded into instinct ... and rage.

"What by the three cities ..." Santon whispered.

Footsteps pounded behind her, growing more distant, and Kyra turned just in time to see Douglass rounding a corner. The sight of him fleeing brought an intense desire to run him down, though she hesitated—the other two were right here. Then Santon and Dalton also turned to flee, and she no longer had to choose between staying or giving chase.

Santon was laughably slow, hardly a challenge at all. She knocked him off his feet; he rolled and jumped back up with his sword drawn. The blade glinted in the moonlight. Kyra hesitated, and Santon took that opportunity to charge. His sword came down on her shoulder, but it felt like a bludgeon instead of a cut as the edge glanced off her fur. Kyra batted the weapon out of his hand.

There was a shout behind her, and Kyra turned to see Dalton running at her with his sword raised. This time, she was faster. Kyra sprang to the side as he swung, and bit down on his sword arm. He screamed, and the sound thrilled her. His blood, warm in her mouth, fueled her growing battle fury. She threw him to the ground with a quick jerk of her neck. He was a large man, but she tossed him around as easily as if he were a child.

Pain exploded in her back leg. Kyra screamed and looked back just as Santon raised his dagger again. She kicked out with her hind legs, catching him squarely in the chest. The dagger clattered to the ground, the clank of metal harsh in her ears. As Santon skidded across the dirt, Kyra felt a wave of disdain. She slashed at him with her claws, opening four ribbons of red along his torso. His cry of pain brought her some satisfaction, and she moved in for the kill. His screams broke off as her jaws closed around his throat. She held on as he struggled, but that didn't last very long at all, and soon he fell still. It had been too easy, and her blood was still hot. Kyra let go of his throat and tore at the now lifeless body, venting her frustration. Then she remembered there were two more. She raised her head and pricked her ears.

"Kyra!"

She heard the words as if from far away. She turned to the sound, teeth bared, but the speaker wasn't one of the wall-huggers who had attacked her. Kyra recognized Tristam even in the midst of her rage, and he was walking slowly toward her, speaking gently, though she couldn't quite make sense of the words. She growled deep in her throat. Even if she didn't want to fight him, he was keeping her from her prey. She turned away, but he said her name again, and his voice pulled at her, calm but insistent.

He kept talking, his hands held placatingly out in front of him. Kyra backed up as he came closer, puzzled at why he was neither fighting nor running away. Slowly, her blood cooled just enough so that Kyra understood she should change back. She gathered the heat, the feeling of her fur, and pushed it back inside, letting out a sigh as her body melted in on itself. Tristam was ready with her clothes as her skin became smooth and she started to shiver. Her nails were covered with blood.

"Kyra?" Tristam searched her eyes as if he was afraid he wouldn't find her there. "Kyra, what happened?"

She shook her head, trying to focus her eyes. It felt as if all the blood in her skull was pounding to get out. "Lord Agan's sons. They came upon me while I was leaving. . . . We fought . . . I . . ." She broke off as she took in the destruction around her.

Dalton was on the ground, moaning and cradling his arm. Douglass was nowhere to be seen. And on the ground behind her . . .

Kyra's stomach reacted instantly to the sight. She jerked away from Tristam and retched, though there wasn't much in her stomach. She could sense Tristam behind her, but he didn't touch her. As her gut stopped spasming, she wiped her mouth and forced herself to look again.

Santon's body was barely recognizable as human. The arms and legs were splayed at awkward angles. The face was covered in blood, the neck torn open. Kyra looked away, unable to reconcile her exultant memories, the bloodlust that still echoed in her veins, with the mangled corpse in front of her. She'd done that to Santon. She'd heard his screams and she'd . . . She couldn't think it.

Tristam grabbed her by the shoulders and shook her. The fear in his eyes was very, very real. That more than anything brought her mind back.

"Kyra, listen to me." He was looking around. Shouts echoed nearby. When he looked back at her, some of the fear was replaced by determination. "You have to go," he said. "Leave the Palace. Leave the city."

Leave the city. Just like that? But they'd had plans in place. When the Palace finally found out, Kyra was going to convince Malikel that she posed no threat. That even though she shared blood with the Demon Riders, she wasn't a danger.

A bloodcurdling scream rent the air. It was Dalton. He had turned over onto his side, and his eyes were fixed on Santon's remains. A dull heaviness weighed down Kyra's chest. How could she think of convincing anyone that she wasn't a danger now? Tristam was right. Fleeing was the only choice left to her.

"What about you?" she asked Tristam.

"Don't worry about me. I'll tell them you ran off."

Tristam wasn't a good liar either. He couldn't quite look her in the eye, and even with her mind muddled as it was, she knew that he was wrong. Tristam was too closely associated with her. They had to convince the Palace that he'd tried to capture Kyra, or he'd take the fall for her.

"Fight me," she said. Even as Tristam was making sense of her words, she reached for her dagger and realized it was somewhere on the ground with her boots. She thought to go back for it, but there was no time. Instead, she tackled him.

Kyra caught him off guard, and Tristam fell backward as she pummeled at his face. He grunted in pain—her blows landed harder than she intended. *Fight back, you idiot,* she thought, even as she struck him again across his cheekbone. That blow split his lip, but her blood still ran hot from the kill, and it was hard to pull back.

Finally, he started to defend himself, raising his hands to block her. A flurry of blows and stinging parries passed between them, then Tristam caught one of her wrists. When she tried to pull away, he captured the other. For a moment, they were locked together, Kyra quivering with battle rage as she leaned into him, both of them breathing in deep, painful gulps. She saw uncertainty and resolve in his eyes, and Kyra realized she didn't know when she would see him again.

"Go, Kyra. Now!"

When Kyra didn't react, Tristam set his jaw, curled his

legs between them, and kicked her off. He wasn't gentle. The kick knocked the breath out of her, and she rolled over twice before she came to a stop. Kyra coughed, then slowly pulled herself to her feet. More shouts. Three Red Shields were pointing and running toward them.

Tristam raised himself to a crouch. One of his eyes was already starting to swell. He launched himself at her again. She dodged him, grabbed her boots, and ran, pushing through the pain in her ribs and her injured leg, hearing his footsteps behind her grow fainter even though she knew he was a faster runner than she. Kyra ducked her head and bent all her energy toward getting away.

Tristam watched Kyra disappear into the darkness. It wasn't hard to feign shock as Red Shields swarmed around him. His jaw ached—Kyra had hit him hard. And he was still reeling from the scene around him.

Red Shields surrounded him and pointed their swords at him. He raised his hands.

"I'm unarmed," he said.

One soldier came closer and patted him down. Tristam winced as the Red Shield hit another spot that Kyra had bruised. She'd been half-wild when she'd changed back into her human shape, more feral than he'd ever seen her. He saw her again, eyes flashing, a hint of a snarl still on her lips. She'd been out for blood, and it scared him more than he cared to admit.

The Red Shield finished his search and nodded to the others, who lowered their weapons. "You were a witness to this?" asked the soldier.

"Yes." Every limb felt heavy. His ribs complained when he drew breath to speak.

"Come with me, then," said the Red Shield, leading him back to the scene.

Santon's mauled corpse lay on the cobblestones. Dalton screamed incoherently, though Tristam could pick out the words "monster" and "girl." He slumped down and rubbed his jaw again, waiting for his mind to clear.

A crowd was gathering now, mostly nobles and guards, though a few brave servants also stopped to stare. A soldier knelt next to Dalton and called for bandages. Nobody came close to Santon's body.

"Make way." The crowd parted, and Tristam's heart skipped a beat as Malikel strode through. The Defense Minister took a long look at Santon, and then at Dalton and Tristam. "What happened?"

"A monster," croaked Dalton, his voice hoarse. "The girl changed into a demon cat." He sounded delirious in his pain, and for a moment Tristam wondered if he could still cover this up. But no, there had been a third brother who'd run.

"What's he talking about?" Malikel directed his question at Tristam.

"There was a demon cat in the Palace, sir," he said. "I was outside my quarters when I heard screams. I came running and saw it attacking these two and their brother." Actually, he hadn't simply been outside his quarters. He'd run out after Kyra, unwilling to let the conversation end the way it had, when he'd stumbled upon that scene.

"And what is he saying about the girl?"

This was it, then. Tristam sent a silent apology to Kyra. "It was Kyra, sir. She...she's a Demon Rider. I saw her change back into her human form after the attack."

Malikel's face clouded over, though he didn't look as surprised as Tristam would have expected. "You saw this with your own eyes?"

"Yes, sir," said Tristam.

"And you had no idea of this. No suspicions."

Tristam hesitated. It was bad enough to lie to any commander, but this was Malikel.

"You knew nothing of this, Tristam. It caught you by surprise," continued the Defense Minister.

Only then did he notice the way his commander looked at him, and a subtlety in Malikel's inflection, as if he was telling Tristam something rather than asking. "Yes, sir," he said hesitantly. He thought he caught a glimpse of approval in Malikel's eyes. "I tried to stop her from escaping, but I couldn't."

The crowd's energy shifted again, and a new voice spoke. "A Demon Rider attack in the Palace? Do I hear this correctly?" Tristam felt the color drain from his face as Malikel squared his shoulders. The people gathered around parted for Willem.

"You heard correctly, Willem," Malikel said.

Willem gave a passing glance to Dalton, who was only semiconscious. "What do I hear about Kyra of Forge being one of the Demon Riders?"

"That is what the witnesses claim," said Malikel. The Defense Minister stood with his feet braced and back straight. *He's preparing to take a fall,* thought Tristam. *There's no good outcome for Malikel here.*

"We had one of our enemies in our midst the entire time, working for the Ministry of Defense?" The Head Councilman spoke more loudly than he needed to, and the look in his eyes was one of a bird of prey who had spotted a rabbit. "This is grave news indeed," he said. "A very bad mistake for someone in your position, Malikel. I'm very sorry, but this will have implications."

The Head Councilman's eyes, however, glinted in a way that didn't look sorry at all.

Someone must have raised the alarm, because the air filled with shouts and the loud rhythms of booted feet. Kyra's leg throbbed where Santon had cut it. It had stopped bleeding, but her trousers kept sticking to the wound. She didn't dare slow down. It would only get harder to escape.

She ran on instinct, too shocked to think out a coherent escape route, relying only on her reflexes to find her the safest way. She kept to the ledges as much as she could to avoid the Red Shields swarming the footpaths. When she had to travel on the ground, she darted from shadow to shadow, more than once diving into a corner to avoid being seen.

Finally, she scrambled up the Palace wall and flung herself over the top. Once on the other side, she ran into a sheltered alleyway. It was as safe a place as any to catch her breath, and she took in gulp after gulp of icy air.

She'd killed again.

Kyra could still see Santon's body on the ground, the angle of his ravaged neck. The memory kept shifting. It was as if she saw the body through two sets of eyes, one that looked upon it with relish and the other with horror. The emotions didn't mix well, and she fought the sickening churn of her stomach. The first time she killed a man, when she'd slit a man's throat in a failed Assassins Guild raid, that had been an accident. But this . . .

A shadow crossed the alley's entrance, and Kyra froze. It wasn't a Red Shield. Just a man, and he continued right on down the street without stopping. But the shock reminded her of her danger. The Palace knew where she lived. There would be Red Shields at her door within a few hours—if not Red Shields, then an angry mob, and Idalee and Lettie were at home. A fresh wave of panic jolted through her. *What had she done?* The mob wouldn't differentiate between Kyra and her family. She had to warn them. Kyra set off again with renewed speed, keeping to alleyways and rooftops since she couldn't blend in with the evening crowds when her clothing was in tatters and her face smeared with blood.

Kyra burst into her quarters to find Lettie, Idalee, and Flick playing a dice game. Flick looked up with a smile, only to have the smile freeze on his face.

Kyra froze as well, staring at the three of them with wide eyes. "We have to leave," she said. "Now. Take everything."

The three of them gaped at her.

"Now!" Kyra said again, louder this time. She could hear the tinge of hysteria in her voice. Giving up on them, she ran over to her chest and started pulling things out. She threw her spare clothes onto the ground and fished out a coil of rope.

"Kyra, wait." Flick crossed the room and took her by the arm. She let him turn her around, and he bent so their eyes were level. "What's going on?"

She was shaking. Even with the pressure of Flick's hands on her shoulders, the tremors came through. She swallowed. "Santon of Agan is dead," she said finally.

"What happened?"

"He—I—" Kyra couldn't say it. "Not now, please. We have to go. The Red Shields will be here any minute." She took a deep breath. "They know what I am. I changed."

Flick's grip on her went slack. "People saw?"

She nodded.

Flick looked down at her scattered belongings with new understanding. "I need to go get my things." The readiness with which he accepted this only served to intensify her guilt. If he'd yelled at her for blowing her cover and uprooting them all, she might have found the energy to defend herself. But perhaps it was better this way. They had no time to squabble.

"Meet us at the spot by the south wall," Kyra said.

After Flick left, Kyra washed the blood off her face and changed into clean clothes. When she turned around, she saw Idalee watching her with a stricken expression.

"Idalee," Kyra said uncertainly. "We need to pack quickly."

The girl looked to be in a daze, but she moved to her own chest and started pulling out belongings with her non-splinted arm. Once Kyra was done with her own bags, she gathered Lettie's clothes. She also jumped to retrieve a stash of emergency coins that she'd hidden in a hollowed-out roof beam. Then she rushed them all out the door.

Flick stood waiting by the south wall with a bag slung over his shoulders. They'd scouted out this spot before, a stretch lined with houses that didn't have windows on their outward-facing sides. Kyra threw a grappling hook over the top—it clinked more loudly than she would have liked—then waited as Flick climbed up and hauled their bags after him. Idalee was next. Kyra tied a loop for the girl to stand on, and she held tightly with her good arm while Flick pulled her up. Lettie followed, and then Kyra came last.

A wide road circled the city wall. Beyond that were houses, not crowded as densely as the houses in the city, but there were still too many people who might see them. The main road led out from the city gates, but that was farther down the wall, and they didn't dare follow it. Instead, they took narrow footpaths that led them between houses. There were others on these roads—farmers returning home, women running errands. The four of them put their heads down and walked as if they belonged.

Flick pulled even with Kyra. "Are you going to tell me what happened?"

"The Agan brothers found me as I was leaving the compound. Started taunting me about Idalee, and then they started threatening me."

"They attacked you?"

Had they attacked her? Flick was clearly willing to believe

that it had been self-defense. And in part, it had been—once they'd laid hands on her. But she'd had a chance to flee—she'd wanted an excuse not to. Kyra shook her head. It was hard even to think back on it. Every time she did, her battle lust crept back like a slow fog. She didn't dare think about what would happen if it took over.

"I don't want to talk about it."

To her relief, Flick didn't push her. "We'll need to figure out where to go."

Kyra watched the ground pass under her feet. "I can't stay in the city. There's too many people looking for me, but it's different for you. There's no manhunt out for you, and you'll have trouble from the Palace if you disappear. You'd be labeled a deserter."

Flick considered this. "They'll likely bring me in for questioning if I stay in the city. Even if they don't, the best I have to look forward to is patrolling the forest with my unit tomorrow. I'll take my chances as a deserter."

She nodded, selfishly relieved. "Is there anyone you can take shelter with out here?"

"I have a friend who lives at the edge of the forest. We can try her."

"What do you think, Idalee? And Lettie?" said Kyra.

Bells started ringing in the city just then, and Kyra's heart nearly jumped out of her throat. She felt Flick's hand on her back. "Keep walking."

Hoofbeats sounded from the direction of the main road. A man shouted commands. Kyra looked around in panic for a place to go.

"The haystack," Idalee said.

The houses had steadily become more spaced out as they walked, changing gradually into farms and fields. The haystack Idalee mentioned was piled taller than a man and cast a significant shadow in the moonlight. They ran for it. Idalee pulled Lettie next to the pile and ducked behind her protectively as Kyra and Flick settled in next to them, crouching in the hard-packed snow. They waited there, listening to the voices until they finally faded.

They continued like this, walking when they could and taking cover when they heard any sign of the search. And though they avoided capture, it was becoming clear that they couldn't keep this up for long. Lettie started to stumble, and Idalee stared blankly ahead as she walked. Kyra found herself watching Idalee out of the corner of her eye. Ilona certainly wouldn't have approved of such exertion.

Finally Flick raised a hand and indicated a small cottage in the distance.

"Is that it?" Kyra asked.

"Aye. Wait while I see if she's there." Flick paused. "I'm going to have to tell her everything, Kyra. I'd not feel right about it otherwise."

"Tell her what you must," said Kyra. "Everybody will know soon enough."

Flick hadn't been exaggerating when he said this house was at the edge of the forest. It would have been possible to throw a stone from the back door and hit one of the trees. Kyra, Idalee, and Lettie crouched in a dip off the road. It was very dark now, and they couldn't see Flick near the house or know if he'd been let in. Lettie leaned on Kyra's shoulder, then slowly tipped into her lap. The girl had fallen asleep.

"Kyra?" Idalee's voice came timidly out of the darkness.

"I'm here," she said.

There was a silence before Idalee spoke. "Did you kill Santon because of what they did to me?"

Kyra wondered if her heart would stop beating. She was glad for the darkness just then, and grateful Idalee could not see her face. "It all happened really quickly."

"You don't have to hide it from me, Kyra. I know how angry you were."

Hearing the tremor in Idalee's voice was like seeing her get beaten all over again. Kyra reached out. It took her two tries, but she found Idalee's hand. "Idalee," she said. "What happened with Santon tonight . . . it was I who did it, not you. Don't ever blame yourself for what they did to you, or what I did to—" She had to stop speaking, as images of Santon's mangled corpse flashed again through her mind. "I lost my temper, and I . . . took things too far. I'm sorry that you have to bear the consequences." *And Tristam and Malikel as well.* She didn't know how far the ramifications would extend.

A long silence stretched between them. Idalee held tight to her hand. Lettie's weight was warm in Kyra's lap. The child's ribs expanded with every breath.

"Will you be all right?" Idalee asked.

Kyra hadn't expected that response, and she marveled at how lucky she was to have Idalee, Flick, and Lettie. She gave Idalee a grateful squeeze. "I hope so."

A small point of light appeared near the house and bobbed

toward them. It was a candlestick held by a very old woman. Her gray-white hair was loosely tied in a braid that hung over her shoulder, and she wore a luxurious night-robe of fine velvet, trimmed with fur.

Flick's voice spoke from behind her. "Kyra, this is Mercie."

The old woman looked them over. "I'll take in the four of you tonight," she said in a rich, throaty voice. "Flick and the sisters can stay until things calm down. But you"—she gave Kyra a pointed glance—"must leave tomorrow. It's too dangerous for me to keep you."

"I understand," said Kyra.

"Well, then, move quickly."

They didn't bother waking Lettie. Flick picked her up, and they all hurried behind Mercie into her house. Kyra couldn't see much by the candle flame, though the floor felt smooth and well polished under her feet. Mercie led them to a back room, where she laid out blankets and furs on the ground.

"In you go, then. We'll talk tomorrow morning."

If Flick trusted this woman, it was good enough for Kyra. She burrowed underneath the pile of blankets, not even bothering to remove her cloak. Idalee pressed her back against hers and they finally surrendered to sleep.

THIRTEEN

There was a rush of cold air as someone pulled the blankets off her. Kyra's eyes flew open, and she reached for her dagger. Mercie took a step back, holding up empty hands.

"It's just me, lass. Red Shields are searching the houses in the area. Someone must have seen you last night. You need to get out. All of you."

That woke her up. Kyra looked around. It was early morning. Racks of shoes, dresses, and hats lined the walls of their room, and the air smelled faintly of perfume. Idalee was shaking Lettie awake, and Flick stood at the window, running his hands through his mussed-up hair.

"They're coming closer," said Flick. Idalee pulled Lettie to her feet and fastened the girl's cloak around her.

"You can go out the forest side," said Mercie. "Quickly."

They stumbled on sleep-heavy limbs through the house. Mercie opened a window and Kyra jumped through, followed by Idalee. Flick lifted Lettie over, then climbed out last. Now that Kyra was outside, she could hear voices in the distance, though the house blocked her view.

"The blankets, Mercie," said Flick. "Remember to—"

"I can handle a dozen Red Shields," Mercie snapped. She pointed to a heavy, flat stone a short distance from the window. "See that stone? When the narrow edge points toward the forest instead of the house, that will mean the soldiers are gone. You can return then."

There was already a trail of footprints from Mercie's house to the trees. They followed it, doing their best to step within the existing prints, and kept going until the road was completely out of view. There, they stopped to catch their breath. Kyra's stomach growled, and she realized she hadn't eaten anything in a long time.

"Think any of the Red Shields saw us?" she asked.

"If they had, they'd be chasing," said Idalee.

She couldn't argue with that logic. "Flick, what does Mercie do? She lives in a cottage but dresses like a wallhugger."

Flick chuckled. "Mercie was a thief, you could say. She charmed well-to-do men and made off with their coin. Doesn't do much of it anymore."

That would explain why she wasn't afraid to defy the law, and why she'd almost seemed insulted when Flick told her to hide the blankets.

"You should go back and hide with her after the search is over," said Kyra. "I'll find somewhere else to go, but there's no reason you must stay with me. There's a cave farther out in the forest where I can take shelter."

Flick shifted uncomfortably. "We can't exactly cut you loose by yourself. Mayhap we could all go to the cave."

"There's demon cats in these forests, Flick. It's not safe for you. I, at least, share their blood."

"I don't know. . . . Mayhap we can think of something else."

Kyra drew breath to respond, but her answer turned into a cry of warning as a demon cat launched itself out of the trees.

It was mind-boggling, how the cats appeared out of nowhere. There had been no sound at all. Only when the cat's shadow fell upon them did Kyra throw herself at the others, sending Lettie sprawling and landing on top of Flick. She got a knee in the ribs for her efforts, and the demon cat pounced onto the spot where they'd just stood.

"Do you know this one?" Flick yelled. He pulled his legs out from under her and hauled Kyra to her feet.

It was a sleek black felbeast. A smaller one, and Kyra guessed it was female. "No," she said. Never had a single word felt like such bad news.

The beast lunged for them. Kyra dove out of the way and rolled. When she regained her feet, she looked in panic for the others. Flick had jumped the other way. Lettie darted for the trees, and Idalee ran after her. The felbeast fixed its eyes on Flick.

"No!" Kyra shouted. Before the beast could leap, Kyra threw herself onto the creature's back and wrapped her arms around its neck. There was a rush of air across her arms as the beast snapped its teeth, and she held on for dear life while the demon cat twisted and bucked. Her grip started to fail.

The cat gave a violent shake of its head, and Kyra fell hard onto the ground. Her head spun. Now would be a good time to change shape, but she couldn't even think straight.

A streak of yellow flew above her, and a cacophony of roars drowned out Flick's yells. Kyra sat up to see a tawny-yellow cat collide with the black one. The two beasts tumbled to the ground, growling and snapping. Was the new cat Leyus? No. The beast was too small, but Kyra recognized it all the same. This was Pashla.

The two felbeasts continued to struggle, but Pashla wasn't going for blood—Kyra had seen enough fights now to know the difference. Pashla used her weight to pin her opponent. She bared her fangs and snapped, but she didn't aim for the other beast's throat. Slowly, the black cat reined in its attack, and the outlines of both cats started blurring.

As the Demon Riders changed into their skin, Kyra glanced at the others. Lettie's mouth hung open, and Idalee stared at the beasts in wonder. Flick stared as well, then raised one eyebrow when he saw Kyra watching. Kyra turned back to see Pashla crouched on the ground opposite a young woman with pale white skin and jet-black hair. The two naked women huddled against the wind as they reached into bags that had fallen at their feet. They must have been wearing the pouches around their necks when they'd been in their fur.

Kyra realized, as she looked closer, that she recognized the other woman. Her name was Adele. She and her friend Mela had once asked Kyra about her life with the humans. Adele had been friendly and curious that time. What had changed?

Pashla caught Kyra's eye and beckoned her closer. "Adele

didn't recognize you. There was fighting this morning, and she mistook you for the hostile humans."

Adele met Kyra's eyes and gave a solemn nod. "I was mistaken. Please forgive me."

Flick came up behind her, eyeing the two clanswomen warily. He looked slightly at a loss for words. At least Pashla and Adele were fully clothed now. Pashla wore a cloak over her leather wraparound tunic and leggings. Adele wore no cloak, and her tunic had no sleeves. Kyra could see goose bumps on the clanswoman's arms, but Adele didn't shiver.

"Is everything all right?" said Flick, looking from the Makvani women to Kyra.

"I think so," Kyra said, and the clanswomen didn't contradict her. Adele eyed Flick with curiosity, looking for all the world like a cat presented with a new insect. "This is Flick, my friend," Kyra said. She turned to him. "There was a misunderstanding. Adele didn't mean to attack us."

"I see," said Flick in a tone of voice that suggested he most definitely did *not* see. Kyra wondered how good the Makvani were at picking up sarcasm. But as strange as things currently were, they definitely could have ended up a lot worse. Now the question was how to proceed.

Pashla's gaze focused behind Kyra. "Those two girls, are they with you as well?"

So much for keeping them out of this. "Those are my adopted sisters. They mean no harm."

"I wish to see them," said Pashla.

Kyra hesitated but decided it was better to trust Pashla.

She nodded to Idalee, who took Lettie's hand and led her cautiously closer. Pashla looked the nervous girls over. To Kyra's surprise, Idalee and Lettie didn't cower, but instead stood taller and calmer under Pashla's gaze.

A branch cracked in the distance just then, and Pashla turned her face to the wind. "There are people coming."

"Soldiers," said Adele. Kyra heard the clank of weapons, and she remembered Pashla's earlier words about a fight and hostile humans. Had the early units out of Forge already clashed with the Makvani? Adele's eyes took on a fierce glint, and she reached to untie her belt. Pashla started to unclasp her cloak, and Kyra realized with horror that they were preparing to change shape.

She grabbed Pashla and Adele by the arm. "Don't," she said. "There's many of them. You can't face them all."

Pashla's face tightened with annoyance, and she shook off Kyra's arm.

"Who goes there?" called a voice.

Kyra's stomach plummeted. For better or worse, the soldiers were here.

Pashla gave Kyra a furious glare. A group of about twenty men picked their way toward them, and the Makvani no longer had the window of time they needed to change shape. Out of the corner of her eye, Kyra saw Flick throw his cloak around Adele's shoulders. It took Kyra a moment to realize what he was doing. Adele's wraparound tunic was the easiest way to identify her as Makvani, and Flick was covering up the evidence. Adele cast a suspicious glance toward him but kept the cloak around her shoulders.

One by one, the soldiers came into view. It wasn't Flick's unit, though like them, these soldiers lacked livery and wore the usual peasant garb of rough tunics and trousers. Despite the lack of uniforms, these men were formidable looking, much tougher than what Kyra remembered from the training fields. They were well muscled, and they carried swords and spears with confidence. A barrel-chested man stepped out to speak to them.

"Your names?"

Flick stepped out from behind her. "My name is Fyvie of Forge, good soldier," he said. "These are my sisters Marla and Isabel, Laurie, and their companions."

The soldier sized them up, and Kyra hoped desperately that Pashla and Adele wouldn't decide to attack. They wouldn't be so rash as to change shape in front of twenty soldiers, would they? Next to her, Pashla lowered her eyes just the slightest bit. Was she trying to hide the amber in them?

"Your business?" asked the soldiers.

"Winter mushrooms," said Flick. "They go for a fortune at the markets, and we used to have a good patch a little north of here. We thought we heard demon cats though, so we're cutting our losses. Best to leave here with our lives and no mushrooms than the other way around, right?" He gave the soldier a self-effacing grin.

The soldier released his hands from his scabbard. "You heard the roars too, then?"

"Aye," said Flick. "Raised the hair on the back of my neck."

The soldier jerked his head toward a man behind him. "Nyles almost got one this morning. Stuck it good in the shoulder, but the beast got away." Pashla stiffened, but the man didn't seem to notice. "Best to pick someplace to forage that doesn't put you in the path of fighting. His Grace doesn't want people in the forest these days."

His Grace, Kyra thought wryly. Not even *the Council.* The soldier was referring directly to Willem as if he were Duke of Forge. That didn't bode well.

The soldier waved them on their way, and Flick started walking in the direction of the main road. The rest of them followed. When the soldiers were no longer in view, Kyra let out a sigh of relief.

"Those are the soldiers you've been telling me about?" asked Pashla. She stared back in their direction, her gaze calculating.

"Aye," said Kyra. The clanswoman didn't seem as dismissive of the troops now that she'd seen them. Kyra wondered if this morning's fighting might have changed her mind. "Pashla, I know Leyus doesn't want to see me, but those soldiers could be a real threat to you. Can you please let me speak with him just once?"

In the ensuing silence, Kyra found herself wishing again that the clanswoman wasn't so hard to read. Finally Pashla gave the slightest of nods. "I'll bring you to Leyus, though he will not be happy with me."

Kyra celebrated a brief moment of triumph before she remembered Flick, Idalee, and Lettie. "I should see my friends safely out of the forest first."

"Bring them," said Pashla. "There are those in the clan who are curious to see more of the humans."

Curious? Kyra wasn't about to risk her family's life to satisfy some Makvani's curiosity.

Her hesitation must have shown, because Pashla spoke again, exasperated this time. "We are not barbarians," she said. "We do not hunt humans for sport. They will be under my protection."

"We'll come," said Idalee. When Kyra looked at her, she shrugged. "Every time we try to go somewhere safer, it just gets worse. At least Pashla says she'll protect us."

Kyra looked to Flick and then Lettie, who nodded in turn. "So be it," Kyra said.

Pashla set off without further comment, leading them through the trees. As they walked, Adele unclasped Flick's cloak and handed it wordlessly back to him.

"You don't get cold?" he asked.

"No," she said.

Kyra bit back a grin as she watched Flick waver between his usual inclination to insist she keep it and his suspicion that Adele would kill him if he argued. He took back the cloak.

After a while, Pashla asked them to wait while she and Adele changed shape. Once in her fur, Pashla threw her head skyward and roared. There was a distant roar in response. Pashla's ears perked toward the sound, and she loped off in that direction. Adele was a slender shadow next to her, almost flowing over the snow. Kyra noticed the black cat's eyes going often to Flick as they traveled, and Kyra surreptitiously inserted herself between the two of them. Pashla might have promised to watch over him, but a few extra precautions wouldn't hurt.

Eventually, Kyra spotted shapes through the trees. She recognized Leyus by his height and commanding posture. In the light of day, he was less frightening, though no more approachable. The clan leader stood talking to Havel and Zora, the Demon Riders who had come upon Kyra in the field. There were others scattered throughout the trees in their skin and their fur—fewer than twenty total, but that wasn't surprising. The Makvani came together only when necessary. Adele sniffed the air as they approached, then left them to join the others.

Kyra looked to see how her friends were holding up. Lettie held tightly to Idalee's hand, staring unabashedly at the Demon Riders. Idalee's jaw was set in a stubborn line, and Flick stayed protectively close to the two girls, one arm loosely resting on each of their shoulders. Around them, the Makvani started to notice the humans. They didn't approach, but they certainly looked, and whispered to each other.

"You'd better be right about us being under your protection," Kyra muttered to Pashla. She thought she saw Pashla's ears twitch in response.

Leyus's mouth tightened in displeasure when Kyra came closer. He turned to Pashla. "Why did you bring her here?"

"I'm here with a message from Forge," Kyra said as Pashla regained her human form. "I'm sure you've seen troops in the forest already. They're just the first step of preparation for a forest offensive meant to hunt all your people down, and it will surely result in unnecessary deaths on both sides. The Defense Minister asks you to consider negotiating peace."

"I've seen one of these so-called units in the forest," said Leyus. "We have nothing to fear from them."

Flick's group hadn't impressed Kyra either, though the unit this morning had looked more formidable. "You're right that many of them are untrained," she said. "But they outnumber you by far, and eventually they'll overwhelm you with their numbers."

Something registered in the back of her mind, and Kyra took a closer look at two demon cats lounging beneath a nearby tree. One beast was lying down, and Kyra saw that blood matted its fur. The other was licking the injured cat's shoulder, cleaning the wound as Pashla had done before for Kyra.

"How did that cat get injured?" asked Kyra.

Leyus followed her gaze. "That is none of your concern."

"He was wounded by humans, wasn't he?" said Kyra, plunging ahead. "Though the humans were weak, their spear struck true."

"Enough." The edge in Leyus's voice was sufficient to make Kyra stop. "The soldiers present no danger, and your city insults us with their quality." Leyus turned to Pashla. "Take them back to where they came from."

Pashla bowed, running three fingers down the front of her throat. Before Kyra could say anything more, Leyus and his two companions disappeared into the trees.

"Leyus has spoken," said Pashla.

"But—" Kyra began. The clanswoman silenced her with a glance. Kyra swallowed her words and followed. The others fell into step behind her.

The injured demon cat growled as they passed. Kyra thought it was growling at them but then realized that its ire was directed toward the beast tending its wound. Adele was with them. She'd changed back into her skin, and she called Pashla's name, followed by a string of words Kyra could not understand. Pashla circled back and nudged the standing demon cat aside so she could crouch next to the injured one.

"The muscle is torn, but it will heal," said Pashla. "Just keep cleaning her wound."

Flick reached into his belt pouch. "I have herbs," he said. "To help with the bleeding and the pain." He held a handful of dried moss out to the clanswomen. Adele eyed the herbs but didn't take them until Pashla nodded her reassurance. The younger clanswoman moved as if to apply the herbs to the wound but hesitated.

Flick spoke hesitantly. "I was taught to crumble some onto the wound and use the rest to press it in." He scooted closer but stopped when Adele jerked away. "Sorry," he said.

Adele handed the moss back to him. "You apply it," she said.

Flick caught Kyra's eye. She shrugged, unsure how to advise him. It seemed unwise to refuse, but tending to a wounded demon cat definitely carried its own risks. Flick drew a long breath, then did as Adele asked, crumbling the moss over the wound and then carefully, very carefully, pressing the moss to the demon cat's shoulder. Kyra slumped with relief when the creature didn't bite Flick's hand off. Flick signaled for Adele to replace his hands with hers, then sat back on his heels.

An older Demon Rider pointed to Lettie and asked Pashla a question. Kyra took a protective half step toward the girl.

"He says she looks like Libena," Pashla said, and gestured toward a very young demon cat in the shadows. Kyra recognized Libena's yellow fur and large eyes and spotted Libena's younger brother Ziben behind her. She'd met these two the last time she'd been with the Makvani.

The kittens stared at Lettie, who stared right back at them. Slowly, Libena crept closer until she stood just a few steps in front of Lettie. The kitten's head came to the same height as the girl's. Kyra watched them carefully, ready at any moment to snatch Lettie back. Libena sniffed at the air, while Lettie continued to stand completely still. Kyra found herself holding her breath. Strangely, it reminded her of the time she'd given Lettie a handful of grain and let her stand in the square for birds to land on her.

Suddenly, the demon kitten whirled around and ran back into the trees. Her brother followed quickly behind.

Pashla watched all this quietly and then signaled for Flick to stand up. "Let us go," she said. "I'll see you safely out of the forest."

FOURTEEN

The magistrate had a way of keeping one eye on Tristam as he wrote, nailing him with a suspicious gaze even as he simultaneously made notes on his desk. It was all Tristam could do to maintain his act under this unnerving scrutiny. He was fortunate, at least, that he was being questioned in the magistrate's study rather than the interrogation rooms, and that for the past week he'd been under house arrest instead of in the Palace dungeons.

The magistrate stopped writing and lifted his parchment up to read, careful of the drying ink. This particular official wasn't one of Willem's lapdogs, though he wasn't overly sympathetic to Malikel's cause either. "I have your official statement, Tristam," he said. "You admit to working alongside Kyra of Forge, but you maintain that you had no knowledge of her identity as a Demon Rider until the night of Sir Santon's murder. Furthermore, you have no knowledge of her current whereabouts. Do you swear to this?"

"I do."

It was clear from the way the men around Tristam exchanged disgusted looks that they didn't believe him—not the magistrate, with his piercing gaze; not the Red Shields by the door, placed there "for his safety"; and certainly not Head Councilman Willem, watching the proceedings from his spot against the wall. But they had no evidence against him and more important targets to go after. The magistrate raised a questioning glance to Willem. "If Your Grace finds no problem with my report, I will declare him free to go."

Willem drummed long fingers on the table. "Your report is satisfactory, but I'll have a private word with Tristam before he's released."

"Very well, Your Grace." The magistrate addressed Tristam. "You will resume your normal Red Shield duties after your release. Any special tasks you've been undertaking for the Defense Minister are, of course, suspended until we are sure of his role in this matter."

The magistrate gathered his things and left, followed by the Red Shield guards. The door clicked shut behind them, and Tristam didn't move as he waited for Willem to speak.

Willem fixed a stern gaze on Tristam. "I won't keep you long. I know you've never been fond of me or my policies." He brushed away Tristam's clumsy attempt at contradicting him. "I simply want to suggest you keep an open mind. You must realize by now that your commander is accused of some very serious lapses in judgment."

Lapses that perhaps could have been avoided had Tristam and Kyra been more forthright about what she was. Something twisted in Tristam's stomach. Had they been wrong to keep the secret from Malikel?

"What direction do you see for Forge?" asked Willem. "Do you share Malikel's goals, giving handouts to the poor, fighting their battles for them? Your father and your brothers patrol your family manor every day at great personal risk. Why shouldn't the common people help defend the lands?"

Tristam gave grudging credit to Willem for bringing up his family. The thought of losing Henril or anyone else was hard even to consider. "We believe it our duty, Your Grace, to take those risks."

Willem gave a hard smile. "That's admirable, but have you ever considered that it might be an empty endeavor? Truth is, we could clear out the Palace treasury and sacrifice all our lives to serve the needy, yet the poor will still remain. Malikel caters to the tenderhearted, but he picks a fight he can't win. Meanwhile, he takes resources from initiatives that could make real change. Forge could be great. We could make Forge a city to be remembered in the history books, and everyone within it would prosper."

Everyone, or simply those in a position to benefit directly? Tristam didn't voice his thoughts.

Willem picked up the parchment from the table. "You may go, but I hope you'll think on what I said. How much will you sacrifice for those who may not deserve it?"

"Thank you, Your Grace."

Right before Tristam reached the door, Willem spoke again. "That's a nasty bruise you have on your jaw, Tristam."

Tristam paused, his hand hovering above the doorknob.

The spot on his chin where Kyra had struck him was still tender to the touch. "It's getting better," he said.

"It's a rare sort of creature who would cause such harm to a supposed friend."

Tristam left without replying. He half expected the soldiers outside the door to tackle him, but they only watched him pass.

The courtyard outside resembled a market more than the Palace grounds. Throngs of citizens lined up in front of harried scribes to enlist in Willem's new army, pushing past one another in their impatience to get through the wait. They were a far cry from the disciplined Red Shields who usually lined up within these walls. Conscripting new soldiers had caused problems in the Palace, and the difficulties didn't just stem from the recruits themselves. Word was that the record-keeping was sloppy as well. Several groups of citizens had already been called back because harried scribes had misplaced their records. The Palace simply wasn't equipped to handle an influx of so many new soldiers at one time.

Tristam hunched his shoulders and threaded through jostling bodies. The noise faded as he left the crowd behind, and he finally gathered his thoughts. He'd been cleared of suspicion. That in itself was a minor miracle. Unfortunately, that almost certainly meant that Malikel was taking most of the blame on himself. Tristam wondered again at the Defense Minister's reaction upon finding Santon's body. The more he thought about it, the more convinced he became that Malikel hadn't been surprised to learn Kyra's identity. The Defense Minister had suspected something about Kyra, but for some reason, he hadn't taken action. Now he would pay the price.

When Tristam got to his chambers, he found that the guards posted there for the past week were already gone. He closed his door, walked into the middle of his room, and surveyed the silent furniture around him. What now?

His breastplate hung on a rack against the wall, polished to Malikel's exacting standards. He could see his face reflected on its surface, and he leaned closer to examine the bruise on his chin. There was a scab on his lip where it had split from Kyra's blow. He saw her again in his mind's eye—confused, horrified, and covered in Santon's blood. Where had she gone? Was she safe? If only he had some way to contact her.

Everything had happened so fast that night. He'd known Kyra's bloodlines and what the Makvani were capable of, but Tristam never expected to find Kyra changed in the Palace courtyard, or see her standing above Santon's corpse. What had driven her to this?

Someone knocked on the door, and Tristam answered to find a servant in the corridor holding a stack of parchments. The servant was an older man whose build suggested a life spent indoors rather than in the fields. "Sir Willem has requested that your armor and equipment be inventoried, in light of the new recruits," the man said.

Now Tristam recognized him. The man was part of Willem's personal staff. "Are all the Red Shields having their equipment inventoried, or just me?" he asked, not bothering to hide the suspicion in his voice. After hearing Willem's speech about Forge and its future, Tristam had thought the Head Councilman was trying to earn Tristam's trust. This seemed a step in the opposite direction.

"Only those that His Grace has listed," the man said in a maddeningly neutral voice. "May I come in? I'm instructed not to touch or take anything at this point, just to take note of any equipment that might belong to the Palace."

Tristam didn't really have the leeway to be difficult right now. He surreptitiously checked the dagger at his belt as his unwelcome guest came to stand in front of Tristam's sword and armor.

"The weapons and equipment are my own," Tristam said, aware that he sounded like a petulant child.

The manservant nodded. "And livery. How many sets do you have?"

"I surrendered anything marking me a knight when they stripped me of my rank." His frustration was rising with every passing moment. "I have two Red Shield tunics that I wear on duty."

The manservant nodded and jotted something down on his parchment. "We may have to take one of those." Finally, he raised his head and looked around. "That will be all. Thank you. My name is Orvin of Forge, if you have further need of me."

He let himself out the door, and Tristam closed it none too lightly behind him. When he turned back around, he noticed a piece of parchment on the table. Had the servant left it there? Tristam unfolded it to find words inside.

I have a message for Kyra, was all it said.

Tristam read the note two or three times. A message for Kyra from Willem's household? If this was a trap, then they were woefully misled. Tristam had no idea where Kyra was, whether she'd fled to the forest or other cities, or somehow found a place to hide within the city walls.

Or could the man be sincere? Not all of Willem's servants were personally loyal to the Councilman. Tristam took two quick steps to his door and pulled it ajar, remembering at the last minute not to throw it open in his eagerness. He peered outside, hoping for another glimpse of Orvin, but the man was long gone.

FIFTEEN

Flick hated the idea of leaving Kyra by herself, but after the near miss with Adele, it was clear that the forest wasn't safe for him and the younger girls. So when the flat stone near Mercie's window turned to signal an all clear, he took Idalee and Lettie back to the old woman's house. Kyra set up camp in a cave nearby with a small stash of food and supplies from Mercie, and Flick left her there with a promise to return soon.

Mercie ran a tight ship. Flick, Idalee, and Lettie posed as grandchildren of a friend of hers who'd come upon hard times. They had chores every day, but the workload was reasonable. After a few days, Mercie went into the city and brought back news, along with a note on a piece of parchment.

"It was left for you at your old home," she said, handing it to Flick.

The message was actually for Kyra. It looked like she'd been using Flick's address without telling him again. Flick didn't mind, though the vagueness of the wording piqued his curiosity. The next day, he packed up some bread and dried meat, and set off into the forest.

He walked quickly, not eager to spend any more time out here than he needed to. Kyra hadn't wanted him to come to the forest at all, but she was such a consummate city lass, and Flick worried about her having enough to eat. He supposed she could have hunted, but she hadn't seemed very eager to change shape.

The bare winter landscape was both a blessing and a curse. It made it easy to see people coming from far off, but also made it harder to keep oneself hidden. He found himself scanning the trees as he walked, wondering if any Demon Riders were watching him. His recent encounter with the Makvani had been one of the most frightening and fascinating experiences of his life—to be so close to death, and then to be granted entry into a world that only a handful of humans had seen. It had been terrifying, yet Flick had also come out of it feeling strangely honored. The Makvani were a brutal people. There was no doubt about that, and Flick had seen humans die at their hands. But his experience in the forest had shown him that there was more to the Makvani. Their culture, their way of being together . . . it made him wonder.

He was mulling this over when two Demon Rider women stepped out of thin air.

Flick stopped in his tracks, feeling a prickle travel down the back of his neck. He knew only one person who could move undetected like that, and that was Kyra—though he supposed he shouldn't be surprised that these women were just as silent. The first woman he recognized as Adele, the one who had tried to kill him. The second woman was a stranger, much taller than the petite Adele, statuesque with a long, graceful neck and chestnut curls. Her arm was in a sling.

As he stood frozen, Adele stepped forward. She walked with the same Makvani grace that he'd grown used to seeing in Kyra, though there was an otherworldly quality about Adele, something about her movements that was not quite human. She regarded him with her head cocked to one side, like a bird. (Flick wondered briefly if he should amend that to a cat watching a bird. But she'd been friendly enough the last time she came.)

"We mean no harm," she said. She held something sizable and grayish brown in front of her like a platter. When she came closer, Flick realized it was a dead rabbit. Newly killed, by the look of it, with blood still matted in its fur. She held it out to him.

"This is for you," she said. "In thanks for the herbs."

"Thank you." Flick took it from her, doing his best to give the impression that he received dead rabbits as presents every day. "This will . . . be a welcome addition to our dinner tonight."

Adele gestured toward her friend. Even that motion seemed smoother on her. "Mela's shoulder is greatly improved."

Mela's shoulder. Of course. The woman standing in front of him was the injured demon cat he'd helped. As if following the direction of his thoughts, Mela met his eyes and inclined her head.

"I'm glad," said Flick. He paused again, wondering how best to proceed.

Adele looked around the forest. Her eyes darted quickly from one thing to the next, giving an impression that she didn't miss much. "You're traveling alone through the forest," she said. "This is dangerous." It wasn't immediately clear whether that was intended as a warning or a question. Flick decided to take it as the latter and hope for the best.

"Aye," he said. "But Kyra's been alone out here for a while. I worry she'll go hungry."

Adele's eyes moved over his features. "Do you share blood with Kyra?"

"Blood? Oh no," said Flick. "We met as children."

"But you are close."

"As close as brother and sister at this point, I'd say."

Adele nodded with something that looked like approval. "It's good that you are loyal to her." She exchanged a glance with Mela. "We will escort you. It will be safer for you that way."

That was unexpected, but it took a weight off his chest. "Thank you," said Flick. "I'd be grateful."

She fell in step beside him, with Mela trailing right behind. Adele asked him questions about Forge as they walked—how many people there were, how they felt about the Makvani, what kind of food they ate . . . If Flick had been the suspicious type, he might have thought she was trying to get information to use against the city. But he didn't think that was the case. Adele had an air of genuine curiosity, as did Mela, who occasionally interrupted with more fanciful inquiries about the colors that humans preferred, or why they wore tunics that required pulling over their heads to remove. Occasionally, Adele gave Mela a reproachful look, as if she thought her friend's question was too silly.

Presently, Adele slowed. "Kyra is there," she said.

It took Flick a while to spot Kyra, and by the time he did, his old friend was running toward him. Kyra's clothes were wrinkled—she'd probably slept in them for several days in a row now—but she otherwise looked healthy. She was about to throw her arms around Flick when she noticed Adele and Mela. Her expression became more guarded.

"We came with him to make sure he didn't get attacked," said Adele. She turned to Flick. "We will rejoin you when you're ready to return."

Neither Kyra nor Flick said anything until the Makvani were out of sight.

"How'd you manage to charm those two?" Kyra asked.

Flick held out the rabbit. "They liked the herbs I gave them. This was their way of thanking me. Feeling hungry?"

Kyra eyed the carcass. "Keep it. My cooking won't do it justice out here."

He handed her the bag of supplies that he'd brought. "The news from the city is bad. There's a price on your head. Malikel's been removed from Council duties and placed under house arrest while the magistrate investigates." Flick wasn't one to follow politics, but even he knew that removing Malikel from the Council would upset the balance of things greatly.

Kyra let the bag of supplies sink to the ground. "And Tristam?"

"Mercie didn't say anything about him, but my best guess is that he's also under investigation."

Her gaze went distant at his words, and Flick watched as conflicting emotions made their way across her face. Flick still wasn't completely sure what had happened between Kyra and Tristam, but he'd eat his cloak before he believed that she no longer had feelings for the wallhugger.

"This is my fault," said Kyra. "I can't just leave them there to take my punishment."

Flick sighed. He'd had a feeling she'd say that. "You won't do them any favors by going back. What could you do?"

She looked at him, her jaw set in a stubborn line.

"Be realistic, Kyra. The Palace would just kill you on sight."

He could tell she wanted to argue, but eventually her shoulders slumped. Flick relaxed slightly when he saw that she'd given up on that line of thought.

"There's one more thing," he said, pulling out the parchment Mercie had given him. "A man named Jacobo says he wants to talk to you."

Here, she perked up. Kyra looked over the parchment with interest. "I asked him about Demon Riders a while back."

"Says he's got news and he's wintering outside the city, if you want to talk to him. Is this about your family?"

She gave a careful nod, and he could tell she was afraid to hope for too much. Flick felt a twinge of compassion for her. He might not be thrilled with his own bloodlines, but at least he knew where he came from. "Will you talk to him, then?"

She hesitated a moment. "Aye," she said. "I'll go tomorrow."

"Want me to go with you?"

Kyra shook her head. "No, I'll be better able to avoid trouble if I travel alone."

As much as he hated to admit it, she was probably right. "Be careful, then, and let me know what you find out." Flick looked out toward the forest. "I should probably be getting back before my . . . escorts get tired of waiting."

Kyra gave him one last hug, coming at him from the side

to avoid the rabbit carcass he still held in his hand. "Good to see you, Flick. Go safely." She took a step back, eyed the rabbit, and then looked off in the direction Adele and Mela had gone. Suddenly, she burst out laughing.

"What?" said Flick.

Kyra shook her head. "I don't know how you do it, Flick. I really don't."

SIXTEEN

Not much news filtered down to the dungeons, but when Kyra killed Santon of Agan and Malikel fell from grace, the Red Shields on duty talked, and James listened. The news came at a time when the assassin sorely needed something in his favor. After weeks of imprisonment, James had fallen ill, and he was running out of time.

In some ways, the illness made things easier for James. It compressed his sense of the passing hours as he hung in his cell and dulled his pain during the interrogation sessions. Over the past few days, his jailers had noticed his illness and had cut their visits short. James was thankful for it. The Palace hadn't yet gotten any useful information out of him about the Guild, but James knew his limits. He'd come close to breaking more than once. The Palace was determined, he'd give them that.

As the fever grew progressively worse, he spent less and less time awake. While before, he had done his best to exercise within the confines of his chains, he now drifted in and out of sleep. He dreamed sometimes of Thalia, her eyes aflame with purpose. She faded in and out, and it was just as well. If she'd stayed longer, he might have been tempted to give up and join her, but he wouldn't give the wallhuggers that satisfaction.

James started receiving visits from a Palace healer, who mixed foul-tasting potions and poured them down his throat. Apparently the Palace thought him too valuable to die. She brought an assistant, a scrawny young man who never quite stood up straight. James paid him no heed the first few times except to note that he stood quietly by the side and did as his mistress commanded.

Today though, James noticed that the apprentice's forehead was covered with a sheen of sweat. Several times, he dropped the herbs he was supposed to be mixing. His mistress was too caught up in examining James to notice, but James made note of it, even as he hung from his chains with his eyes half-closed. The apprentice was nervous, and that was interesting. Very interesting.

James had developed a grudging respect for the Defense Minister during his time in the dungeon. Malikel was smart. Much more competent than his predecessor, and he'd acted decisively and quickly to counter any possible attempts to break James out. The guards who watched over him had proved hard to blackmail or bribe. But with the current trouble in the Council, maybe, just maybe, there were now some holes in the Palace's precautions.

James kept his body heavy and his movements lethargic. It wasn't hard to do, with the fever pounding in his brain. The healer was finishing up now. She made notes on a piece of parchment as the apprentice packed up her jars of herbs and gathered soiled bandages. He came to stand in front of James and inspected a bandage on James's arm.

"Sloppy wrapping," the apprentice muttered. His words were tight and clipped, and his eyes darted between James and the healer. He unraveled the bandage partway and pressed something hard and flat against James's arm before rewrapping. Then he lowered his voice even more. "Two days from now. Second watch."

James wondered how Bacchus had gotten to this one. Bribery? Threats? He suspected the former. There was a glint of avarice in the young man's eyes and not enough fear for the latter. He hoped Bacchus had an adequate plan. To break someone out of the dungeons was no small task.

As the apprentice returned to his mistress's side, James flexed his forearm and felt the pressure of the blade against it. It was small. Its shape suggested that it didn't even have a hilt. But if he was careful and quick, it would be enough.

SEVENTEEN

Kyra knew where the trade caravans wintered. There was a cluster of clearings west of the city, and she'd run across trade caravans there a few times when touring the woods with Tristam. It would take a while to get there because she'd have to avoid the main roads, and there would be some risk. Could this be a trap by Jacobo to lure her in for the reward money? She didn't think so. Jacobo hadn't seemed the type to sell people out to the Palace. And this was one circumstance under which Kyra refused to be careful. If Jacobo did have more information about her past, then she would learn what it was.

She set out early in the direction of the trader camp. It took her the better part of the morning, but eventually she noticed wagon ruts on a side path. A few more steps, and she smelled smoke. She started to hear voices through the trees after a while, and shapes around what were now clearly several campfires.

A voice called out. "Stop there, stranger. What's your business?" A man stepped out of the trees. Between his fur hat and his thick cloak, Kyra couldn't see much of his face.

"My name is Kyra," she said. "I'm looking for Jacobo. Is he wintering here?"

The sentry looked her over, then waved her past. Kyra noticed other sentries in the shadows, both men and women, warmly bundled and holding spears like they knew how to use them. She kept a mental note of where they were and the gaps in their formations.

Kyra broke through the trees and into a clearing where ten wagons circled a fire pit. When she walked through to the center, she saw Jacobo and four other men and women sitting around the campfire. The trader was much as Kyra had remembered, though he looked more at home here, reclining at the fire, than he'd been in Forge. It took him a moment to recognize her.

"Kyra of Forge," he said, extending a hand to her. "I'm glad I found you. It seems I'm not the only one looking these days."

His words gave her a jolt, and she hesitated a split second before taking his hand. If Jacobo knew there was a price on her head, then he must also know what she was. But Jacobo's handshake was firm, and his gaze didn't waver.

"I've run into some trouble lately, but I mean no harm to your camp," she said.

"I certainly hope not." He indicated the spear bearers. "We do travel the Aerins, and we have experience defending against dangers." He smiled, and his eyes crinkled. "But I didn't call you here to deliver threats, and you needn't look like we're going to knock you over the head and deliver you to the Palace. There's someone who would like to talk to you." He indicated another trader sitting by the campfire. The man's hair was mostly gray, and his face was lined with wrinkles that told of a lifetime in the sun, but he stood up with no difficulty, and his stance was sure. Kyra stopped dead in her tracks when she realized whom he must be. Jacobo had mentioned a survivor of the caravan attack fifteen years ago....

Jacobo cleared his throat. "Craigson, this is Kyra of Forge."

The older trader dismissed Jacobo's introduction with a wave and swaggered over to where they stood. He then proceeded to look Kyra over from head to toe, as if evaluating a packhorse. Kyra was just about to make a rude comment when the man crossed his arms and nodded in satisfaction.

"She's not Kyra of Forge, Jacobo. She's Kyra of Mayel." Then he looked Kyra in the eye, and his gaze softened. "Your face brings up many memories, lass."

Did he recognize her? Though this was why she had come, she couldn't shake the feeling that this was impossible. She was an orphan. Her past was unknowable. To accept his words would be like putting on a glove that belonged to someone else.

Craigson took a step closer. "I've startled you. I apologize." He reached for Kyra but lowered his hand when she flinched. He spoke again, his voice thick with regret. "In fact, I must beg your forgiveness for many things. You were under my care when I lost you to the Demon Riders, and I was never able to find you."

Kyra's tongue was dry in her mouth. She felt dizzy, and she probably could not have formed words even if she'd known what to say. The most she could do was nod when Craigson suggested they go somewhere quieter to talk and follow him until they found a fallen tree some distance from the camp. As she sat and looked more closely at his face, she remembered a dream she had the first time she was in the forest with Tristam. There had been demon cats all around her, and a man had been carrying her and running away.

This man, Louis Craigson.

"I was on your caravan when it was attacked," she blurted. "You fled with me, and you smeared my face and clothes with some kind of pitch."

Craigson sat as well, holding one of the fallen log's protruding branches for support as he lowered himself down. "You remember, then," he said, eyes trained on her face. "What else do you remember?"

Kyra shook her head slowly. "I don't remember much else."

He let out a bark of a laugh. "Of course you would only remember the worst moments. You did have some good times with us, you know. You used to climb around my textile wagons and burrow under the blankets."

Kyra imagined burying her face in pungent silk as he said this, but who knew if it was a memory or just something she'd conjured?

Craigson continued. "The pitch you remember was to hide your scent from the felbeasts—demon cats, as you call them here."

"You're from across the Aerins?" Kyra asked.

"I hail from Edlan, but I was a Far Ranger much of my life, as I never had much use for dukes or cities. I crossed the Aerins often and traveled a route that went as far as your mother's village."

Her heart skipped a beat at the word "mother." The one person she'd forbidden herself from thinking about because she'd seemed so out of reach. "Who is my mother?" She was light-headed with the eagerness to know. And there was a second question, one that frightened her with its possibilities. "Is she alive?"

Craigson let out a long breath, looking down as if having a hard time picking the right words, and Kyra feared the worst.

"The answer to your second question is that I don't know," he finally said. "She was alive the last time I crossed the Aerins a decade ago, but we lost touch after I stopped traveling. But let's start from the beginning. You were born in a desert village called Mayel, about as far from here as you can get. Your mother's name was Maikana."

"Maikana," Kyra repeated, sampling the syllables. "It sounds like a different language."

"It is, but the leaders of her village speak our language too. They call it the trader tongue." Craigson paused again. "Your own name is actually Kayara," he said gently. "Though it's not hard to see why it might have turned to Kyra over the years."

She felt an irrational panic rising in her chest. For some reason, that revelation knocked her off balance more than even the mention of her mother. All these years as an orphan, she'd had at least her name. With effort, Kyra fought the panic back down.

"What was my ma like?"

"She was a strong woman. A leader of her people, and she loved her village dearly." Craigson looked at Kyra, and suddenly chuckled. "I hear you're quite a climber."

"Climber?" It was such a random thing to say. "I do climb walls when I need to. I'm a thief." She felt surprisingly ashamed at that admission, now that Craigson had just told her how respectable her mother was, but Craigson didn't react to the revelation at all.

"If you ever cross the Aerins and see your mother's village, you'll see why it amuses me. They are all well-practiced climbers. You look a great deal like her people—small, slight of form. And your face is the spitting image of your aunt." He braced a hand on his knee. "Maikana bore you and raised you for two years, but there was a drought that you couldn't weather. She put you in my care until the rains came again. I wasn't planning to take you across the Aerins, but your father somehow got word that I had you."

"My father. He was Makvani?"

"Your mother was human. Your father was a member of a Makvani slaver clan that attacked your mother's village."

Pashla had told her before about the Makvani's history as slave traders. But if her father had been a slaver who'd attacked her mother's village... It raised a horrifying implication. "Did he ... force my mother ..."

Craigson furrowed his brow. "To be honest, I don't know what happened between your parents. She never spoke of the specifics, and I never asked. I know that things were not simple between them and that it didn't end well. Maikana didn't want him to know about you, but somehow he found out. We crossed the mountains when we learned he was seeking you, but he and his companions pursued us. We managed to evade them for a while because we knew this land better, but they caught up to us near Forge. I stowed you in what I thought was a safe place and led them away." Here, Craigson paused and eyed a spot on the ground in front of him with distaste. "They left me for dead, but some travelers found me. It took me two days to get coherent, and several more until I could go search for you. And by then..." He spread his hands. "You were gone. Along with the rest of my caravan. I figured they'd taken you, or that you'd died." Kyra was surprised to hear a slight tremor in Craigson's voice. The trader seemed so gruff.

"And my da. Do you know what happened to him?"

"Aye, I kept track of his whereabouts, and I made sure to avoid him and his clan. He crossed back over the Aerins, and after a while it got too dangerous for me to travel, so I found a quiet place outside Edlan and settled down. I didn't hear of him for many years, though there was news of fighting among the Makvani and rumors that some clans were searching out new lands. So it wasn't a surprise to me when I heard he'd come back, this time with his entire clan. He must know by now that I'm here. I'm sure he keeps an eye on travelers."

It took Kyra a moment to realize the implications of Craigson's words, but when they sank in, she found it hard to breathe. Thus far, only two clans had come across the Aerins, and she'd met both their leaders. Could it be...

"Who is my father?" This time, her eagerness was mixed with dread.

Craigson hesitated then, and that space between two breaths felt like an hour. But then he met her eyes. "Your father is the leader of the first clan that came over the mountains. His name is Leyus."

EIGHTEEN

The door to James's cell opened. He could tell from the footsteps that two Red Shields had entered, and he didn't spend any strength to look. The Palace interrogator preferred working after dark, and the guards often came for James at this hour, the second watch of the night.

"It's a dangerous line they're walking, bringing him in so often when they want to keep him alive," said one.

"Our job is to obey orders, not ask questions. He asleep?"

The first guard put a hand under James's chin and lifted. James returned his gaze with half-closed eyes.

"Naw, he's awake. But we might have to carry him." They spoke with a careless air. As the once famed leader of the Assassins Guild had sickened like any other prisoner, the guards gradually lost their caution around him. James did his best to encourage this. It made what he had to do just a little easier.

James slumped against the chains, letting his body fall heavy. He flexed his fingers just slightly, feeling for the strength in his arms, and then did the same for his torso and legs. He didn't have much left in him. It would have to be quick.

The guard's key clicked to unlock the shackles around one of his wrists, and then the other. James crumpled to the ground and landed on his knees, bending so that his body blocked his right arm from the guards' view. The faint outline of the blade was visible beneath the top layer of bandages. He coughed and used the spasms to hide his movements as he ripped those layers loose. A small blade with no handle dropped into his hand, and James gripped it, careful not to cut himself on the satisfyingly sharp edge. The guard swore and hauled James to his feet.

Now.

James brought the blade up, threading it between the guard's arms and slicing it across his neck. He didn't stop to check his work but turned to the other guard, who stumbled back in alarm. James closed the distance between them, thrust his elbow into the guard's ribs, and slit the man's throat as he fell forward. The whole thing happened in the span of two heartbeats. Neither guard had made a sound.

He stumbled then, and reached for the wall as a wave of nausea overtook him. That burst of speed had cost him. When he could move again, he examined the two guards on the ground. One man was much bigger than he, but the other had a similar build to James. He knelt and removed this guard's tunic. It was slick with blood, but thankfully, Red Shield livery was crimson, and it was dark. He also took the guard's sword and dagger.

He caught two other guards unawares on the ground floor of the dungeon. He'd hoped to walk right past them, but the prison guard force was small, and they knew each other by name. Another of Malikel's precautions, most likely. The first guard, he dispatched cleanly. The second called for help and opened a gash in James's thigh before James was able to drive a dagger through his stomach. As the man fell to the ground, James heard answering shouts. The door at the end of the corridor flew open, and two Red Shields appeared. James pivoted to run but stopped when another guard came up the stairs at the opposite end. They had him hemmed in.

James put his back against the wall and turned so he could see the men coming at him from either side. His initial flood of energy from the escape was ebbing away. Still, better to die fighting than wasting away under the interrogator's care. He eyed the lone guard between him and the stairs and willed one last bit of strength.

The door burst open again and two men with covered faces ran in. Two glints of metal flew through the air, and James flattened himself against the wall. There was a thud, a clink of metal on stone, and a gurgling gasp. The Red Shield closest to the door pitched forward, a knife buried in his back. His comrade pressed one hand firmly to his side as he turned to face the new threat, only to be run through as he raised his blade.

As the third Red Shield struggled to make sense of the scene, James attacked. He feinted to the left, then stepped in to close the distance. Pain lanced through his leg—he'd forgotten about that. As he collapsed, a knife flew over his head and grazed the Red Shield's arm. The soldier grunted, and James brought his knife up into the man's gut. The man fell. James heard footsteps behind him and turned just as one of the masked men came up close. A carrot-colored lock of hair had escaped the man's mask.

James smiled.

Rand peeled off his mask and offered James a hand up, which he accepted with a muffled groan. Bacchus, also unmasked now, looked James up and down. They were standing close to a torch, and its light was bright enough to illuminate James's many cuts and bruises.

Bacchus shrugged. "You were always too fond of that pretty face of yours."

Rand spat on the ground. "Never mind his face. We've got to bind that leg."

Bacchus was already cutting strips from a Red Shield's livery. As he wrapped it around James's wound, James noticed that Bacchus favored his left arm. "You're wounded," he said.

"So are you," Bacchus retorted.

James looked at Rand. "And you?"

"A few scratches and bruises," said Rand as he retrieved the daggers he and Bacchus had thrown. "We couldn't get past the guards all quiet like your thief lass, so we'd best get out soon." He wiped off his dagger and tucked it into his belt. James noticed that both Rand and Bacchus had swords as well, though they hadn't drawn them in the cramped corridor. He didn't bother to ask whether any others from the Guild had come. Loyalties didn't run very deep in an organization like his, not when the Guildleader's position seemed so close to opening up again.

Bacchus pulled back to inspect James's newly bound leg. "You able to put weight on it?"

"I'll live."

Rand pulled James's arm over his shoulder, and they made for the exit.

Once outside, they ran. Or tried to. James's time in the prison had taken its toll, and his injured leg threatened to give way. Shouts came from the direction of the prison, followed by more shouts and the ringing of bells. Bacchus gestured toward a building that was partially sheltered by bushes, and they ducked into its shadow. Rand leaned against the wall, alert but breathing heavily. Bacchus held his blade at the ready and peered around the corner, back toward the prison.

"You're trailing blood," he said to James when he turned back. "Hard to see in the dark, but someone will spot it soon enough."

Rand tore a strip from his tunic and handed it to James, who pressed it firmly to his leg. They all went still as three Red Shields ran down the path in front of them. At first it seemed they would pass without noticing what hid in the shadows, but then the last soldier slowed and squinted in their direction. "Wait," he called to his comrades. "I think there's someone—"

The soldier's words choked off as Bacchus's dagger buried itself in his stomach. Before the man hit the ground, Bacchus and Rand had drawn their swords and charged. James moved to follow and bit back a curse as he fell against the wall. When he looked up again, the two remaining Red Shields lay on the ground. Wordlessly, Rand and Bacchus dragged the bodies into the bushes. There was a fresh cut across Rand's chest.

"It in't deep," said Rand when he saw James looking at it. "Stings like a banshee's scream though."

"You shouldn't have come to break me out," said James calmly. The three ducked farther out of sight.

Bacchus snorted. "And let the wallhuggers win? Not while I draw breath." Nobody mentioned that, at this point, it wasn't very clear how much longer any of them would be drawing breath.

"What do you think?" said Rand. "West wall?"

James thought over their options for escaping. Two sets of walls stood between them and freedom. They would either have to fight their way through two guarded gates or find some way to scale the walls. But now that the alarm had been sounded, guards were lighting torches and patrolling the perimeter. He tested his injured leg again and suppressed a grunt as pain lanced through his thigh. It would take him a while to climb in this condition. Rand and Bacchus had a decent chance of getting out if luck was on their side. With James in tow though, their odds became much more dire.

"I've got news that I couldn't entrust to a messenger," Bacchus said suddenly. "I followed up on the hunch you had about that lass. You were right about her—what she knows and what she can prove."

"You mean Kyra?"

"I mean Darylene."

James went completely still. He turned his gaze to Bacchus. "Are you sure?"

"One of my crew heard her confiding to a friend. Seems she's suffering from a crisis of conscience."

Rand snapped at them to be quiet. They fell silent as more Red Shields ran past.

"This is what we've been waiting for—if she can be

convinced," said James after they'd gone. "Have we got any leverage?"

"In't that what your boyish charm is for?" said Bacchus.

James tuned out the shouts of guards around him, weighing the risks. Rand and Bacchus stood alert on either side of him. Neither interrupted his thoughts.

"Change of plan," said James. "I talk to her now."

Rand dusted off his hands. "To her quarters, then?"

"No, I go alone," said James. "Her quarters are close by. I can get there fine, but I'll need a diversion."

Rand and Bacchus exchanged a look.

"You sure you've got your wits about you?" asked Bacchus.

"Aye," he said. His tone left no room for argument.

Bacchus gave James a long, calculating look, then drew his dagger. "Well, Rand, I've always thought those ministers' houses got too chilly in the winters. What do you say?"

"I'm in," said Rand. He looked to James. "Good luck."

"I'll see you when it's done."

As Rand and Bacchus sprinted away, James crouched down behind the bushes and settled to wait. Now that he wasn't moving, the chill from the air seeped into his bones, and he hoped Rand and Bacchus wouldn't be long. Thankfully the alarm bells soon started ringing a new pattern, and new shouts arose on the grounds around him. Once the shouts moved into the distance, James gritted his teeth and made his way as quickly as he could.

James knocked on her door and claimed to be a member of the guard force. When the girl opened it a crack, he forced his way in and shut the door behind him, ensuring her silence with a hand over her mouth and a knife to her throat. She went rigid under his blade, though she didn't weep or scream.

"I mean you no harm," he said. "I wish to talk. You'll want to hear me out, if you care for this city."

Her eyes fixated on his face at the last few words, and some of the tension left her frame. He took a gamble and removed his hand, then slowly withdrew his dagger. The room they were in was not as opulent as its counterparts in the outer compound, but the furniture was well crafted, and fine blankets and silk pillows lay piled atop the bed. The girl straightened and smoothed out her gown, regathering her dignity as best she could.

"If you're here to take a hostage, you'll have to find someone the Palace actually cares about," she said.

"You undervalue yourself. But I'm not here to take a hostage."

Her eyes flickered over him, lingering on his wounded thigh, taking in the labored rhythm of his breaths and the way he leaned against the wall. He was weak enough now that she had a chance of overpowering him if she was fast. James could see her considering this, but when she moved, she backed away and sat down on a carved wooden chair.

"What do you have to say?" she asked. She spoke calmly, with her hands folded carefully in her lap.

He spoke his piece, and she listened almost without breathing, weighing every word.

"How can I be sure of you?" she asked when he was done.

"You can't be sure of anything," was his only reply.

211

Rand and Bacchus stood back-to-back, swords drawn, as Red Shields closed in on either side. Scattered at their feet were the bodies of men they'd already cut down. Those bodies were illuminated, as was everything else in the courtyard, by the flickering light of hungry flames. Even as soldiers regrouped around them, the flames climbed higher. Occasional cracks rent the air as roof beams buckled and walls caved in. The bleary-eyed wallhuggers who'd fled the fire had long left for a safer part of the compound.

"Think he made it?" shouted Bacchus. His voice was barely audible over the flames and shouts.

"Aye," said Rand. "He always does."

Bacchus smiled then, a dangerous smile that made the advancing Red Shields slow in their approach. "You know, he probably meant for us to do something smaller and get our hides out of here."

"Selfish bastard," said Rand. "Trying to steal all the credit for himself. But I reckon we've done enough. Time to clear out?"

"Agreed," said Bacchus. And he raised his blade to meet yet another soldier.

The girl didn't speak to James for very long, but it was enough time for him to get his point across. Nevertheless, she didn't agree to his request—it was too great a thing—though she promised him that she would consider it.

After they finished, she watched as he laboriously pushed

himself to his feet and let himself out. She remained sitting, staring at the door after it had closed behind him.

Sometime later, triumphant shouts sounded as the alarm bell rang clearly three times in a row, signaling that the escaped prisoner had been recaptured. Darylene blinked, and some sort of emotion flickered across her face. She hid it quickly behind her usual mask of calm. Then she took out her handkerchief and scrubbed away the smear of blood he'd left on the door.

NINETEEN

Lettie was missing.

Flick was halfway through his morning chores when he noticed that the girl was nowhere to be seen in Mercie's small cottage. Between the kitchen, Mercie's bedroom, and the workroom where the three of them slept, there weren't many places a young girl could hide.

"Did she go into the city with Mercie?" Idalee asked when Flick told her.

"No," Flick said. "I saw Mercie leave alone this morning."

The two of them looked at each other, then flew into action. Flick swept the house one more time while Idalee called Lettie's name outside. It was unlike the girl to wander off by herself, and he feared the worst. But why would anyone kidnap Lettie, yet leave no word or demand?

Still no luck in the house, so Flick ran outside. Mercie's house was slightly set off from the road, between two farms on either side, with the forest at the back. He had a clear view of the neighboring farms as well as the road in the distance. He saw no one.

"Flick," called Idalee from the forest. "She's over here."

There was an odd tone to Idalee's voice. Flick found her just a few trees into the forest. Idalee pointed to the ground in front of her, and Flick looked down to see Lettie curled up... asleep...between two demon kittens.

"Lettie, what are you—" Flick strode toward them, but Idalee yanked him back.

"I don't think you want to surprise those two," she whispered.

Fair point. The two of them stood watching for a while, unsure what to do. Then the larger yellow kitten stirred. It sneezed, opened its eyes, and fixed them on Flick and Idalee. The next moment, it was on all fours with legs splayed out and hair standing on end. This woke the other two. The gray kitten opened its eyes and stared. And Lettie's face took on a perfect mask of guilt.

"Lettie," Flick said again, keeping his voice low lest he startle the kittens more. "What are you doing?"

Lettie shrank down and leaned a little closer to the gray kitten. "They wanted to play."

Play? These kittens were as big as she was, and their fangs looked sharp. "You've been *playing* with them?"

"When you and Idalee were busy around the house," Lettie said, raising her eyes to his reproachfully.

"How long has this been going on?"

"Today, yesterday, and the day before."

Flick took a step back, ran a hand through his hair, and forced himself to take a few deep breaths. Lettie was safe. She didn't look to be missing any limbs. *But what by the three cities had the girl been thinking?*

"Come here, Lettie." He took the girl's skinny wrists in his hands and rolled up her sleeves, then spun her around in front of him. She had a scraped elbow and a few bruises on her other arm. Her dress was torn at the bottom.

He opened his mouth to berate her when a familiar voice spoke from the forest. "She has been in no danger. I've been watching."

Flick supposed he was getting used to seeing Adele pop out from between the trees. The clanswoman seemed more sure of herself this time, less shy. "Flick, Idalee," she said in greeting.

"Lady Adele," said Flick, wondering briefly what the proper way to address a Makvani lass was. The day just kept getting stranger and stranger. Though he had to admit that part of him was glad to see her. The clanswoman intrigued him.

"The kittens mean no harm," said Adele. "It's play for them. That's all."

"Lettie's rather scratched up for a bit of play."

Adele cast a glance at the girl. "How do your small ones grow strong if you don't let them tumble?"

"I'll wager our small ones don't heal as quickly as yours," said Flick.

Adele held out her arm to Flick and traced a faint scar on her skin. "These marks make me a better sibling to my litter-mates, and a better fighter for my clan. But I know that your young are more delicate than ours. I made sure that Libena and Ziben were careful." She crouched next to the kittens and rubbed each of their heads in turn. "The kittens are curious about humans," she said.

"As are you," said Flick.

Adele looked at him, taken aback. Flick was beginning to notice that she startled when he stepped too close, whether physically or in conversation, though she recovered more quickly each time.

"Our elders mixed more with humans before Leyus pulled us out of the slave trade," she said. "But we younger ones have only been among our own kind."

She mentioned the slave trade without any self-consciousness, as if it were just a matter of fact, which Flick supposed it was. Kyra had mentioned something of the sort. "And what do you think now that you've spoken to us?" he asked.

"You *are* weaker, in some ways. But you are not helpless. And you solve your problems by very different means." Well, that was certainly honest. Flick got the impression that Adele rarely lied.

Adele looked up then, to some sound Flick couldn't hear. "One of my kin is close by. Stay here, and stay quiet."

She untied her tunic and let it drop to the ground as she walked to the trees. Flick caught a glimpse of her (admittedly shapely) backside before propriety prompted him to avert his gaze. Well, propriety and the fact that Idalee was smirking at him. In theory, the prospect of shape-shifting women who shed their clothes at a moment's notice had very few downsides. Of course, theory didn't include two younger sisters watching his every reaction—Idalee with noticeable amusement, and Lettie with her usual wide-eyed interest.

"Just try not to get yourselves killed, all right?" said Flick, trying his best to hold on to his dignity.

Idalee was still smirking. Flick raised an eyebrow at her,

though it warmed his heart to see Idalee's spunk returning. The girl hadn't really joked around with him since the beating.

Adele returned in her fur, and this time accompanied by a larger brown cat. They stopped a few paces away and changed back to their skin. The brown cat was a muscular young man, and this time it was Idalee's turn to blush. The only thing keeping Flick from shooting her a wide grin was the presence of the two Demon Riders. He did keep his eyes averted as they dressed themselves, and this time Adele noticed.

"We change in front of you to show our trust, but you look away," she said. "Does it frighten you?"

"I, uh . . . it's not that. We just don't customarily go without clothing." Sometimes honesty was the best approach.

Adele cocked her head, then seemed to dismiss the idea as strange. "This is Stepan, my clan mate. He wanted to meet you."

Stepan came forward and extended a hand, which was a relief because Flick didn't really know how the Makvani greeted each other. He had seen a few variants of bows, but had a feeling that there was much more complexity to them than Flick could figure out. The Demon Rider's handshake was firm.

"Idalee," said Flick, catching her eye. "Mayhap you could bring out some food to share."

Idalee tilted her head, trying to discern if Flick's request was a real one or a signal to run for her life. Flick gave her a subtle nod. If the Demon Riders were being friendly, they would be friendly as well.

As Idalee gathered her skirts and hurried back to the house, Stepan looked around and inhaled deeply. "Livestock," he said.

Flick froze. "You're not going to ..."

"What would you do if we were to raid these farms?" asked Adele.

Flick swallowed and took some time to consider his response. Was Adele testing him? She was certainly watching him with interest, and he didn't think she was bluffing about raiding the farms. But neither did he think she was toying with him.

"I suppose there's not much I could do," he said. "I can't outrun you, so I wouldn't be able to warn them, and I can't fight you without any weapons. I might follow, to see if I can help get the farmhands to safety." He watched the Demon Riders' expressions carefully, alert for any sign of offense. "I wouldn't try to stop you, but it would sadden me. I've enjoyed your company, and I imagine it would drive a wedge between us, if you were to raid the nearby farms."

Adele cast her gaze down as she thought this over. "Are most humans like you, using their words to fight instead of their claws?" she finally asked.

Despite the tension, or perhaps because of it, Flick had to laugh. Kyra would have appreciated that description of him. "Can you blame me, since I don't have claws?" Flick curled his hands, with their stubby nails, into his best claw impression and showed her. He thought he saw the corners of her mouth creep up. "But no. There are many in Forge who prefer 'claws' over talk."

"We won't take anything from the farms," Adele said. She seemed to be talking as much to Stepan as to Flick.

Idalee arrived just then with a platter of bread and cheese

and a wool blanket to spread over the snow. Flick hoped that the girl didn't pick up on his residual nerves from that last exchange. Adele and Stepan took their time with the food, savoring each bite and stopping to inhale the bread's aroma. "We have not been able to cook in the past year, since we've been traveling," said Stepan.

"Czern tells me that we used to have cheese often, back when we raided more villages," said Adele.

Idalee choked on her bread, and Flick himself had a hard time keeping a calm demeanor at yet more talk of raids. Again, Adele noticed.

"It bothers you to speak of raids," said Adele. Flick would have laughed at the magnitude of the understatement, but Adele looked genuinely concerned.

He wondered how to respond. "A good friend of mine, like a mother to me, was killed in a raid. It's hard for me to think about them."

To his surprise, Adele's features softened in understanding. "I lost two brothers and a sister to raids. It saddens me still."

Idalee looked up from her bread, dropping a piece of cheese on the blanket. "Your clan was raided?"

Adele nodded, surprised at Idalee's surprise. "By another clan."

"Did this happen often?" asked Flick.

"There were many of us over the mountains," said Stepan.

"And you were constantly at war?"

"There were many of us," said Adele again, as if that were the answer to his question.

Flick chose his next words carefully. "Did anyone try to

put a stop to the fighting? I imagine it would have been taxing on your people."

Adele and Stepan looked at each other for the length of several breaths. "That is not the way we do things," said Adele.

At that moment, both the Demon Riders looked toward the road. Flick had been around Makvani enough times now to realize that they were hearing something he couldn't. He turned and saw a rider in official Palace colors coming from the city. News from the Palace, and it must have been important if a herald had come to announce it. Flick exchanged glances with Idalee. The last courier to be sent out like this had borne a description of Kyra and an announcement for the bounty on her head.

"Mercie will know the news when she comes back," said Idalee.

"It might be too late by then," said Flick. Idalee didn't argue, and Flick stood. "I'm very sorry, but I must go."

"I understand," said Adele. The two Demon Riders dusted the bread crumbs from their clothes and left with little ceremony.

Flick looked back toward the city. The heralds traveled the main roads, stopping to announce their news at crossroads, squares, and inns along the way. "There's an inn up the road," he said. "If it's important news, the people there'll be talking about it."

"Will you go by yourself?" asked Idalee.

He nodded. "I'll be careful."

The fields were quiet, and every farmhouse he passed had smoke coming out of its chimney. Folk were holed up inside, where it was warm. It was a long walk past the farms, but as he came closer to the inn, he noticed more people than usual about on the road. Flick slowed and listened for snippets of conversation.

...A Palace building burned down....

... magistrate make an example of him...

His pulse quickened, and he ducked into the inn's dining room. It was a small establishment compared with the ones in the city, but it should be busy enough to get him the news he needed.

The energy level inside was certainly high. While the dining room was usually divided into separate tables, the majority of the patrons were seated near the center, participating in one big, disorganized discussion.

"They say he single-handedly took out a dozen Red Shields," one potbellied man was saying. "And his lackeys killed even more with that fire."

Flick took a seat near the side and settled down to listen.

TWENTY

Leyus was her father.

Even after she said good-bye to Craigson and started making her way back to her cave, the knowledge sat awkwardly in her mind. Kyra circled it warily, afraid to delve too deeply, yet unable to forget it.

You don't choose your family. Kyra had known this. Yet in her imaginings, she'd still conjured the warm, loving parents that every orphan wanted. This hope had taken a blow when she learned she was half Makvani, but even then, she hadn't completely given it up. She'd just re-created the picture into someone like Pashla—dangerous yet gentle.

Kyra would not have chosen Leyus. He was distant and intimidating, and he frightened her. Yet it all made more sense than she cared to admit. Leyus had always been a little too lenient with her. He'd had reason to kill her many times when she'd lived among his people, especially after he found out she worked for the Palace. But instead, he'd always sent her off with a warning.

And then there was the way the clan kept track of her

movements in the forest. Pashla had made it sound as if they watched all comers, but with Kyra it was more than that. Kyra thought back to that time Leyus rescued her from Zora's attack, and the two times Pashla had saved her, once when Zora threatened her in the clearing, and once when Adele attacked. No, Leyus wasn't just having her watched. He was having her protected.

It was that thought that spurred her into action. Even now, Kyra could sense someone watching her, and the questions became too insistent to ignore. Why would he do this, yet stay so cold and aloof? How long had he known?

"I know someone's watching me," Kyra called out into the trees. "Pashla? I need to speak to Leyus."

The forest went quiet at her voice. She cast around, alert for any response, but nothing came, and slowly the sounds of the forest returned—the fluttering of a winter bird's wings, the high bark of a fox. Kyra leaned against a tree, swallowing her disappointment and trying to make sense of everything Craigson had told her. Her mother was a woman who led a village an unfathomable distance away. And her father . . .

Something shifted around her. "Anyone there?" Kyra asked. She definitely sensed someone coming toward her now, someone quiet enough to keep her from zeroing in on a specific direction. It might have been Pashla, but it didn't *feel* like her. Kyra fell still, ready to run or fight if needed.

Leyus stepped out from between the trees as naturally as if Kyra had been waiting in the antechamber to his throne room. She looked at him, really looked at him this time. He was tall, larger than life, bronze-skinned, and strong despite his age. She didn't resemble him at all. His face was square and angular, his nose and eyebrows pronounced, in contrast to Kyra's heart-shaped face and softer features. But something stirred within her when she studied his eyes. They were amber, just like hers, and the arch of his lids felt familiar.

Craigson's story just seemed so unlikely. How could this imposing Makvani man possibly be her father? He certainly wasn't looking at her like she'd imagined any long-lost father would. Leyus regarded at her as he always had, with the same distant, proud gaze, and a touch of wariness or disdain.

"I met a trader," said Kyra, glad that her voice didn't shake. "Or he used to be a trader. By the name of Louis Craigson."

There was a flash of something dangerous in Leyus's eyes. "And what did he tell you?"

Kyra couldn't do it. Couldn't come right out and ask him if he was her father, like some waif in a talesinger's ballad. "Why did you protect me when Zora tried to kill me?"

Leyus gave a grunt of disgust. "The caravanner should watch his tongue. I spared his life once, but I may not do so again." He looked at Kyra. "You're Maikana's child—is that what he thinks?"

It was surreal, hearing the same name coming out of Leyus's mouth. "Aye."

He looked her over carefully, just as Craigson had, though Leyus's scrutiny was more severe. "You have the look of her people, as well as some of their...peculiarities. Though your face resembles her sister more than her."

That repeated detail about Kyra's aunt drove it home for her, made it clear they had moved beyond her childish daydreams to a reality that was so much bigger than two imagined parents. There was an entire world Kyra didn't know about, with implications and echoes that she was just starting to feel. Kyra realized she was trembling, and she pressed her arms to her sides in an attempt to stop. It was suddenly important to her that Leyus not see her shaken.

Leyus gazed into the distance, as if looking into the past. "Maikana trusted Craigson. When I heard rumors about a halfblood in his caravan's care, I immediately suspected."

How had this Makvani man, the same one who looked at her and other humans with such derision, ever been intimate with a human woman? "What did you do to her?" Kyra whispered.

Leyus turned furious eyes to her. "Is that what you think it was? That I ravished her like some base human bandit? Watch your words carefully, Kyra. I will not be insulted again."

The strength of his outrage caught her off guard. Had he actually cared about her mother? "I don't understand."

"It is not for you to know," he said. Under the anger in his voice, there was a layer of pain. Kyra stared at Leyus, drawn to this crack in his mask. But he looked away, and when he turned back, there was no more trace of that pain on his face. "Take care you do not put too much stock in your bloodlines, Kyra. And do not expect to hide behind your parentage. Blood relations are earned. Respect is earned. Do not expect any special treatment from me."

She widened her stance, as if somehow it would lend her strength. "Why haven't you let me die, then? You've had plenty of chances."

The smile he gave her had very little humor in it. "Misguided hope, I suppose. Maikana was a capable leader and stronger than any human I'd met or have met since. She knew who she was, and she knew what she wanted. She didn't run from her troubles." He said the last part as if it were a rebuke to Kyra. "It looks like that trait was not passed on to her daughter."

The judgment in his words was unexpected and so harsh that her uncertainty turned to anger. Heat flooded through her. "I've known my mother's name one day, and you're expecting me to live up to her example?"

"As I said, blood relations are earned. It shouldn't matter who gave birth to you, though it's a disappointment that you are so different from what you could have been. Physically, you have the strength of our people, but you shrink away from your fights, worrying about what you are and wavering between choices. Your mother would never have done that."

He was being unfair. She knew this even in the midst of her confusion, but knowing that a knife had an ill-made edge didn't make its cuts hurt any less. "You speak of my mother as if she were some heroine. But wasn't she your enemy? If you thought so highly of her, why are you on this side of the mountains?"

"She knew her duties, and I knew mine," he said. "In the end, it came between us." He looked at her again. "You're a child of mixed fates. Our blood could bring you strength, but instead it feeds your fear. That does not make you someone I would be proud to call my own."

Leyus left Kyra after their conversation, disappearing into the forest without a second glance at the daughter who stared after him, gutted by his words. When it became clear to Kyra that he wasn't coming back, she gathered herself together and headed to her cave. She wasn't aware of much of the rest of the journey, just that it was dark by the time she arrived.

She longed for Flick, Idalee, and Lettie desperately that night, but of course they were safe at Mercie's house. To make it worse, the temperature dropped and she woke up shivering violently, her limbs stiff and her toes going numb despite the layers she'd wrapped around herself. She realized that she either had to stay active all night like her Makvani kin or find a better way to keep warm. Her pouch of supplies with her flint inside lay enticingly within reach, but the cave had no good outlet for smoke. Of course, there was one other way she could keep warm, one that she had thus far been avoiding....

Our blood could bring you strength, but instead it feeds your fear. That does not make you someone I would be proud to call my own.

Leyus's words were sharp thorns, digging themselves into the tender places of her chest. Kyra peeled off her clothes with something akin to anger, throwing them against the cave wall, hardly able to breathe as the icy air burned her skin. Soon enough though, she felt the familiar warmth of her fur forcing its way through her body. The cave around her settled into a crisper version of itself, and the air that had felt so bitterly cold a moment before no longer touched her flesh. Kyra turned a few circles on all fours before she curled back onto the ground. Sleep came more easily after that.

She was in her fur, still half-asleep, when she heard Flick approaching. She knew the cadence of his footsteps well enough to recognize him, and she hurriedly changed back before he arrived. She didn't think she would harm Flick, but she wouldn't take the risk.

"Kyra, I've got news," he said. But then he stopped when he saw her face. "Are you hurt?"

"No, I'm not hurt. I..." She fell silent, trying to get her thoughts in order. "Can we sit?"

"Of course." Flick was still looking her up and down with concern as they settled themselves at the mouth of her cave. "What is it?"

It took some time for Kyra to get her thoughts together. In bits and pieces, she related everything Craigson had told her and then recounted her conversation with Leyus. Flick let out a low whistle when she finished. "Leyus, of all people. What do you make of all this?" he asked.

Kyra took a while to answer. "I don't really know," she said. "I didn't expect my first conversation with my da to go quite like that."

Flick gave her a crooked smile. "Fathers aren't always what we wish them to be. I should know."

Flick's words triggered a loosening in her chest, and she smiled back despite herself. "I suppose we've got something new in common, then."

"High-ranking fathers who can't stand the sight of us?"

Kyra couldn't help but feel a twinge in her stomach. Leyus's words had hurt, though they shouldn't have. Why should she care what the leader of a clan of barbarian invaders had to say about her? But apparently she did, when that leader was her father. "Do you think he's right, about me living in fear of what I am?"

She was glad Flick didn't respond right away. If he had, Kyra wouldn't have believed him. "I do see you afraid of your Makvani blood," he said carefully. "But I don't think it's as bad a thing as he thinks. In fact, it gives me comfort that you're afraid. It tells me that you're still the same thief girl I met on the street years ago. You might be able to grow claws now, but I'd still trust you to watch my back."

She nodded, comforted slightly by his thoughts. "Though mayhap he has a point about running from my fights," she said. "I'm out here in the forest when things are happening in the city."

And here, Flick's expression darkened.

"What is it?" Kyra asked. "Are we found out?" She looked around her, half expecting to see soldiers in ambush.

Flick shook his head. "Nothing like that. It's about James."

"What of him? Did he escape?" She felt a shiver of fear. What would James do if he was free again?

"He did . . . almost," said Flick. "They say that he somehow got ahold of a weapon and overpowered his guards. Two of his men were there to help him."

The men were almost certainly Rand and Bacchus. But Flick had said he'd *almost* escaped. "Did they recapture him?"

"Aye, but not before they'd killed several dozen Red Shields and burned one of the Palace buildings to the ground. His two accomplices escaped, though both were gravely injured. The Palace recaptured James alive."

Kyra let out a sigh of relief, though she wasn't sure if the relief was because James had been recaptured or because he was still alive. "So they have him again." But there was more to the story. Otherwise, Flick wouldn't have looked so disturbed.

"They did nab him. The magistrate was furious, as was the Council, as you might expect. They've decided to stop trying to get information out of him and to make an example of him instead." Flick took a breath. "They've sentenced James to torture and a public execution in two days."

A chill spread over Kyra's skin at Flick's words. For a long moment, she didn't say anything.

"In the city square, as usual?" she finally asked.

"That's the news."

Kyra was familiar with the type of spectacle planned for James. The Palace reserved it for its most notorious criminals, to make an example of the very worst and warn others away. Kyra had gone once out of curiosity, and she'd had nightmares for a solid week afterward. The criminal hadn't been recognizable as a man by the time they'd finished with him, and he'd screamed until he was no longer physically able to continue. She swallowed against the bile suddenly rising in her stomach.

"You're certain of this?" she asked.

"It's all anyone was talking about."

It shouldn't have surprised her. After the Demon Rider raids and the latest escape attempt, it only made sense that the Palace would choose a public and painful way for James to die. But that didn't stop her gut from twisting at the prospect.

"Kyra?" Flick put his hand on her shoulder, forcing her to look at him.

She shook herself. "Sorry."

"What are you thinking?"

If only she knew. Her thoughts about James had always been an inscrutable mass. "I've every reason to hate him," she said slowly. "But his ends were not completely unjust." James had done some inexcusable things. She wouldn't romanticize him as she had before, but they'd come to some sort of understanding in that dungeon, and it didn't feel like the naïve infatuation she used to hold.

"I need to get back into the city," she said.

Flick sat up. "Kyra, you can't let one comment from Leyus push you into risking your life. He might be your father by blood, but he's never done anything for you."

"I in't doing this because of Leyus. Tristam and Malikel are in trouble with the Palace on my account. I need to speak with Tristam, to see if there's any way I can help, and I'd like to—" She'd been about to say that she wanted to talk to James one more time. "I'd like to see if I can learn anything more about the Guild before James dies."

Flick shook his head, massaging the knuckles of one of his hands. "I won't try to stop you. Never does any good."

Was she really that hardheaded? "I'll be careful. I promise."

He smiled at that, and tugged on a strand of her hair. "The problem is, you have a funny idea of what it means to be careful."

TWENTY-ONE

Getting back into the city wasn't hard, but moving around without being recognized was tricky. Kyra waited until it was dark to scale the city walls. Once inside, she kept her cloak low over her face. She weaved her way through the evening crowds, taking care not to attract anyone's attention. Parchments with her likeness were posted in the larger squares, and Kyra had a nervous moment when a maidservant squinted at her, trying to see beneath her cloak. Kyra affected her most unconcerned expression and walked on. No one chased after her, and she soon found herself staring at the Palace wall.

Perhaps it was her fate to always be sneaking in. She'd had a brief period of legitimacy, when she'd walked in through the gates as if she belonged. But she'd never felt comfortable out in the open, not like she did now. Even her fear of discovery was a thrill of excitement in her veins as she pulled herself over the ramparts and dropped to the ground.

It was still early enough in the evening for people to be about their after-dinner business—guards making their rounds, noblemen and their families out for strolls—so she climbed the closest building to escape the torchlight below. The icy wind whipped around her, buffeting her ears. She could feel her fingers getting numb, so she broke into a run to keep warm.

She was making decent progress along the ledges until her foot slipped out from under her. Kyra gasped and splayed her limbs out wide. She landed lengthwise along the edge, one leg hanging over empty space as she scrambled to grip the stone. Soft conversation and chatter floated up to her from below, and her heart pounded in her ears as she slowly hauled herself back to her feet. She'd thought that the sun had melted all the ice from the buildings, but she'd obviously been wrong.

Kyra proceeded more slowly from there, testing the surfaces before she stepped and sticking to walls that faced the sun during the day. The difference between smooth granite and slick ice was subtle but important. Finally, she stood atop the wall of the inner compound. The prison building was a barely visible shadow in the night sky. As she made her way closer, she passed the burned-out shell of what had once been noblemen's living quarters—Rand's and Bacchus's handiwork. The sight brought uncomfortable memories of The Drunken Dog, and she hurried past. Finally, she looked down on the prison from a nearby ledge and took in the entire scene.

The building was on lockdown. Red Shields stood guard all around the building's perimeter, with six more blocking the doors. Extra torches had been lit along the paths and hung on the walls so that only the very top of the building was dark.

Make no mistake, Kyra. Someday I'll call in a favor from you, and I'll hold you to it.

Kyra thought of the Demon Rider raids that James had

instigated, the fire, the injured along the street, the countless left without homes. Those people deserved justice, didn't they?

She counted the guards again and imagined ways of getting past them. Just a game, a thief's mind exercise, as she'd done before with hundreds of other buildings. There were too many Red Shields up front. A diversion might take a few away, but they were probably alert for one. Maybe with some luck she could get into the prison, but getting out with a gravely wounded James would be near impossible.

Another column of guards walked in through the gate. Kyra started to count them too but stopped. She knew in her bones that she wouldn't be going into the prison tonight. Her debt to James did not extend that far. When she finally admitted this to herself, Kyra wasn't sure whether the tugging at her chest was pity, guilt, or grief for the people James had taken from her.

She stood there a while longer, until the chill made her spring into motion. There was one more place she wanted to go. Her heartbeat quickened in anticipation as she approached the building that housed Tristam's quarters. Was he even there, or was he still being held somewhere else? His room was dark through the windows, but he might have simply been out for the evening. Kyra found a spot where an outcropping offered some shelter from the wind. She'd been up there for about half an hour when she heard his voice down below.

It was Tristam, dressed in one of his finer embroidered tunics and a fur cloak. And with him, on his arm, was a woman. Kyra couldn't see her very well from that height, but she could tell that the woman was young and that the luxurious furs lining her cloak were fit for a nobleman's daughter. The two of them stood for a while on the path outside the building until a courtier arrived. Tristam bowed then and kissed the girl's hand before she left with the courtier at her side.

The moment his lips touched her hand, Kyra's chest turned to ice. She'd assumed, with all the upheaval in the Palace, that something like the marriage negotiations would have been suspended. How naïve she'd been.

Tristam watched the girl leave and went inside the building. A short while later, a soft glow came from the window as he lit a lamp. Kyra pressed herself flat against the wall. She'd planned to knock on his window, but she couldn't let Tristam know what she'd seen. She lingered outside until her skin was numb from the wind and finally admitted to herself that she was being ridiculous. She'd come all the way here from the forest. She wasn't going to leave without speaking to Tristam.

It took a couple raps on the shutters for Tristam to notice, but then he pulled them open and peered out the window. His eyes focused quickly on Kyra—he'd gotten much better at spotting her on ledges, though he still did a double take before he moved to make room for her to jump in.

There was such relief in his eyes when he looked at her, and it felt so good to see him alive and well, that for a moment Kyra forgot the noblewoman she'd seen. As soon as her feet touched the floor, he pulled her into a hug, and she gladly returned it, squeezing him as tightly as her frozen limbs would allow. He was blissfully warm, and the fine silk of his tunic was soft against her face. He smelled like warm bread and spices. After a moment, hc held her out again at arm's length.

"I've missed you," he said softly, his eyes scanning her. "And you're freezing." Tristam motioned for her to sit down at the table and moved to check the latch on his door. He lingered there for a moment, alert for noises in the hallway.

"I don't hear anyone," said Kyra.

He pulled a blanket from his bed and draped it over her shoulder. It wasn't nearly as warm as his arms had been, but Kyra pulled it tight around her. He scrutinized her, and she did the same to him, studying his face, his posture. He seemed healthy. There was a tired slump to his shoulders, but he was alive and not imprisoned.

"Where have you been?" he asked. "Your landlady had no idea, and neither did Flick's roommates."

"I'm still alive," she said. She filled him in on her flight from the city and where she'd been hiding. "And things at the Palace. How are they? Have you been cleared of suspicion?"

A crease formed between his eyebrows. "I have, but not Malikel. They're still questioning him, and Willem means to drag this out as long as he can."

He didn't direct any accusations at Kyra, which somehow made it worse. "Is there any way I can help?"

He shook his head heavily. "Not unless you can control the minds of the Council." But then he raised his head. "Does the name 'Orvin' mean anything to you?"

Kyra blinked. "Willem's manservant?"

"He came to me with a message for you soon after you disappeared."

Orvin had approached Tristam? She wondered what had persuaded Orvin to trust him. "He was an informant for the Guild. He gave me information a while back, and I asked him to get word to me if he had any more. I was trying to find some way to discredit Willem but didn't get anything before I had to . . . leave."

There was just the slightest flicker of confusion across Tristam's face. He was wondering why she hadn't told him until now. "Orvin must have decided I was the best way to reach you. I was worried it was a trap, but I finally spoke to him. He says Willem is expecting a messenger eight days from today."

Kyra leaned forward. "One of the private messengers?"

Tristam nodded. "It would be too dangerous to confront him inside the Palace, but Orvin says the messenger stays at an inn when he visits Forge and that he comes into the Palace compound and leaves through the private gate near Willem's residence. I was considering tailing him myself, but I'm not as good at it as you are."

Kyra was finally warming up, and she let the blanket fall from her shoulders. "I'll do it," she said. "I'll have to think about how best to track him. It's a pity I didn't learn more about James's crew of spies during my time with the Guild."

"You heard about James, then?" said Tristam.

"Aye, Flick told me. Is it . . . certain?"

"The executioner's wagon is set to leave the compound gates at the eighth hour tomorrow."

The executioner's wagon . . . There was still something she might be able to do for James, though she wasn't sure if she had the stomach to see it through. "Is it taking the normal route from the Palace to the city center?"

"As far as I know." Tristam eyed her suspiciously. "Why do you ask?"

"Just curious." She stood. "I should go. I'm...glad that you're all right, Tristam. Flick and the girls are taking shelter with a woman named Mercie just south of the city. If you need to find me, they'll know where I am."

He wrapped her hands in his own. "Take care, Kyra." This time, the thoughts of his betrothed *did* come into her mind, but Kyra pushed them away. There were bigger things at stake.

"Thanks for letting me warm up." She studied his face again as she handed him the blanket, fixing his features to memory.

"I don't think I've ever seen you shiver so much," he said, smoothing the blanket back over his bed. "And you must have scaled walls on colder nights than this."

"It was windy," Kyra said.

"True. Well, maybe you can run extra quickly to stay..." His voice trailed off. The look he turned on Kyra was a little too keen. "You've not been running, have you? Did you have to stay out in the cold somewhere?"

"I..." Kyra trailed off, distracted by the memory of Tristam and Cecile. No sooner after she faltered did she realize that she should have kept talking. Tristam's brow furrowed, and she could see him trying to figure out why Kyra was slow to answer what she realized now had been an innocent question.

Then his eyes widened in a mixture of comprehension and dread. "You saw her, didn't you?"

It wasn't the first time that Kyra wished Tristam weren't quite so observant. Her silence spoke more clearly than any affirmative, and Tristam let out a soft groan. "I'm sorry you had to see that."

"I wasn't spying. You weren't here when I came to find you, and then I saw you return with her." She didn't want to argue with Tristam over this, not when she didn't know when she'd see him again. "She seems nice," Kyra finished lamely, belatedly wondering if it came across as sarcastic.

There was a grim humor in Tristam's eyes as he took in her words. He sat down heavily on his bed. "I have very little to complain about," he said. "She's pleasant and close to me in age."

Kyra didn't want to hear this, but he was staring past her without seeing her.

"Cecile is lovely and talented, and clearly cares about her family." Tristam shook his gaze from whatever he'd been looking at and focused his eyes back on Kyra. "I feel nothing for her," he said simply. "Nor does she feel anything for me. We're both well trained in the courtly arts. We can exchange pleasantries for an hour, and we can smile at each other over dinner. I suppose marriages have been built on less."

Though it pained her to hear about this girl, Kyra also realized now how self-centered she'd been. She'd painted herself as the victim in this scenario, the city girl who would be tossed aside by a nobleman. But she hadn't considered how hard it would be for Tristam. He wasn't some fatpurse who took and discarded women at his whim. He was bound by his family and his duties in a way that Kyra never would be.

She crumpled the hem of her tunic. It was time to grow up. "I said some things I shouldn't have, when we last spoke of your marriage." *Right before I turned into a felbeast, eviscerated a man, and had to flee the city,* she thought ruefully. How had so much happened in so little time? "It was unfair of me to be so upset with you. I understand that you have duties to your family."

He met her eyes with gratitude. "I'm sorry I didn't tell you earlier. I shouldn't have hidden it from you."

Kyra looked to the window. She needed to go. There were preparations to make if she was going to attempt her new plan. But her conversation with Tristam didn't seem quite complete. She swallowed. "Do what you think is best, Tristam. Whatever you decide, I'll still be your friend and comrade-in—"

She didn't get to finish the last few words, because he closed the distance between them, threaded his arms behind her back, and kissed her.

Kyra drew half a breath in surprise before his lips met hers and her mind went blank. They had kissed once before. That had been a stolen moment, shy and uncertain. This time, it was also a stolen moment, but it was far different. There was an urgency in the way he pulled her close, an insistence in the way his lips sought hers, as if they might never do this again. Kyra understood it, because she felt the same. She returned his kiss with equal fervor, her world shrinking down to just the two of them, his hands in her hair and hers tightly clutching his waist. His tongue parted her lips, and she gasped as a shiver danced down her spine and her knees went weak. She could lose herself like this, forget about betrothals and marriage negotiations, forget about what she was going to do right after she climbed out the window.

But, of course, she couldn't. Even as she reached up to cup his face, even as she wished she could pull him even closer, she knew this. They weren't some lovers from a talesinger's ballad, about to run off into each other's arms. The next morning, Tristam would continue his negotiations with the family from Parna, and Kyra would go back into hiding. That is, if Kyra survived the night.

Perhaps Tristam sensed the direction of her thoughts, because he pulled back. He looked as if he wasn't quite sure what had happened. And neither was she, for that matter. Kyra's heart still pounded in her chest, and she was sure her face was just as flushed as his. She couldn't look away from his eyes. Tristam was watching her as if convinced she was about to disappear.

And Kyra supposed she was. She gathered her resolve before it could weaken any further and pushed him away.

"I can't," she said quietly. "And neither can you."

He accepted her words without argument, closing his eyes in resignation. "I'm sorry."

She wasn't sure what he was apologizing for. The marriage negotiations? The kiss? She wasn't sure if it mattered, and she wasn't sure she wanted to know. "I really should go," said Kyra.

He watched her silently as she pushed open the shutters and climbed back out. When Kyra peered back in from the ledge, he'd sunk down into a chair, his forehead resting on his hand. His eyes were open, but his gaze was focused on something Kyra couldn't see.

TWENTY-TWO

As always, the darkness cleared her mind, and the task before Kyra forced her to focus. In that way, she was grateful for the danger. The need to maintain her balance on the ledges and make plans for her next step was the only thing that could keep Tristam from her thoughts.

The first things she needed were supplies. Here, her knowledge of the Palace, her *thief's* knowledge, proved useful. She broke into a minor storehouse and pilfered some twine, some leftover biscuits, Minadan hot pepper powder, and a few strips of cloth. She wrapped the pepper powder into four loosely tied cloth packets and stowed them in her belt pouch. Then she made her way toward one shack she'd never entered before, one that reeked with the smell of old blood. The guard here was uncharacteristically light for the inner compound. There was no one at the door, and only the occasional patrol. Kyra supposed it made sense. What sane intruder would voluntarily make for the torture master's storage house? The lock gave way without much problem, and Kyra felt her resolve weaken as the door swung open. There were things here that she didn't want to look at or think about, wicked-looking knives and racks, other implements she didn't even recognize that were still crusted with blood. It would not be good to be caught here.

Kyra waited for her eyes to acclimate to what sparse moonlight filtered in through cracks around the door. There was only one wagon, and she recognized it immediately from previous execution marches. It was a platform on wheels with a single pole and crossbeam on top for the prisoner to be lashed to. She had never followed the execution parade, but she knew its path. The wagon would come out of the Palace and wind through the streets, making its way to the merchant's ring before circling back to the city center. People would be gathered on either side, jeering and throwing refuse. It was always very crowded.

Kyra crawled between the wheels and felt around with her hands, hoping for some shelf underneath she could cling to, but she found nothing. She supposed it was too much to wish that the wagon would come ready with a hiding place. She crawled back out and wondered if she was taking too much of a risk. But then she imagined James stretched on a rack in the city square, skin flayed open, and bile rose in her throat. She would try this.

It was too dark to see. Kyra brought out her flint, some dried moss, and a stick, listening carefully for footsteps outside. There was always a chance someone would see light leaking from between the slats of the shed, but she couldn't do this blind. She struck her flint until a spark caught in the moss she'd laid out on the floor, then coaxed the flame to life. In its light, she could barely make out the contours of the wagon. She scanned its surface, looking for slots between planks where she could thread some twine. When she found what she was looking for, she blew out the flame. The rest she would do by touch.

Kyra reached into her belt pouch for four pieces of twine and threaded each one around a plank, tying them into loops. They'd be visible from the side of the wagon, but the wood was rough and uneven in color, and she hoped that everyone would be paying more attention to the prisoner than to the execution cart. She crawled underneath and pulled the loops through, then threaded cloth through them so that two long strips ran along the length of the wagon. She tested whether the strips could hold her, hooking her feet over them and spreading the weight of her chest and torso over the length of her arms. It wasn't comfortable, but she'd be able to hold on long enough. With those preparations in place, Kyra let go again and settled in for a wait. She didn't dare sleep, but she curled up under the wagon and tried to make herself as comfortable as possible on the hard ground.

Gradually, light started to filter in from outside. The padlock securing the outside door clanked, and Kyra hurriedly pulled herself up so she was flat against the bottom of the wagon. She saw a pair of boots walk in. Metal clanged as the boot's owners walked around, rearranging equipment. A few times, he threw something on the wagon, and Kyra felt the thud vibrate throughout the frame. Finally, he pulled the wagon outside. If he noticed the extra weight on the wagon, he gave no indication. He hitched a horse to the front. Then a group of soldiers marched toward the wagon—four sets of booted feet surrounding a pair of bare feet in tattered trousers.

The wagon rocked to and fro as soldiers lashed James to the wagon. The planks above Kyra warped with the extra weight, and she eyed the knots in the cloth that supported her, hoping they wouldn't unravel. James made no noise, and Kyra's stomach tightened as a drop of blood landed on the ground.

It was an agonizingly long wait before the wagon finally started rolling. As they came closer to the Palace gates, Kyra heard the roar of the crowd, the anticipating energy. Then they were past it and surrounded by jeering onlookers.

The cobblestones rolled beneath her, about two hand-widths below her nose. Kyra had to be careful not to stare too long at them, lest they make her dizzy. It would be easy enough to get sick here, with her stomach tight as it was. Though she tried to spread her weight along as much of her body as possible, she felt a light numbness through her arms. Kyra flexed her fingers and shifted her weight, doing her best to loosen up. She was waiting for a certain street just outside the merchants' district, where the road became narrower and the rooftops leaned in close. That was when she would make her move.

It was hard to navigate when she could see only gutters and the occasional building foundation, but she managed to keep track of where she was. The wheels in front of her tossed up stones as they turned, and though she managed to dodge most of them, a few left stinging imprints on her skin. The mud was harder to evade, and Kyra soon gave up on avoiding splatters. Slowly, the wagon neared the bottleneck. Three turns away, then two turns, then one.

Ahead of her, the street narrowed and the Red Shields on either side moved to the wagon's front and back, though there was still enough room along the sides for someone small to squeeze through. Kyra took one last breath. Then she dropped to the ground, scrambled between the still-moving wagon wheels, and pulled herself over the edge.

The scene hit her all at once. The wagon was in a narrow alleyway. Red Shields stood ahead of and behind it, facing a crowd of men, women, and children along the road. The bystanders pressed in on the soldiers, though their screams quieted as Kyra stood up to her full height. She got her first glimpse of James as she drew her dagger. He was, as she'd expected, lashed to the crossbeams on top of the cart. He was thinner than she remembered. There were fresh bruises on his face, and a patch of blood seeped through his tattered trousers above his knee. But his gaze was still quick. In a split second, he took in Kyra's dagger, the Red Shields around them, the hanging rooftops, and the hungry crowd around them. Comprehension lit his eyes.

Why should they dictate how we live and how we die?

"Would you choose the way you die?" Kyra's question came out breathless. With the roar of the crowd around her, there was no way he could have made out her words. But she could see that he understood nonetheless.

"Do what you came to do," he said. His gaze was as intense as she'd ever seen it. Was he angry at her? Grateful? Kyra didn't have time to wonder. Red Shields were pointing at her and shouting, and she had to make her move. She closed the distance between them. He caught her eyes as she raised her knife to his throat, and such was the strength he projected that Kyra could not look away. The edge of her blade nicked his skin, and still their gazes remained locked. One stroke, then it would be over, quick and clean. But Kyra couldn't move.

The wagon rocked. Kyra cursed her hesitation and whipped around as a Red Shield pulled himself onto the back edge of the cart. She grabbed a pepper pouch and threw it at him. Her left-handed throw went wide, but the second try caught the soldier square in the face, and he fell backward onto his comrades. Kyra pivoted and threw her remaining pouches at the guards on the other side.

Then, as red pepper dust still hung in the air, Kyra turned, gritted her teeth, and buried her blade in James's stomach.

He shuddered once, the muscles of his throat tightening and his jaw clenching against the pain. As warm blood washed over Kyra's hands, a memory came to her. She was on the floor of James's study, convulsing around his blade as she bled out onto his floor. *You could have gone far,* he'd whispered. The scar on her own abdomen throbbed in recognition.

She heard James's voice again, and it took her a moment to realize that this wasn't from her memory. He was speaking, though Kyra couldn't make out the words. Her body was tangled up with his. She still held her dagger, buried in his stomach, and she'd grasped the back of his neck for leverage. Kyra could feel a layer of sweat on his skin, his pulse growing erratic under her fingers. As he struggled to draw breath, she tilted her head to let him speak into her ear.

"Choose your fight," he said.

Then he slumped into his bindings, and the life left his eyes.

TWENTY-THREE

There was no time to pause, to wallow in what she had done. No time to clean her dagger, wipe James's blood off her hands, or search his face for any remaining message. The crowd was screaming. The dust had cleared. Two Red Shields, one on either side, jumped onto the wagon. Kyra thrust her knife into her boot and leaped for an overhang, pulling herself up and away as the soldiers reached to grab her.

She sprinted down the row of rooftops, jumping between uneven levels and rolling when she took a long drop. But even as she pulled farther away from the wagon, Kyra realized she'd miscalculated. She'd traveled these rooftops before and knew a path that would take her to the city wall, but she'd underestimated the crowds. They were everywhere, and already, she could hear people shouting to stop the lass on the rooftops. She skidded to a stop at the last house and looked down into the faces of wide-eyed watchers below, packed so tightly she couldn't even see the ground. Kyra turned around to see Red Shields climbing up awkwardly after her. Then the first arrow struck by her feet.

Kyra scrambled away from the edge and crouched as another arrow soared over her head. The way forward was closed to her. Behind her, three Red Shields gained their footing and raced toward her. Kyra hesitated a brief moment, then ran straight at them. The houses along this street had courtyards, and Kyra dropped into one, pressing herself between a row of hedges and the wall. She wasn't very well sheltered here. The hedge was only slightly taller than she was, about three hand-widths from the wall. An overhang from the roof offered some coverage from above, but there was plenty of open space between the roof and the top of the hedge through which someone could see her.

Kyra struggled to calm her breathing as the footsteps above came closer. Her blood ran hot with the battle rage she was coming to expect every time she killed. Her fur called to get out, and Kyra knew instinctively that to change form right now would take no effort at all. She thought for a moment about succumbing to the change, of exploding out of the hedges and onto the soldiers who chased her. But there were so many bystanders around, and she didn't know what she would do to them.

The shouts were all around her now, accompanied by thuds as men dropped onto hard dirt. Kyra peered through a gap in the leaves and counted eight Red Shields, though they moved in and out of view so quickly that she couldn't be sure. It would only be a matter of time before they found her.

She drew her dagger once more. But then, was she really expecting to fight eight swordsmen with a knife? No, there was only one way she could take on all of them. Kyra could feel the heat within her, eager to come out. Could she simply change form and run for the walls? She didn't hate these men like she'd hated Santon. Maybe she could control it this time.

A shadow fell across her. A soldier hung his head and shoulders off the rooftop, looking down at her hiding place. He opened his mouth to call the others.

Before he could speak, Kyra climbed, using the wall and the hedge for footholds, and gripped his tunic. He made an ill-fated grab for the roof but missed, and they both fell, stripping leaves and branches from the hedges. Kyra landed in a crouch. The soldier landed face-first and groaned.

Before he could move again, Kyra jumped on his back and snaked her arm around his neck. A wave of battle fury hit her, the thrill of it as strong as the smell of his fear. Kyra had an overwhelming urge to tighten her grip further, to hold the choke and not let go.

"There's something moving back there," said a voice on the other side of the hedge.

Kyra jumped back from the fallen soldier, trembling at how close she'd come to wringing his neck. As the man fell forward, coughing, she drew his sword and threw it away from both of them.

"Go," she hissed. "Tell your comrades to flee. This in't worth dying over."

She was ready with her dagger as he regained his feet, but he took one last look at her and fled around the hedge. Yells sounded from the other side. Commands. They were planning the best way to surround her. Kyra heard the scrape of swords being drawn, and she cursed the discipline of Palace troops. Soldiers appeared at the ends of the hedge.

"Stay back," she yelled again, but they only raised their swords.

Kyra tossed out one last desperate wish for control before she pulled off her shoes and threw her cloak to the ground.

When the shouts and screams first started, Tristam held rank with his fellow Red Shields. They stood at attention along the side of the road, scanning for any signs of resistance and bracing themselves for the rush of people that would surely come when the execution cart passed their stations. He didn't pay much attention to the ruckus at first. It was an execution, after all—a fair amount of rowdiness was to be expected. And frankly, he didn't have much energy left in him for alarm. He hadn't exactly slept well the night before.

Tristam had stayed awake long after Kyra left, unable to forget how she'd felt in his arms and how desperately she'd kissed him back. It had been such a relief to act on his feelings for once, to stop being the responsible son if only for a moment. But once the dust had cleared, things remained the same.

I can't. And neither can you. He saw Kyra saying that, her eyes still bright, but grounded now with regret.

Kyra was right, of course. Tristam was to have dinner again with Cecile in another week, and he had no idea how he would look her in the eye, let alone discuss their marriage. Tristam had been brought up with the expectation of serving his family through this type of alliance, and he'd long made his peace with it. But he'd never realized just how hard it would be. He shouldn't have kissed Kyra last night. It only made things worse. But somehow, he couldn't quite bring himself to regret it.

Tristam might have remained lost in his thoughts, but gradually the commotion around him increased until he could no longer ignore it. Tristam pushed his worries aside and peered up the street. The execution cart wasn't here yet, though it should be close if everything was running on schedule. He exchanged a glance with the soldier next to him, who was also starting to look around.

"Think they need reinforcements?" asked the Red Shield.

"I've not heard a call for them," said Tristam.

Then he started to make out words. "Girl...rooftop... monster..."

"Kyra," he whispered. And he knew something was horribly wrong.

"What did you say?"

Tristam stepped out of formation and ran up the road.

Getting to the cart was easy. The road had been cleared, and his fellow soldiers were holding the crowd at bay. Quite a few Red Shields turned in confusion as he ran by. Someone shouted his name, asking him what he thought he was doing, but he just ran faster. The orderly ranks of soldiers broke down as the wagon came into view, and the shouts of the crowd grew deafening. Tristam caught a glimpse of James, hanging limply from the crossbeams. Dead.

Tristam stopped in his tracks, staring in disbelief. Shouts of "girl" and "monster" still rose up at random around him. "Girl crawled out from under the wagon," said an old man. "Gutted him like a fish."

Had Kyra done this? Had she planned to? And *why*? Tristam grabbed a man in the crowd. "Where did the assassin go?"

The man pointed—at the rooftops, naturally. Tristam gritted his teeth and pushed his way into the throng. It was slow going. Even with his official livery and his height, the mob could only part so quickly. He took a rougher approach as he grew more impatient, throwing elbows and ignoring angry comments.

Red Shields ran along the rooftops and dropped out of sight farther on. They had the right idea—the crowd wasn't going to get any thinner. Tristam gave up on the street and pushed his way to a nearby wall. He jumped for an overhang and pulled himself up. Most of the Red Shields he'd seen were gone by now, but he had a vague idea of where they'd disappeared to. Tristam ran, his steps landing too heavily for comfort on the well-crafted roof tiles. He'd heard enough from the crowd to know that they'd recognized Kyra for who she was and what she was. There was no way this could end well.

Tristam was halfway there when he heard the roar, and the blood drained from his face. No. She wouldn't.

He redoubled his speed. His way was once again directed by screams and shouts, and it was easy to find the courtyard where chaos was breaking loose. He skidded to a stop dangerously close to the roof edge and took in the scene below.

She was there. Tristam had seen Kyra twice in this form now—dark brown fur, slender muscular body—and she was backed into a corner by four Red Shields. Tristam's first reaction was relief to see that they wielded swords rather than spears.

But then Kyra growled, a deep-throated snarl that sent shivers down his spine, and he wondered if he was worried for the wrong party.

He lowered himself off the roof and crept closer. *Jump over them, Kyra. Knock them aside and make for the forest.*

Just then, two of the Red Shields attacked. One of them managed to cut Kyra's flank, and she roared in fury. She leaped into their midst, scattering them like pebbles. There was murder in her eyes.

"No!" Tristam shouted. He ran in front of Kyra, holding up his hands. "Kyra, it's me. Don't do this."

She fixed his eyes on him, and what he saw froze him to the core. Last time, after she'd killed Santon, Tristam had still been able to see some humanity in her. He'd spoken to that, and he'd reached her. But this time, he saw none of it. No sign at all that Kyra recognized him. No hint, as she advanced on him, teeth bared, that she even knew who he was.

Tristam drew his sword. Bad idea. At the first flash of steel, Kyra launched herself at him. He dove out of the way and turned to find her engaging now with the other Red Shields. Things were spiraling out of control.

Tristam tossed his sword to the side. It would only make things worse. And then, without stopping to think lest he realize his foolishness, he ran and threw herself onto her back.

Kyra's reaction was immediate. She twisted and snarled as Tristam looped his arms around her neck and hung on for dear life. "Don't do this, Kyra. It's me."

Kyra gave no sign of understanding. She rose up on her hind legs, doing her best to toss him off. Tristam continued talking to her, shouting words he couldn't even make sense of himself. But finally, his grip failed, and she tossed him onto the ground. The impact knocked the breath out of him. He groaned, willing the spots to clear out of his vision. The courtyard had gone quiet. Kyra was staring at him, still growling, tail swishing.

"Leave the city, Kyra," he said. He breathed in dust from his fall and coughed. "Get out of here." Was she that completely gone? Would she kill him right here and now?

A door opened into the courtyard, and new soldiers rushed in, some with spears this time. Kyra whipped around to face them, and Tristam braced himself for what was to come. But then she turned abruptly and ran up a tree. It bowed under her weight, and just as Tristam thought something would snap, Kyra launched herself onto the rooftop and ran for the city walls.

TWENTY-FOUR

Kyra ran with a speed born of madness. As she leaped off the rooftop and onto the street, people screamed and scattered in her wake. She was tempted to chase them, but Tristam's voice lodged in her mind and she kept running. She cleared the city wall by climbing another tree, then tumbled down the other side. She landed on her feet.

Houses changed to farmland, then gave way to the shelter of the forest. She dodged branches and tree trunks, zigzagging her way through. A pent-up frustration drove her on, a feeling that if she stopped or slowed, she would explode. Kyra spied a raccoon and gave chase, killing it with a snap of her jaws and tearing into its flesh. Only then did her blood cool. Only then did her wits return. She couldn't stay in this shape, but she would freeze if she changed back now.

She limped her way to her cave. The winter air swirled around her as she finally shrank back into her skin. Her limbs ached, and she was covered with cuts and bruises, including one long gash across her ribs. Nothing life-threatening, but they made every movement painful. Kyra stumbled inside, shivering violently, and dressed herself as quickly as she could. This was her last spare tunic.

She crumpled against the sandy cave wall as the memories came back to her. The fight against the guards—had she killed any of them? Then there was Tristam. *Tristam.* How badly had she hurt him?

Kyra's hands were still crusted with James's blood. Somehow, through all the transformations, fighting, and fleeing, it had stayed on. Kyra stared at her fingers until her eyes blurred. What had James been to her? At different times, he'd been a Guildleader, an infatuation, an enemy, and a co-conspirator. And now he was dead at her hands. He'd wanted her to be an assassin. Today he'd been her mark.

Kyra saw again the pain in his face as he'd died. Why had she stabbed him in the stomach? She'd meant to cut his throat, but then the Red Shields had come after her, and she'd simply acted. Kyra had thought to kill him as an act of mercy, but had there been a part of her that sought revenge? Maybe she hadn't been ready to let James forget the pain he'd caused her.

Snow crunched nearby, and Kyra held her breath. Outside, the forest had fallen unnaturally silent. She grabbed her dagger and ran to the cave mouth. Someone stepped out of the trees.

"Tristam?" Kyra asked. Her voice shook.

He stepped fully into view. "You left a trail. I tried to obscure it as best I could." He held out a cloak and a pair of boots—hers. "I don't think anyone saw me grab these."

"Thank you." She came out of the cave and took her things, tucking them under one arm. Tristam's eyes flickered over her, taking in her ragged appearance. He didn't look too good himself. There was dirt on his tunic, and the skin on one side of his face looked raw. But the worst was the caution in his eyes, the way he stood as if he expected her to change shape at any moment.

"I'm so sorry." Kyra's voice broke.

He didn't respond right away, and Kyra wondered if this had finally turned him away from her forever.

"Are you... back to yourself?" he finally asked.

She nodded, closing her eyes. "The Red Shields. How many...?"

"Four had minor injuries to be treated. One lost a great deal of blood but should survive."

Her knees buckled with relief, and she touched a tree for support. "Thank you for stopping me." When she'd faced the soldiers, they'd seemed nothing more than nameless enemies, helpless targets. But they'd had families and children.

"You're shaking," Tristam said. He took her hand and led her back to the cave. She was grateful for his touch and that he didn't refuse to be close to her. But still, he was so careful in the way he moved, so on his guard.

"I thought I could control it," she said. But was that even true? She'd been scared, hemmed in by soldiers, and taking her other form had seemed her only way out. Her life or theirs. She'd made her choice, though there had been eight of them and one of her. "I don't think I should change shape again," she said.

He didn't argue. They sat just inside the cave entrance. The afternoon sunlight came in at an angle and illuminated the dust in front of them.

"How many people have you killed, as a soldier?" she asked.

"Two," he said quietly. "The first time, we happened upon brigands attacking a trade caravan. The second was near my manor. It was the same thing, except they were looting a farm."

"How did it . . . make you feel afterward?"

He took his time answering, as if he knew how much hung in the balance. "It was hard, looking into the eyes of someone who was dying and knowing it was my doing."

Did he feel a rush of power when he killed? An overwhelming desire to draw more blood? She couldn't ask, but she suspected she knew the answer. "James held my eyes when I killed him," she said. "He wouldn't let me look away." Of course James would know what those last moments were like. Of course he'd insist on that last connection.

"Why did you do it?" asked Tristam. "That much planning, that much risk, just to spare him the last few hours?"

"I couldn't let him die like that." It didn't make sense. Even Kyra didn't quite understand the common thread of purpose that bound James and her together. They'd hurt each other so many times, yet some part of her had felt she owed him this. "He said something to me before he died. He told me to choose my fight."

"Your fight?" Tristam echoed. "And what is that?"

She rubbed at her fingers to get the blood off. "I don't know."

"I don't believe you."

He was right. Kyra wasn't as naïve as she used to be. She knew more about the city now and its workings. James had wanted to bring down the entire Council. She wasn't sure what he'd had in mind after that. Anarchy? Establishing himself in

260

power? He hadn't seen fit to share his plans with her, and Kyra suspected she wouldn't have agreed with them. But neither was she happy with the way things were.

"Willem's got to go. It's not enough simply to stop the Demon Rider offensive. I want him out of power."

Tristam was silent for a long moment before he finally spoke again. "I'll help you in any way I can."

He'd spoken so calmly that it took a while for Kyra to recognize the implications. But when they finally sank in, she looked to him in alarm. "Tristam, this is high treason. You've been working so hard to get back to good standing in the Palace, and you've got your marriage negotiations to think about." He'd given up so much for her already.

Tristam stared at the dust swirling in front of them. "You know, before I met you, I never gave much thought to my station in life. I knew I was fortunate, but I didn't really know what it meant. But I have to think now that my good fortune comes with some measure of responsibility, whether it be taking up arms to protect the lowborn or trying to make changes where we can." He paused then. "I suppose we all have to make our choices. This is mine."

It was the type of decision that should have been announced with trumpets and rousing speeches, but instead it was just the two of them hiding in the mouth of a cave, bruised, dirty, and exhausted.

"I won't stop you," said Kyra. "But if you have doubts at any point, you need to tell me."

"What next, then?"

She looked up at him, and their eyes met briefly. It seemed

she was always looking at the space between the two of them. Measuring it, wishing she could bridge it. "James told me once that Willem must be disgraced before he's brought down. I think he's right. We need to discredit him."

"Orvin's mystery messenger, then?" said Tristam.

Kyra nodded. "We'll need to think how best to do it. Flick might be able to help. He's good at flipping pockets." She started going through the possibilities in her head, but her mind wouldn't cooperate. Too much had happened in too short of a time. She wasn't ready to get back on the warpath just yet. "We'll make plans, but can you give me a moment? I can't think straight."

He looked her over again, and there was a softness in his gaze when he nodded. She leaned her head against the cave wall and closed her eyes. She'd only meant to rest a little, but a while later, she was groggily aware of him laying her down on the cave floor and tucking his cloak around her. She reached out and took his hand. His grip felt so comfortable, so solid. And yet, there was caution in his manner that hadn't been there the night before.

"Tristam," she said. "It's not just Cecile that stands between us, is it? Even if I were higher-born, it wouldn't matter. You're scared of what I am."

He didn't answer right away, and his hesitation spoke more than any words he might have said. For a moment she could see it in his eyes, his lingering fear and mistrust of the Demon Riders, something he'd done an admirable job of hiding from her but was nonetheless still there. Kyra looked down, trying to ignore the tightness that had arisen in her chest. "I'm not completely blameless in Santon's death. I hoped he would attack me, and I pretended to be vulnerable so they'd give me the excuse I needed. Part of me liked tearing Santon apart. I'm not proud of it, but I won't hide it from you. I owe you that much."

Tristam looked down at her hand. When he finally spoke, his voice was heavy. "I don't envy you, Kyra. I might have done the same or worse had I been in your shoes."

He was offering her empathy, understanding, friendship. And though a selfish part of her wished for more, Kyra supposed that they didn't have that luxury. Tristam brushed her hair away from her face with the back of his fingers. The featherlight touch left a pleasant tingling on her scalp, and she let her eyes close. "Should you be getting back to the city?" she asked him.

"They won't notice my absence for a few more hours. Sleep for now. I'll be here."

TWENTY-FIVE

Flick was getting better at spotting Demon Riders in the trees. Or at least he thought he was. He caught hints of movement in the corners of his eyes when he walked near the forest, though when he turned and looked, he never saw anything for certain.

He was out behind Mercie's house this afternoon. There had been a lot of activity on the roads earlier, and Flick suspected something had happened in the city. Mercie had gone in to hear the news, and Flick watched the road, eager to know what had occurred.

But there was that thing that kept moving in his periphery. He supposed he should have been more nervous, but he suspected he knew what it was. Or rather, who it was. Finally, his curiosity got the better of him. "Is anyone there?" he called.

Adele stepped out. Flick grinned. "I'm glad to see you."

She smiled serenely in return, her amber eyes sparkling against her pale skin. That was a first. He couldn't remember her giving him a full smile before.

"Are you well?" she asked.

"I am. Thank you."

They stood looking at each other for a few moments. Finally, Flick gestured to the forest. "I was just taking a walk. Would you like to join me?"

"To see Kyra?"

"No, just watching the road. But there's no reason I must do it alone."

Her eyes brightened at this, and she fell in step beside him. They strolled just inside the line of the forest so Flick could catch glimpses of the road. It was his fourth time meeting Adele now, yet he still felt off balance around her. He'd had his share of sweethearts in the past. Flick never had trouble talking to girls or making them laugh. But then, none of girls he flirted with back in the city had been capable of turning into giant beasts. Not that he thought he was flirting with Adele. Who knew what these people's customs were? It was enough of a triumph that he hadn't yet been mauled to death. But something about this lass fascinated him. Her quick eye and curiosity, her uninhibited openness in expressing her opinion, her never-ending stream of questions for him.

Speaking of which, she was about to ask him another one. He could tell. Flick interrupted her. "You're always asking me about me and my people," he said. "I think it's my turn, don't you?"

A few meetings ago, this sort of question might have made her jump back in alarm. But this time, she simply tilted her head, then nodded. "What would you like to know?"

"Well..." Flick paused. He hardly knew where to start. "What do you do most days?"

"Nights," she corrected. "I hunt at night, and I wander the forest. Sometimes I gather with the others."

"What do you do with them?"

"Talk, tell stories, sing." She reached out and touched a tree branch with her finger as they walked past.

Sing? The idea of Adele as a songbird piqued his interest. "Will you sing something for me?"

He thought he'd have to coax her further, but she launched right into a quick song. Her voice was high and steady. The melody itself was unusual. It went up and down in finer increments than the songs he was used to hearing. It almost reminded Flick of Minadan pipe tunes, the ones said to lull a sleeper into strange and curious dreams, but Adele's tune was livelier and happier.

"You sing beautifully," he said when she finished. "Can you teach me this song?"

She sang a phrase for him to repeat, then covered a smile at his attempt.

"No good?"

"Your pronunciation is not the best," she said gently.

He tried several more times until she deemed his performance satisfactory enough to move on. They continued like this, phrase by phrase, laughing at his mistakes and sending wayward phrases into the trees. He'd almost made it through what he thought was the first stanza when Adele stopped him with a touch to the elbow. She was looking into the forest again.

"Some of your kin?" he asked, suddenly tense. Adele, he was always happy to see. But the others . . .

She stared in that direction, then shook her head. "It's Kyra. And someone else."

Kyra came into view a few moments later. Her face was smudged with dirt, and she moved like it hurt to do so. And was that blood seeping through her tunic?

"Kyra, what happened?" Then he saw Tristam a few steps behind her, looking equally beat-up and still wearing his Red Shield livery.

Kyra looked between Flick and Adele, confused for a moment, and then seemed to put the matter out of her mind. "Have you had news from the city?" she asked.

"Not today. But Mercie went in to find out what the excitement was."

Kyra lowered her eyes. Flick could tell from the way her brows knitted together that the news was big, that it had to do with her, and that he wasn't going to be pleased.

"Out with it," he said.

She spread her hands apologetically. "Things have happened," she said. "And we need your help."

Flick knew that the Palace compound had two main gates, one in the north, and one on the south wall. These were the only ones opened on a regular basis. What he hadn't noticed until tonight was the presence of smaller gates. According to Kyra, these were usually double-locked and guarded, although select noblemen living within those walls had keys. A few hours past midnight, a man had entered through one such gate, and now Flick waited in a nearby alleyway for him to leave.

He heard a faint metallic creak, followed by quick footsteps that echoed down the empty street. Flick ducked deeper into the alley as the man walked past. A few moments later, a shadow passed overhead—Kyra was trailing him on the rooftops. Flick pulled his cloak tighter and settled down to wait.

Kyra dropped off the roof a short while later, landing softly in front of him. Though Flick could not see her face clearly in the darkness, he could hear her panting from exertion. Kyra was dressed for work in a dark tunic and trousers, with her hair tied back in her characteristic ponytail. He'd seen her like this hundreds of times, and after all the craziness of the past few weeks, it was nice to see her back to form.

Flick had been . . . less than pleased to learn what had happened at James's execution. But somehow, after berating Kyra for her harebrained, risky scheme, he'd immediately agreed to help her with another one. Kyra had argued that this new mission was important, and this time, Flick agreed. If there was any way to stop Willem's Demon Rider offensive, they had to try. Flick's conversations with Adele had convinced him that peace with the Makvani was possible, but only if Forge didn't embark on such a disastrous attack.

Kyra dusted off her hands. "The messenger's staying at an inn called The Drowned Cat," she said. "Not the most auspicious name for an inn, is it?"

"Mayhap it refers to the contents of their stew," said Flick.

Kyra stifled a giggle as they made their way to the inn. The windows were dark, and the road was completely silent. They slipped into an alleyway across the street, where Tristam was already waiting.

"I'm guessing he'll leave tomorrow morning to blend in with the other travelers," Tristam said.

Flick handed Kyra a large bag. "If he breaks his fast in the inn's dining room, I'll flip his purse then. And you, my delightful assistant, will need these."

Kyra reached into the bag and fished out a long black wig, a trader's tunic, and a pair of shoes, examining each in turn. Flick grinned when he saw Tristam eyeing the props with curiosity. The wallhugger would be getting quite the education in undercity tactics today.

Kyra rounded the corner with the props. When she came back, she looked taller, thanks to the shoes' well-concealed heels, and she boasted a head of luxurious ebony curls instead of her usual brown ponytail. In the darkness, Flick could barely make out the intricately patterned leather knots decorating her tunic in the style of the southern traders. Trader women were some of the few who might actually eat or stay at an inn. It wasn't the best disguise, but it was the best Mercie had. Flick didn't bother with a costume himself, thinking instead to blend in among the countless tavern-going men. Though he'd grown out his beard since he fled the city. It always made him look quite a bit older.

They took turns watching the inn until light started to shine on the horizon and the city started to stir. When the innkeeper came out to sweep the doorstep, Kyra looked to Flick. "Better if you're already in the dining room when he comes in. Remember what he looks like?"

"Black hair down to his shoulder, a few years older than

me. Small eyes. Mustache." Flick wiped the dust off his cloak. "You're paying for my drink, right?"

Kyra rolled her eyes and handed Flick a few coppers.

"The messenger came in late last night, and he might not be up for a while," said Tristam. "Do you think it'll be suspicious for Flick to be in there so long?"

Flick and Kyra exchanged a glance, and Kyra's lips twitched. "Flick always thinks up something to do." She turned to Flick. "Just, uh, try not to attract too much attention, all right?" The last time Flick had done a day-long stint at an inn, he'd invented a drinking game where each drinker had to be at a higher physical location than the last. The fallout had involved a crowd of people on the roof, multiple bruises, one broken limb (not Flick's), and a warning never to step foot in The Bow-Legged Canary again.

Flick grinned. "Who, me?" And he sauntered off.

After a night out in the cold, the warm air of the inn's dining room felt lovely, and the smell of freshly baked bread wafting out from the kitchen made Flick's stomach growl. The room was about half full as the earlier-rising patrons broke their fast, and Flick settled near a window. The serving girl was a friendly lass with dimpled cheeks who laughed at his jokes. She brought him a plate of sausages, and he tucked into the meal.

He'd just about finished his sausages when he saw his mark. The messenger entered alone and sat down with the bristly body language of someone who didn't want company. Flick washed down his last bite of breakfast with ale, then put a little unsteadiness in his stride and strolled to the messenger's table.

"Fine morning, in't it?" said Flick, sinking onto a stool next to him. The messenger didn't so much as glance at him. Flick had been about to recite some platitudes about delicious food and beautiful serving girls but changed his mind when he saw the man's scowl. "Of course, can't quite enjoy it in this type of establishment. Second-rate food and lazy serving lasses." Flick sent a mental apology to the nice serving girl, grateful she was out of earshot.

Flick studied the man with a careful eye. The messenger was grumpy and standoffish. His clothes were unremarkable in style and color, but his tunic was of surprisingly thick and soft wool, and he wore a finely crafted ring. Flick also noticed that the man's hair and mustache were meticulously trimmed. Most importantly, he carried a small leather bag across his shoulder. That was likely where his message would be.

"That's a fine ring you've got there," Flick said. "Impressive detailing. Must have been made by a master."

The man straightened just the tiniest bit.

"What's the design? Looks like one of the newer fashions out of Parna."

It was just an educated guess, since everything seemed to come from Parna these days. But the messenger regarded him with new consideration. "That's right."

Flick smiled and extended a hand. "I'm Taylon of Forge."

"Robert," said the messenger. No city, no house. Still being careful.

The door opened, and Flick saw Kyra come in and sit at a back table. He averted his eyes and launched into an elaborate story about getting cheated by a trader over a fake silver brooch. Robert's lips curled slightly as the story progressed—the messenger didn't have a high opinion of Flick's eye for goods—but Flick knew he had him. Robert was listening intently, and he'd forgotten all about his earlier attempts to stay aloof.

Flick patted Robert on the shoulder. "I'll wager someone like you wouldn't be fooled by such a simple trick." The pat was a little rougher than it needed to be, and Robert scowled at Flick's drunken clumsiness. As the messenger pulled away, Flick undid the clasp on Robert's bag, looking out the window as he did so. "You've far to travel today?"

Robert followed Flick's gaze. They always did, if he led confidently. "Not too far," the messenger said, oblivious to the fact that Flick had just lifted a piece of parchment from his purse.

Flick tucked the parchment up his sleeve and continued to chatter on. Someone brushed past him—Kyra's scratchy wig tickled the back of his neck. Her fingers skimmed his palm, and he let the parchment drop into her hand.

He spoke to the man a while longer and then pushed back from the table. "Pity that ale never stays with us very long," he said with an embarrassed grin. He made a show of asking for the privy before he went out the door.

Flick found Kyra and Tristam crouched in the alley behind a stack of crates. Kyra had already opened the parchment, and Flick noticed with pride that she'd managed to keep half the seal intact, though the other half had broken into pieces.

"Find anything?" he asked, bending down to join them.

Tristam handed him the opened note. The message inside was written in neat, elegant script.

All our soldiers are in position and ready for the forest offensive,

*though the Council is volatile and our plans are far from secure. I
need more funds to gain the cooperation of Palace scribes, as well as
key members of the defense forces. The more of our own that we have
within the Palace, the safer our position will be.*

"That's Willem's handwriting," said Tristam.

Flick read it over one more time, then returned it to
Tristam. "Certainly seems underhanded, but what's it mean?
Care to enlighten us on the ways of the court?"

Tristam rubbed his temples. "Willem's trying to ensure the
success of the Demon Rider offensive—that's clear enough.
And looks like he's using bribes to do it. The Council members look to the scribes and army leaders for advice. If Willem
controls what they hear, he controls what they think."

Seemed a roundabout way of pulling strings, but Flick supposed everything in the Palace was roundabout. "Who do you
think is providing this coin?"

"Hard to tell. My best guess would be some of the minor
families outside the city. They'd have the most to gain from an
offensive against the Demon Riders."

They were silent for a moment, then Kyra spoke. "If the
Council's decision to attack the Demon Riders was influenced
by bribery, would that be enough reason to stop the offensive?"

"It might be enough to delay while they investigate further,"
said Tristam, "and it might be the first step we need to discredit
Willem himself. But I'm not sure we have enough proof. This
is only one letter, and it's not even signed. Willem's handwriting could easily be faked. And we don't even know who his
co-conspirators are."

Flick drummed his fingers against his thigh. "What if you

had the testimony of the messenger? He'll find his purse empty soon enough and come looking for me. Might there be some way to, ah . . . persuade him to cooperate?" He almost felt guilty for suggesting it. Though really, Robert was a rather unpleasant fellow. . . .

Tristam squinted in the direction of the street. "Depends on how his loyalty measures up to his self-preservation. But we'd need someplace to keep him. We can't exactly interrogate him here."

"I could guard him at my cave," said Kyra.

"It'd be better if you had help," said Flick. An idea came to him, and he made a quick decision. Why should Kyra be the only one to come up with harebrained schemes? "I might have friends who could keep an eye on him."

"Are these friends trustworthy?" asked Tristam.

"They've no love for Willem. I'll introduce you and you can decide for yourself."

Tristam looked to Kyra. "What do you think?"

She stared at the parchment. "We've only seven days until the offensive starts. Think we can get the messenger to crack that quickly?"

"Can you think of a better way?" said Tristam.

A vendor on the street outside hawked his hotcakes as the three of them thought this over. Kyra gave a decisive nod. "Let's do it."

They sketched out a quick plan, then Flick returned to the inn, bypassing the dining room this time for the living quarters in back. He climbed the stairs in a rush, as if he were making a hasty exit. No one stopped him, so he ran through the hallways several more times, wondering how long he could keep this up. Finally, Robert stepped around the corner. The man grabbed Flick's collar and forced him against the wall.

Flick raised his hands. "Whoa there, friend." One of the doors in the corridor opened, and a bewildered lodger peered out, only to duck back into his room when Robert glared at him.

The messenger bent his face close to Flick's. "Where is it?"

"Where's what?"

Flick felt the sharp point of a dagger against his side. "The parchment," said Robert.

"I've no idea what you're talking about." Flick bit back a curse as cloth ripped and the dagger skimmed his skin. He was pretty sure Robert had drawn blood. "Search me if you want," he said through gritted teeth. "I've nothing on me." *You owe me, Kyra.*

Flick stayed absolutely still as Robert patted him down. Robert searched him twice, then narrowed his eyes. "It was in my purse when I stepped into the dining room, and gone after you left. No one else came near me except for you." Robert raised the dagger to Flick's throat.

"All right, all right, I took it." Flick didn't have to work hard to sound convincingly panicked. "It's outside. I can give it back. Just—keep that dagger to yourself."

The messenger spun Flick roughly around so they were facing the same direction. A moment later, the knife reappeared at his back. "Slowly," said Robert. "If I suspect anything, your life is forfeit."

They walked in lockstep down the stairs. The lodgers they passed didn't even notice anything was amiss. Once out the door, Flick headed for the alley, and Robert tightened his grip. "Don't try anything."

"Do you want the parchment or not?" said Flick under his breath.

Flick felt a layer of sweat forming over his skin as they stepped into the alley. There was no sign of Tristam or Kyra as they walked past the stack of crates, and he dearly hoped that nothing had gone awry. Flick's gaze settled on a pile of rocks next to the wall. "There, under the rocks."

Robert nudged him closer. "Move them aside slowly."

Carefully, Flick got to his knees and began slowly shifting the rocks in the pile. *Any time now, Tristam...*

Robert grunted behind him, and Flick felt the man's grip go slack. He turned around to see Tristam carefully lowering the messenger's body to the ground. Kyra dropped off the roof, eyed Robert, unconscious on the ground, and breathed a sigh of relief.

"He's alive," said Tristam. "He'll have a headache when he wakes though."

"Cutting it a bit close?" said Flick, shaking out his arms and shoulders. He hadn't realized how tense he'd been.

"Sorry," said Tristam. "With that knife drawn on you, I wanted to make sure he didn't see me coming."

Flick plucked Robert's dagger off the ground and wiped the dust off the blade. "I'm keeping this," he said. "For my troubles."

TWENTY-SIX

They bound Robert tightly and gagged him while Tristam hurried back to the Palace for a wagon. When the messenger awoke, Kyra showed him her dagger.

"You'll be quiet," she said, conjuring her best imitation of James in his more dangerous moments. "And you won't cause any trouble." The messenger's glare could have sparked kindling, but he made no noise.

A short while later, Tristam pulled up with a wagon full of the fake demon cat heads. "I told them I was going to set up some exercises outside the city," he said. "I suppose I'll have to do that now."

By pulling the wagon right to the alley, they loaded Robert without attracting too many wayward glances. Flick lay down behind him, holding tight to the ropes that bound Robert's wrists. Kyra took her place in front of the messenger, and Tristam covered all three of them with demon cat heads. The hemp sacks smelled like mold, and Kyra could feel Robert's eyes on her in the cramped semidarkness. The messenger exuded fury, and Kyra wondered how they would possibly get him

277

to cooperate before the start of the Demon Rider offensive in seven days.

After a bumpy and stuffy ride out of the city, Tristam pulled the wagon off the road. Flick left to find his friends, and Kyra and Tristam marched Robert to Kyra's cave. Their captive walked stoically in front of them, with Tristam's knife at his back. He was obediently quiet, but his eyes were a bit too keen, and it was with great relief that Kyra saw her cave appear ahead of them.

Kyra scouted it first, then waved Tristam in when she found it empty. Not much light came in from the mouth, and it took a moment for their eyes to adjust to the darkness. It also smelled slightly of cat, and Kyra wondered if Tristam noticed.

Tristam ungagged Robert. "You may sit if you'd like," said Tristam, motioning to the cave wall. The messenger glared at them but carefully lowered himself onto the ground. He pulled his legs away from Kyra when she tried to retie them, but relented after a moment.

"You're from the Forge Council?" said Robert. "I didn't peg that fellow for a Palace man."

"We'll be asking the questions," Tristam said calmly. "Who sent the message to Willem?"

Robert's laugh had a sarcastic edge. "And you expect me to simply lay it all out for you?"

"No, not immediately. But you will. You looked competent with that dagger, but you're a messenger and not a soldier. You aren't sworn to die for your master, and I don't think you mean to. It might take some time for this to sink in, but you'll come around."

Kyra had been on the receiving end of Tristam's interrogations not long ago, and it was strange to be on the other side. Tristam didn't yell or raise his voice, but there was a quiet intensity to the way he spoke that commanded attention. He was also incredibly calm. All their plans hinged on this messenger, but Tristam acted as if he had the upper hand.

"I don't believe you'll kill me," said Robert.

"I won't have to," said Tristam. "The Council will gladly execute you for me. But if you give us useful information, we might be able to speak on your behalf. I can't promise you any specific terms to your sentence, but I can promise you far better than what you'll receive if I turn you in without an admission of guilt. Just tell me which house employs you and whom the message was for."

Kyra heard footsteps outside a few moments before Tristam did. They exchanged a glance, and she slipped out. Flick waited a short distance from the cave mouth, shifting his weight from foot to foot. She could have sworn he looked guilty.

"My friends can help," he said. "And they're right behind me."

"I see." Kyra took a few steps closer, wondering at Flick's manner. "That's good news, in't it?" She stopped as Adele, Pashla, and Mela and a man she didn't recognize came into view. "Flick, that's—"

At that moment, Tristam stepped out of the cave. He took one look at the newcomers and reached for his sword.

"There's no need, Tristam," said Flick. "These are the friends I mentioned."

Tristam had gone rigid. He drew breath sharply to speak, then looked back at the cave mouth. His voice was low when he spoke again, but no less angry. "You didn't mention that your friends were Demon Riders."

"I know," said Flick. He spoke carefully, though there was no hint of apology in his manner. "They're good to help, but you don't have to accept it."

Kyra looked from Flick to Tristam and back again, trying to ignore a feeling of betrayal that was trickling into her consciousness. She wasn't sure what bothered her more, that Flick had obviously hidden this plan from her, or that he'd been the one to think of it when Kyra shared their blood.

Pashla nodded to Kyra in greeting, then looked at Tristam. "I didn't know the knight would be here," she said to Adele.

"I have a name," said Tristam, his voice taut.

"Tristam of Brancel," Pashla said lightly. While her tone didn't exactly convey disrespect, neither did she assign much importance to the utterance. The tension in the circle was palpable, and Kyra couldn't quell the feeling that things were about to unravel. She didn't know what Flick's game was, and the thought of her old friend doing anything behind her back bothered her more than she cared to admit.

It was Adele who spoke first. "Flick tells me that we need this prisoner if we want to stop Forge from sending soldiers into the forest. We will guard him for you. You have our word that he will not escape," she said.

"Your word?" said Tristam. "And what's that worth?" Kyra had to look away at the raw animosity in his voice. If she'd had any doubt as to how he felt about her kin...

"We're skilled at watching prisoners, and we're skilled fighters," said Pashla. "This, you should know, since you've been one of our captives, and you've seen how easily we can kill your kind."

Kyra looked to Pashla in disbelief. Was she deliberately goading Tristam, or did she simply not realize what effect her words would have?

Tristam took a step toward Pashla, drawing his sword. "I stood by while you murdered two of my comrades. I will not stand by while you mock their deaths."

"No!" Kyra reached for him as Pashla took a step back. The Demon Riders to either side of her untied their belts.

"Stop now!" Flick could be deafening when he wanted to be, and his shout reverberated through the trees. Everybody froze, and he planted himself between Tristam and Pashla. "We've got the same goals here and enough at stake so that we can't afford to fall apart amongst ourselves."

Tristam's sword hovered a finger's width from Flick's throat. Adele's features blurred and re-formed as she looked between the two of them.

Kyra finally found her voice. "Tristam," she said softly, almost apologetically. "I think Flick's right. The Makvani could do a better job of guarding him than I could by myself."

Tristam's face was still tight with anger. "Can I have a word, Flick?" he said.

"Aye," said Flick, resigned.

Tristam lowered his blade, and the two walked into the trees with the wariness of men about to start a duel. Kyra wondered if she should step in. Both Tristam and Flick knew how high the stakes were. They wouldn't come to blows over this, would they?

"Your friend holds long grudges," came Pashla's low voice at her ear.

Kyra could feel a headache starting to form right in the middle of her forehead, and she found she didn't have the patience for caution or tact. "You killed two of his friends, Pashla. That's more than a grudge to get over."

"They were killed in battle," said Pashla calmly, as if that settled the matter.

Flick and Tristam were arguing and gesticulating, though Kyra couldn't make out the words. At one point, Flick gestured in their direction, and she got the clear impression that he pointed to her rather than the Demon Riders near her. A short while later, her friends returned. Tristam's eyes still flashed, and Flick had the look of someone who'd just weathered a hard storm.

"Everything all right?" Kyra asked. She'd have her own words with Flick later, but right now she just wanted to keep everything from falling apart.

"We accept your help," said Tristam to the Demon Riders.

"We are, in fact, grateful for it," added Flick. Tristam's expression remained stony. "And I have clothes for the guards to change into. Seems it would be prudent not to let"—he jerked his head toward the cave—"know about, uh"—he gestured toward the Makvani.

Things progressed quickly after that. Kyra set up a guard schedule with the Demon Riders while Tristam questioned Robert further. The messenger didn't give him any useful information, but Tristam didn't seem surprised.

"He needs some time to think. They always do," Tristam said to Kyra as he prepared to leave. He'd calmed down since the confrontation earlier, and Kyra had seen him thank Adele for the Makvani's help.

"I certainly needed some time," said Kyra, thinking back to her interrogation and imprisonment at the Palace.

Tristam's eyes went cautiously over her face, and only after searching her features did he relax and meet her eyes. "You know, I still feel guilty about how I treated you," he said.

She smiled wryly up at him. "Why ever for? We've been through enough together. No reason to dwell on past misunderstandings."

They looked at one another, sharing for a moment the memory of when they'd faced off over the interrogation table. And though they had hated each other at the time, thinking back on it now brought Kyra comfort. It was a reason for hope, she supposed, that two people at odds could come so far.

Finally, Tristam looked down. "I should go," he said. "I'll be back when I can. Keep him well fed and sheltered. We need him to believe us when we say we can protect him."

Kyra let out a long, slow breath as she watched Tristam walk away. When he finally disappeared, she covered her eyes with the heel of her hands and arched her back, trying to loosen up her muscles. Footsteps crunched in the snow, and she opened her eyes to see Flick walking toward her, for all the world looking like a dog who'd been caught ransacking the family kitchen.

"So," he said. "Are you ready to yell at me now?"

That was all the encouragement Kyra needed.

"What were you thinking?" She rounded on him, venting all the tension and betrayal she'd been feeling. "They could have slaughtered each other in front of that cave."

Flick bore her words, making no attempt to interrupt her.

"Why'd you do it?" she asked, throwing up her arms. "Why didn't you tell me?" She looked back toward the Demon Riders by the cave. "And have you become bosom friends with Pashla, too?" She finally admitted it. She was jealous of her friend, who picked up allies wherever he went, while it seemed she herself only found more enemies.

She ran out of words and settled for glaring at Flick, who stirred when he realized she was done.

"I'm sorry I didn't tell you," he said, subdued. "I knew Tristam wouldn't agree if I asked him beforehand, and if I'd told you, you'd have been forced to decide whether you wanted to hide it from him. This way, the blame fell squarely on me." He took a breath. "I don't know Pashla well at all. Adele was the one I asked for help, and she found the others."

"And you just decided this was the right thing to do?" Kyra said.

"Can you think of anyone else who could have helped us?"

She couldn't, really, but she wasn't ready to let him off the hook. "Just because things didn't explode today doesn't mean they won't tomorrow."

"I know. But it's worth it." Flick spoke with surprising conviction, and Kyra wondered at it. He sank down onto a fallen log. After a moment, Kyra grudgingly followed his lead.

"Why?" she asked.

Flick stared down at his hands, massaging the knuckles of

his right hand with his left. "Call me foolish, I suppose, but I think it might do some good to work together with these people. I've had a few run-ins with the Makvani now. Truth is, they do look on us humans as something below their regard. But I'm realizing that it's different when they see you face-to-face. That's why I don't think those folk by the cave will hurt me, even if their clanmate was wounded by a soldier this morning. I'm no longer a nameless human to them. And I wonder, if more of them actually spent time with us, maybe something could come out of it."

"You think we could avoid a war?"

Flick sighed and absentmindedly broke a twig off the fallen tree. "I don't think Adele's eager for a fight, and some of the others aren't either. I mean, I'm not naïve. I know this will only make a small difference. But it's better than nothing, in't it?"

His face had such an optimistic cast that Kyra found it hard to hold her grudge. "I hope you're right," she said. "And I hope Tristam can get over what happened today and trust us again."

"Tristam, in particular, needs to get over his fears."

There was a layer of meaning in Flick's tone that caught Kyra's attention. "Why? What do you mean?"

"Oh." For the first time, Flick stumbled on his words. "I just mean..."

And Kyra remembered how Flick had pointed at her when he argued with Tristam. The pieces fell together, and she looked incredulously at Flick. "You're not trying to put me and Tristam together, are you? You've been against it from the beginning."

"I was wrong," Flick said. "I admit it. Tristam's a decent fellow. He's not my da, and you are not my ma. I probably should have realized that sooner, and I worry that something I said might have swayed you against him."

Kyra put a hand to her temple. Of all the times for Flick to come around ... "You *were* wrong about him," she said. "But it doesn't matter. He's still a nobleman, and he has duties to his family."

"That might be true," said Flick. "But he in't married yet, and who knows what might happen? Things are changing, Kyra. I don't think we can take anything for granted anymore."

Kyra wondered if the fight with the messenger had muddled Flick's brain. But then she followed Flick's gaze to where Adele stood arm in arm with Mela, and she finally understood.

She jabbed her elbow into his rib cage. "Someone's changed your mind, Flick. And it wasn't Tristam."

He saw where she was looking and gave a sheepish smile. "I suppose one's view on forbidden romance changes when it no longer concerns other people."

Even though Kyra had suspected something, it still surprised her to hear Flick confirm it so readily. It hadn't been that long since they'd met, had it? "Is it ... mutual between the two of you?" she asked.

He shrugged, eyes still on her. "I'm only now learning their ways. I don't even think they all 'take mates,' as they call it. She'd need the permission of the clan leader. But she enjoys my company, and I've grown rather fond of hers. She's been bringing her friends to meet me. It's been ... quite an adventure."

"What will you do?" Kyra asked.

He shrugged. "Who knows what will happen tomorrow or next week, with things the way they are. But we'll live things out day by day. It's all we can do, really." He had a gentleness to his voice that tugged at Kyra's heart.

As if sensing Kyra and Flick talking about her, Adele turned and gave a slight smile. Flick waved.

"In that case, I wish you two the best," said Kyra, giving Flick's shoulders a quick squeeze. Kyra stood and dusted off her clothes, then turned a mischievous eye back toward him. "I do have one question though."

"What?"

"Are you sure you're not smitten with Adele simply because you saw her without her clothes? She does have a lovely figure."

"All right. That's it." Flick rolled up his sleeves and lunged for Kyra, ignoring her squeals as he caught her in a bear hug from behind. "I think you need some lessons in respecting your elders." And he methodically began to turn her upside down. Kyra yelled something about things dropping out of her pockets, but she was laughing too hard for any coherent words to come out. She scrabbled at Flick's legs behind her head, wondering at how the trees looked so much taller from this angle, when she saw the Demon Riders making their way toward the commotion.

"Everything's fine," said Flick. "This is how we show love in our family."

And Kyra didn't have the breath to contradict him.

TWENTY-SEVEN

Tristam tried not to worry as Robert held out, but the calendar was not on his side. As the date of the offensive ticked closer, units started taking position outside the city, and news of clashes with the Demon Riders came in daily. On his third trip to the cave, Tristam noticed that some of the Demon Riders had dyed the skin of their fingers red. When he asked Kyra about it, she coughed uncomfortably and told him that it was their tradition to do so before battle.

"That bad?" said Tristam.

"They're expecting a war," said Kyra.

The one good result of the approaching Demon Rider offensive was that Malikel resumed his duties with the Council. The magistrate's reasons for reinstating him had more to do with the city's need for wartime leadership than with his own investigations, but any change that got Malikel back on the Council was a good one in Tristam's book. On the first day of Malikel's return, Tristam hung near the Council Room, hoping to speak with the Defense Minister, but Malikel's movements were still closely monitored, and he couldn't get a word with him alone.

Three days before the Demon Rider offensive, Robert finally folded. "I serve the Whitt house," he said. "I've been carrying messages between Lord Whitt and Head Councilman Willem." His well-tailored clothes had become wrinkled and dirty after his days in the cave, and his hair and beard were unkempt.

It took some effort on Tristam's part not to let his relief show. "And what do they discuss?"

"They tell me very little," said Robert. "I simply carry the letters."

He might have been lying. He might have been telling the truth. But Tristam was running out of time. The Whitt household was one of the smaller houses of Forge, halfway to Edlan. They certainly would have had plenty of reason to encourage a Demon Rider sweep. "Will you testify to the Council that you ran messages between Willem and Lord Whitt?"

Robert didn't answer right away, and Tristam allowed the silence between them to stretch. It was like a game of cards, interrogating a hostile prisoner, always trying to hide one's own hand while guessing the opponent's.

"I'll testify," Robert said. "But I want a guard around me at all times. I fear for my life."

"I can arrange that," he said. "We'll take you to the city tomorrow."

He kept his walk at a dignified pace until Robert could no longer see him, then he rushed out to find Kyra. The cave was surrounded by Demon Riders. Each time Tristam returned, it seemed more Makvani loitered in its vicinity—four the first time, then five, then seven. Only one or two at any given time were actually serving a shift. The rest had no obvious reason for being there.

He finally spotted Kyra farther out, walking aimlessly through and around the trees. She looked a little worse for wear these days—her clothes were dusty, and her ponytail had several escaped strands, though she still walked with that graceful, easy stride. She came toward him when he caught her eye, and something must have showed in his expression, because a cautious optimism crossed her face.

"Do you believe him?" asked Kyra after he told her.

"We can't afford not to," he said. "If we want to stop the offensive, we must do something now."

"And you're set on taking it before the Council? It could be bad for you, if they don't believe you." There was real worry in her eyes. The strands of hair that had escaped her ponytail blew across her face. Tristam was tempted to brush them away but thought better of it. He was to have dinner again with Cecile tonight. "It's less dangerous for me than it would be for you."

Kyra pursed her lips but couldn't argue with his reasoning. "Very well, then," she said. She squeezed his hand. "Rest well."

The voices of the Makvani drifted after Tristam as he walked away. As much as he hated to admit it, Flick had been right about asking the Demon Riders to help. The guards had been very helpful. There was no way Kyra could have watched and sheltered Robert nearly as well on her own. He thought back again to his argument with Flick. They had primarily exchanged words over the Makvani, but it was what he'd said about Kyra that stuck in Tristam's mind.

You think you can keep her separate in your mind from the others. You think she's different, Flick had said. Or, more accurately, yelled. *But don't you realize Kyra doesn't see it that way? It's killing her to see you hate her kin like this. You'll never truly care for her if you despise her blood.*

Tristam could have argued with Flick. There were many things that made Kyra different from the others. But even if he'd brought those up, he couldn't argue with the look in Kyra's eyes whenever he made his true feelings about the Makvani known. He'd seen it many times, but he'd looked away.

Distracted by his thoughts, Tristam was slow to react when a yellow blur shot out from between the trees and knocked him to the ground. Before Tristam could grab his sword, whatever attacked him had disappeared back into the trees. He climbed to his feet, holding his sword in one hand and his dagger in the other. Had that been a demon cat? No, too small. Whatever had hit him had run into his legs.

He heard some scuffling around him, then saw a gray blur in the trees, circling him. Tristam dropped into a defensive crouch. Footsteps sounded behind him. He turned and almost dropped his sword in shock.

Lettie stood ten paces away from him, as surprised to see him as he was to see her. The girl was bundled up in a wool tunic, trousers, and a cloak. Her cheeks shone red from the cold, and she was taking in big gulps of air, as if she'd been running very hard.

"Lettie!" Tristam said. "What are you doing here?"

The girl gave him a shy smile. "Ho, Tristam."

"Does Kyra know you're out here?" he asked.

"Aye," Lettie said, wiping her nose with the back of her hand. "I'm playing with my friends."

He was about to ask her to explain further when two young demon cats, the yellow blur and the gray blur, crept out and did their best to hide behind Lettie—not incredibly effective given their size. The yellow one peeked out occasionally to stare at Tristam but retreated whenever Tristam looked back.

"And these are your... friends?" Tristam asked.

Lettie blinked up at him. "Flick was worried too, but he still lets us play. All the Demon Riders watch us." She pointed to the yellow one. "This is Libena, and her brother is Ziben." Lettie turned to address Libena. "Tristam's nice. You can let him pet you."

He really would have preferred not to, but Lettie was beaming up at him and he couldn't bring himself to refuse. It did help that these cubs had features clearly marking them as babies—large head and eyes, and soft, downy fur. The gray one crept closer, step by step, and finally rubbed his flank against Tristam's knees. Ziben was about three times the size of a house cat, and Tristam reached out carefully to stroke his back. The kitten yawned, revealing tiny, sharp fangs.

"I told you Tristam was nice," said Lettie smugly.

Following her brother's bravery, Libena circled closer. She was considerably larger, standing as high as Tristam when he was on one knee. When she leaned against Tristam's back, it took some effort on his part not to be knocked over. Both cats sniffed at him, sticking their noses in his face. Ziben's chest was rumbling. Was that a *purr*?

Eventually, the two kittens lost interest. Libena moved away first, and Ziben soon followed suit. Libena stepped toward the trees and looked expectantly at Lettie.

"Good-bye, Tristam!" said Lettie, and ran off after them.

He watched them disappear, feeling as if he had come out of some bizarre dream. His cloak was covered with strands of gray and yellow fur.

"It is interesting, isn't it?" said a new voice behind him. "How easy it is for the younger ones to fall into new patterns."

A prickle passed over the skin of Tristam's arms and neck, and he turned around to face Pashla. He didn't reach for his weapon—that would have violated the unspoken truce between them. But it was hard to be civil to the woman who had stood by calmly while her companion killed Jack, and who had wounded Martin and delivered him to his death.

"I won't lie," he said. "I worry about Lettie's safety."

"As do Kyra and Flick, but the girl is stronger than she looks," said Pashla. "Lettie and the kittens have become fast friends. There are some among our own number who object to this, but others urge them to let Libena and Ziben pick their own companions." Pashla paused. "Kyra and Flick hope for peace between our peoples. Do you share that hope?"

It would have been safest to lie to her, but to do so seemed a betrayal of Jack's and Martin's memory. "I hope for peace," said Tristam. "But I cannot see how it could come to pass, if your people view us as mere animals to be slaughtered."

"And your people, how do they view us?" asked Pashla. "Are we worthy of friendship and understanding, or are we simply monsters to be destroyed? Virtue does not solely reside with your people, nor does brutality reside solely with mine. We live and die by our honor, courage, and loyalty. Can you say the same for Forge?"

"I won't deny your courage," said Tristam. "But your people take pleasure in bloodshed. I've seen what you do in battle when your rage overtakes you."

"And what about Kyra?" asked Pashla. "Do you shun her because she succumbs on occasion to her instincts?"

Pashla's question silenced him. To have yet another person bring up Kyra like this . . . Tristam swallowed and couldn't think how to respond.

Pashla took a step closer to him, and then another, until the two of them stood almost toe to toe. She was tall for a woman, and their eyes were almost level when she spoke again. "If you can trust Kyra, then you can learn to trust us. If you cannot trust us, then perhaps you do not really trust her."

Tristam met her gaze and finally found his voice. "Fair point," he said. And he stepped away.

Pashla stayed where she was, and her gaze seemed to go right through his skin. "I do understand what it's like to lose a friend in battle," she said quietly. "I do have sympathy for your loss."

Was she trying to make amends? Even now, Pashla's words brought back the sheer horror of those fateful encounters. Jack had died silently, but Martin's screams would forever be etched in Tristam's memory.

"Thank you." He couldn't give her more than that. Not yet. Pashla inclined her head at his words. "Our ways are different," she said. "But perhaps we can learn from the kittens."

And then she too disappeared into the forest.

"I understand it's been a trying week for all of us," said Cecile of Routhian. "But I do require a minimal amount of effort from you, Tristam, if we are to carry on a conversation."

The impatience in Cecile's voice was mild, but it jarred Tristam to attention nonetheless. It was the first time he'd seen anything but perfect poise from her. The two of them sat in a private dining room on the Palace grounds. A servant had just brought them each a small bowl of lemon curd to finish up the meal.

"I'm sorry," he said, rubbing his forehead. He'd struggled all evening to be present with her, but there were simply too many thoughts going through his mind: his conversation with Pashla, Robert's confession, tomorrow's Council meeting... "I've been inexcusably rude. Forgive me."

Cecile was quite pretty, with flax-colored hair and large green eyes that shone with intelligence. She usually held herself and spoke in a way that projected serenity, though now there was strain around her eyes and a tightening at the corners of her mouth. She placed her spoon back onto the table and looked him in the eye.

"Kyra of Forge is alive, isn't she?" she said. "And you've been in contact with her."

It was only by a small miracle that Tristam didn't drop his own spoon.

Cecile smiled sadly at his surprise. "When you're alone in a foreign court, you pay attention to the gossip, especially when they concern your prospective husband. I've known from the very beginning that your heart wasn't in these negotiations."

Tristam lowered his spoon into his bowl. He felt like the lowest kind of human being, and he couldn't find it in himself to keep up the pretense. He looked Cecile in the eye. "I have a great deal of respect for you, my lady, so I won't attempt to deny anything you've said. And I have no excuses for myself. Though you should know that Kyra and I do not intend to . . . pursue our relationship, if you and I were to marry."

Cecile took a delicate bite of lemon curd, eyeing him thoughtfully. "I believe you," she said finally. "And that says something about my regard for you, as I would not believe those words from many other men."

It surprised Tristam how calmly she was taking this. Sure, he'd known that she wasn't in love with him, but it still must hurt one's pride, if nothing else, to learn that one's betrothed already had feelings for someone else. "If you . . . find that you no longer wish to continue the negotiations, I can send word to—"

Cecile stopped him with a hand on his wrist, touching him in a way that was authoritative rather than flirtatious. "Do your feelings for Kyra change your family's need for help against the Demon Riders?"

Tristam grimaced. "No. I suppose not."

She withdrew her hand. "Nor does it change my family's ambitions. I was raised in the court just as you were, and I know my duties. I believe you to be good and honorable. There's no reason to believe another match for me would turn out better." She met his eyes with a wry smile. "We're both affected by things out of our control. But we make the best of it, don't we?"

Her candor was refreshing, even if her words contained unpleasant truths. "You're a better woman than I deserve, Cecile."

She inclined her head, smiled, and did not contradict him. The door opened, and a servant announced the arrival of the courtier who would escort Cecile back to her quarters.

Tristam left dinner with Cecile's words circling in his head. He found he respected her more after that frank exchange, though the open-eyed pragmatism of her words seemed sad. But she was right. The circumstances surrounding their marriage alliance remained unchanged.

Tristam was marginally successful in focusing his thoughts as he made his way to the Red Shield barracks, where a few quick inquiries led him to Fitz. The young man blinked when Tristam asked for a private word with him but agreed readily enough.

"I have a favor to ask," said Tristam when they were out of earshot of the barracks. "It would help Malikel and Forge, but it's of questionable legality."

Fitz's eyes widened. "Looking to get yourself demoted again, milord?"

Tristam thought back to his earlier conversations with Fitz and hoped that his impression of the Red Shield's character and loyalties was accurate. "I have a prisoner who has information about Willem's misdeeds. I need someone to guard him while I speak to the Council. If things go wrong, I'll do my best to ensure any blame falls on me, but I can't promise I'll succeed."

Fitz leaned back on his heels and considered Tristam's words. "If it'll help Sir Malikel, I'll do my part." Then he grinned. "What's a soldier's life without risk, right?"

Tristam took Robert back to Forge early the next morning and left him in Fitz's care. Then he attended the Council meeting, carrying the message that he, Kyra, and Flick had confiscated from Robert. At the end of every Council meeting, the Head Councilman traditionally announced an opportunity for any citizen to raise an issue before the Council. It was an old law, and admirable in its designation of the Council as a government that listened to all. In practice though, because only a very special portion of the population was even allowed in the Palace compound, much less the Council Room, the definition of "any citizen" was much narrower than the wording suggested.

Nobody paid Tristam much mind as he slipped into the Council Room. Malikel had taken the stage to discuss preparations for the forest sweep. When the discussion ended, Willem gave the customary closing. "If any citizen of Forge would like to make a petition before the Council, he may take the stage now."

It was now or never.

"I have a petition," he said loudly, getting to his feet. He was painfully aware of the Council members swiveling their heads to look at him. Tristam walked up the aisle with as much dignity as he could muster. Willem looked at him with thinly veiled annoyance. "A petition, Tristam of Brancel?"

"Some information has come into my possession, and I would like to present it to the Council."

"It is your right," said Willem drily. "Go ahead."

"I received word of a messenger carrying a private missive into the Palace compound. I, along with some companions, intercepted this message and found that a leader of Forge was conspiring to unlawfully influence the decisions of the Council." In the corner of his eye, he saw Malikel sit up straighter. He dearly hoped that his commander would approve of what he was about to do.

"That's a very vague report," said Willem. "Who was your informant?"

"My informant wishes to remain anonymous, Your Grace, but the note itself requests gold to sway scribes, soldiers, and other people within Forge. It suggests that the Council's vote to attack the Demon Riders was corrupted by bribery." Tristam produced the parchment out of his pocket. "Here is the original note, if the Council would like to inspect it."

Willem held out a hand. "Give it here."

"I'm afraid I can't do that, Your Grace." Willem shifted in surprise, and Tristam felt his heart pound against his rib cage. Even after all this, he wasn't used to direct insubordination, and his body was letting him know it.

"You refuse?" asked Willem.

"I refuse because the messenger entered the Palace compound from your private gate, and the note is written in your handwriting."

The Council Room erupted in shouts. Willem pounded his gavel to regain the floor. "Let me see if I understand you,

Tristam. You are accusing me of treason against Forge, the city in which I already hold the highest office."

Tristam raised his voice. "With all due respect, Your Grace, you are indeed Head Councilman, but the Demon Rider offensive was a close vote, and there was plenty of motivation on either side to sway it."

Lord Perce of Roll, a Council member who had voted against Willem, raised his hand. "These are serious allegations you bring against the Head Councilman. Do you have any evidence?"

"I will gladly hand over this note to a neutral third party."

"May I see it?"

Tristam handed the message to Perce, who looked it over. "The note reads as Tristam says, but it contains no signature, and the seal is not one I recognize." He looked back at Tristam. "Do you have any stronger evidence?"

Tristam nodded to a manservant waiting near the door and hoped that Fitz was still outside. "I have the testimony of the messenger."

This time, he did see a flicker of worry across Willem's face. A moment later, Fitz stepped into the room with Robert in tow. The messenger faltered when he saw Willem, and Fitz had to drag him the remainder of the way. *Don't lose your nerve*, thought Tristam.

"This is the messenger whom I followed from the Palace walls to an inn not far away. He has confessed to taking messages between Head Councilman Willem and Whitt Manor."

Tristam could see observers in the Council Room looking around, probably trying to see if Lord Whitt had any representatives in attendance. Tristam doubted he did. Whitt didn't have a strong presence within the city.

Perce addressed the messenger. "What is your name?"

"Robert, sir. Of Forge." The messenger couldn't seem to take his eyes from Willem, who was studying him with an intense, cold gaze.

"And do you confirm what Tristam of Brancel has said? Did you, in fact, receive this message from the Head Councilman to deliver to Lord Whitt?"

The messenger was still staring at Willem. His jaw worked, but he didn't speak. Tristam focused everything he had on Robert, willing him to follow through.

"Please answer the question," Perce repeated.

The messenger licked his lips. "No," he said. "The parchment that Tristam claims to have found on me was a plant that he created himself. He tried to pay me to testify against Willem."

Tristam struggled to maintain his composure as the room once again dissolved into murmurs. Of course that was what Robert would say. What did Tristam have to threaten him with that didn't pale against the Head Councilman's influence?

Willem sat back in his seat. "I believe we've taken care of that," he said. "I will be requesting a full investigation into Tristam for bringing false charges against me."

Malikel cleared his throat. "May I suggest that the messenger might not be trusted to give a truthful testimony in front of the accused?"

"How much longer must we put up with this nonsense?" said Willem. "We have preparations to make. Tristam of Brancel has already wasted enough of our time in a clear effort to delay our attack on the barbarians. I move to dismiss discussion of this subject to a later time."

It was a close vote, but it came out in Willem's favor. Willem looked pointedly at Tristam. "You are dismissed, soldier."

There was finality to that command, and there was nothing Tristam could do except bow and walk away. Robert, still in Fitz's grip, avoided Tristam's gaze as he passed. Tristam tried his best to hold his head high on his way to the door, fighting the despair that was starting to take root in his stomach. They had staked so much on this. What could they do now?

Tristam was so caught up in his own frustrations that he didn't notice that someone was trying to talk to him. When he finally realized someone had spoken his name, he turned to see a young servant girl looking urgently up at him. He returned her gaze, surprised to be approached so by one of the staff. She looked familiar.

"Lord Tristam," she said, her voice low. "Can anyone speak in front of the Council?"

"Anyone?" he echoed dumbly before he finally made sense of her question. "Anyone, yes. But only before Willem closes the meeting."

She nodded then, and her face took on a mask of determination. Tristam watched in bemusement as she made straight for the herald. The two exchanged a few words, and she seemed to be arguing with him, though Tristam couldn't make out what was said.

Finally, the herald drew breath for an announcement. "Darylene of Forge would like to make a statement before the

Council." His voice lacked his usual confidence, and he glanced uncertainly at the serving girl behind him.

"What is the meaning of this? We've had enough oddities today," said Willem. Tristam was surprised to hear alarm in Willem's voice, given the cool disdain with which the Head Councilman had responded to Tristam's accusations. Then Tristam recognized the girl. Darylene of Forge was Willem's mistress.

"We haven't closed the Council meeting yet," said Malikel. "The lady has a right to speak."

Darylene didn't look at all at ease in front of the Council. She glanced from Councilman to Councilman, though she seemed to studiously avoid Willem's gaze. "I'm sorry, milords," she said. She sounded younger than she looked. Tristam had thought her older because of her association with Willem, but he now realized she was probably close to his own age, if not younger. "I've been listening to the young lord's testimony, and I can tell you that he's both right and wrong.

"I am . . . privy to some of the Head Councilman's private dealings," she continued. Some knowing glances passed between the Councilmen, and a few snickers sounded from the observing benches. It took no small amount of courage, Tristam thought, to brave such scrutiny.

Darylene waited for the room to quiet. "The messenger Robert of Forge is, in truth, Robert of Edlan. He lied about working for Whitt Manor. He has actually been carrying messages directly between Sir Willem and Duke Symon of Edlan. They have been working together to overthrow Forge's Council."

Pandemonium. Willem shouted something about the girl having lost her mind, and Malikel called for order as Tristam struggled to understand what he'd heard. Had he misread the message from Willem?

"The girl tells lies," said Willem. "She must be in the employ of my enemies."

"Lies or not, they must be investigated," said Malikel. "Darylene, do you have any evidence?"

Darylene looked to Willem, who was staring at her with barely controlled rage. "There's a compartment in the floor of his sitting room, next to the fireplace. You can access it if you pry up the floorboards. You will find other messages there from those he's been contacting in Edlan."

"This is preposterous," said Willem. "A clear attempt to distract from the coming offensive. I move to dismiss this Council meeting."

"Not yet, Willem," said a Councilman in the second row. "The girl gave us information that can be easily confirmed. It is only reasonable to do so." Tristam began to feel some hope. At least the Council members were taking these accusations seriously now.

"I agree." Malikel raised his voice. "Seal the doors. Don't let anyone come in or out of this room until we've verified Darylene's claims. I'm sure you'll agree, Willem, that the best way to dismiss these claims beyond doubt is to verify them now."

Willem gave Malikel a long, measured look, and then nodded. "Very well, if you are to accuse me, then let us go investigate these charges. Do you claim this investigation under your purview, Malikel?"

"I will verify the allegations as Defense Minister. I believe protocol also requires the presence of the accusers, Darylene and Tristam."

"Will you take guards too, lest I turn violent upon discovery of my misdeeds?" A layer of scorn laced Willem's voice.

"The usual escort of Red Shields should be enough," said Malikel mildly.

Willem nodded to the Red Shields lining the side of the room, and four stepped forward. The Head Councilman turned his eye to Tristam and then to Darylene, who stood braced against Willem's fury as if it might knock her over. "Let's get this farce over with."

Willem led the way across the Palace grounds to his private living quarters. It was a small, detached building in the inner compound, unremarkable on the outside, though the inside was luxuriously decorated with tapestries, carvings, and marble statues. Nobody spoke. The Head Councilman exuded an aura of fury and kept a few steps in front of everyone else. Malikel trailed behind him, calm but focused, and Darylene followed after. Tristam wished he could talk to her, find out more about what she was thinking, but she studiously avoided his gaze.

"Are we headed to my bedchamber?" asked Willem.

"Is that correct, Darylene?" said Malikel.

She gave a barely discernible nod.

Willem led them up a flight of stairs, where a manservant opened a pair of tall oak doors. The suite within was large and opulent. A four-poster bed took up the center of the room. The walls, the rug, and the linens on the bed were all decorated in maroon with gold accents.

"By the fireplace," said Malikel.

One of the Red Shields bowed and knelt near the fireplace, running his hands along the floorboards. "I don't feel anything," he said.

"To your left," said Darylene. "Feel for a raised portion along the floor."

"By all means, search your best, soldier," said Willem. "There's nothing to be afraid of."

The Red Shield paused in his search, fingers curving against an edge Tristam couldn't see. The soldier jiggled something, and then there was the clear sound of a wood panel sliding away. Tristam's breath caught. He'd believed the girl, but somehow he still hadn't expected the Red Shield to find anything.

"What is that?" said Malikel, walking toward him. The Red Shield was frowning at a box in his hands. "It's a compartment, just as the lass said."

"Let me see," said Malikel, reaching for the box.

"Now," said Willem.

The Red Shield handed Malikel the box. And then, as the Defense Minister's hands were occupied, the Red Shield drew his dagger and thrust it toward Malikel's stomach.

TWENTY-EIGHT

Darylene screamed. Tristam shouted Malikel's name and took a step forward, so intent on his commander that he almost didn't see the man coming at him from the side. Tristam ducked out of the way just in time to avoid being gutted. He pivoted to face his attacker. It was another of the Red Shields who had accompanied them. Had Willem managed to turn them all? Tristam drew his dagger, extremely grateful that he'd kept it on him this morning. When his attacker came at him again, he stepped around the Red Shield's knife hand and grabbed his wrist, pulling the man past him and sinking his own blade deep between his opponent's ribs. He pulled his dagger free and threw the man to the ground.

Tristam cast about, breathing heavily, trying to get his bearings. The man who'd attacked him lay on the ground in front of him. Darylene stood pressed against the wall. There were blood spatters on her face and gown, but she looked otherwise uninjured. Malikel crouched with his hand pressed to his side. The mysterious box sat on the ground not far from him, and next to the box lay the body of the soldier who had attacked the Defense Minister. The room was otherwise empty. Willem and the remaining two Red Shields were nowhere to be seen.

"Malikel!" Tristam ran to his commander's side.

The older man groaned. "It's not as deep as it could have been," he said. "Must have glanced off one of my ribs. Help me bind it."

Darylene came forward with a strip of fabric she'd torn from the bed linens. Tristam thanked her and set about wrapping Malikel's chest.

"Quickly, Tristam," said Malikel. "Did anyone see what happened to Willem?"

"He ran, with the two Red Shields after him," said Darylene.

Malikel exhaled sharply through his nose as Tristam pulled the makeshift bandages tight. "All four of the guards were loyal to Willem?"

"I don't think so," said Darylene. "Three of them were, and the fourth chased Willem when he fled."

Tristam secured the bandages, and Malikel gripped his arm. "A hand, please." Tristam had doubts about whether his commander should be standing and moving, but he obeyed. The Defense Minister regained his feet and nodded toward the door. "We need to get word to the Council."

Darylene took the hard-earned box of evidence, and Tristam ducked under Malikel's arm. They slowly made their way out, Tristam sneaking surreptitious glances at his commander to see how he fared. Malikel moved as if it pained him, but at least he was supporting much of his own weight.

Tristam drew his dagger as they stepped into the corridor. It was eerily silent in Willem's house. As they made their way down the staircase, Tristam caught sight of a few servants running away. As he neared the front door, Tristam heard noises from outside—shouts, yells, and the clash of weapons. Malikel frowned.

Tristam stopped. "With your permission, sir, I'll go scout."

Tristam wished he had his sword. The dagger wasn't going to do much good against enemy soldiers. Willem's doorman was long gone, so Tristam reached for the doorknob and hoped for the best.

He opened the door to a battle in full swing. Soldiers clashed swords while Palace staff did their best to flee the fighting. Tristam looked around in confusion as battle cries and screams assaulted his ears. Were they invaded? Had the enemy breached their walls so easily? But then he realized what had really happened. The three Red Shields who'd attacked Malikel were obviously not the only traitors in the compound.

There was a cluster of four soldiers fighting just a short distance away. At first, Tristam had trouble distinguishing sides because they all wore Forge livery. Then he saw that two of the soldiers had blue armbands. Edlan blue.

I need more funds to gain the cooperation of Palace scribes, as well as key members of the defense forces, Willem's note had said. Tristam had thought it a roundabout way of swaying Council votes, but Willem had actually been using the bribes to hide Edlan troops within Forge. There had been such confusion in the Palace lately, with the extra conscripts from the city. A few well-placed bribes to scribes and Red Shield commanders, a few altered documents... *The more of our own that we have within the Palace, the safer our position will be.*

A body sporting a blue armband lay beside one of the pathways. Tristam swallowed against his disgust and took the man's sword. Its balance was different from his own, but it would have to do.

The men outside Willem's house were still fighting. One of the true Red Shields had fallen, and his comrade was backed against a shrub, trying to fend off two enemies. Tristam cut one of the traitors down from behind. The remaining Edlan soldier turned to gape, and the cornered Red Shield ran him through. For a moment, Tristam and the Red Shield stared at each other, catching their breath.

"Thank you," said the soldier.

"That was an impressive fight. I'm Tristam of Brancel," said Tristam.

"Claren of Forge."

They looked to the neighboring courtyard. There, five Red Shields closed in on three Edlan fighters. A line of soldiers rounded the corner, and Tristam raised his sword, only to cautiously lower it again when he saw no sign of Edlan blue. Forge soldiers still outnumbered the Edlanese, at least in this part of the Palace.

"How widespread is the fighting?" asked Tristam.

"All over the Palace grounds. There must have been some kind of signal."

"The Defense Minister is wounded," Tristam said. "Can you help?"

They rushed back to Willem's house. Tristam had just thrown the door open when he heard new shouts.

"Forge men, to the city wall! Edlan's army is at the gates!"

Kyra waited out the morning as close to the city as she dared. She climbed a tree overlooking the main road and ducked behind the trunk whenever a traveler passed by. She tried not to dwell on her worries, but it became harder as the sun climbed steadily overhead. What had become of Tristam? Would the Council believe him? She had ample time to think up worst-case scenarios, but she didn't dare go into the Palace, at least not until dark. The last thing they needed was for her to create more trouble by getting impatient.

She heard footsteps approaching, not from the main road, but from the forest below her. Kyra froze stock-still. There wasn't nearly as much cover for her in the winter. She hoped whoever was coming would not think to look up.

It turned out to be another one of Willem's forest patrols. Kyra stayed silent as the men passed below her, and they were none the wiser. She watched them gather on a plot of farm-land just outside the forest boundary. There they stood, wait-ing. Some tended to their weapons, while others simply milled about. After a while, Kyra turned her attention away from them and resumed watching the main road.

It wasn't until a second group came and joined the first that Kyra began to wonder. And then a third, fourth, and fifth group came as well. Soon there were a hundred men standing on that field. Kyra watched as a man came walking from the opposite direction—the owner of the farm, Kyra guessed, and she was suddenly scared for him. The gathered soldiers had also noticed the farmer, and one of them went out to meet him. Words were exchanged. Kyra couldn't hear them, but they were obviously not friendly. The soldier drew his weapon and Kyra stifled a gasp, but he didn't strike. The farmer retreated.

As the one soldier rejoined the rest of the group, Kyra gave up completely on watching the main road and focused on these men. They were taking tunics out of sacks now and putting them on. The tunics were colored deep blue. Edlan blue.

This time Kyra did gasp, and it was only the men's lack of attention that kept her from discovery. Puzzle pieces fell in place in her mind. She remembered the group of soldiers who had stumbled upon her family with Pashla and Adele in the forest. They'd looked like seasoned soldiers instead of peasants. One had told Kyra that "His Grace" didn't want people in the forest. It was a funny way to put things, since Forge citizens almost always referred to the Council as a whole. The man had been an Edlan soldier hiding under the guise of Willem's Demon Rider offensive. Did Willem know about this? If Willem had betrayed the city, what had happened to Tristam and Malikel?

The gathered soldiers were dressed now, and they began to march toward Forge. Kyra waited until they had gone some distance, then came down from her hiding place and trailed them. When she came out of the trees, her heart almost stopped. From her vantage point, she had only seen one group of soldiers. But now that she was in open farmland, she could see multiple companies taking up formation and converging on the main road. The muted thuds of their boots carried over the fields.

Kyra shielded her eyes and squinted toward the city. The gates still looked to be open. Did the Palace have any idea what was happening?

No, they likely did not.

In front of her, the soldiers marched at a quick pace, and people took notice. Those on the road and fields ran, some retreating into their houses and others running for the city gates. One older man shouted defiantly at the troops. Two Edlan soldiers cut him down.

Finally, the call of bugles drifted from the city, and the gate began to close. Soldiers, just dots from this distance, ran along the parapets. Kyra breathed a sigh of relief. Someone had sounded the alarm.

But the Edlan troops continued to march.

◻ ◻ ◻

Disgraceful. That was how Malikel had described Forge's response to the attack. Yes, they had been betrayed. Yes, they'd had little warning of Edlan's approaching troops. But still, the Palace's forces had been far too slow to react. Messages between wall sentries and the Palace had gone astray. Commands had been dithered over and questioned. Tristam himself had been shocked at how greatly the forces' discipline had fallen short of what it should have been. Part of it was due to Malikel's removal from command. Part of it had been the confusion sowed by Willem's schemes. But whatever the reason, the city was in dire straits.

The watch had barely managed to close the city gates in time, and archers were still running to their stations. Tristam stood on the parapets next to Malikel, surveying the scene outside the city. The main road led out from the gates. On a normal day, Tristam would have been able to follow it with his eyes as it passed houses, then farmland, until it disappeared into the forest. Today though, the road was blocked by Edlan soldiers. Rows of them, lined up in formation on the road and spilling into the farmland on either side. Scouts had confirmed that Edlan had blocked the roads to the south as well. Groups of people fled their homes with hastily wrapped bundles on their backs, some running for the protection of Forge's walls, and others for the forest.

"Edlan could have taken the city," said Malikel. "If they'd wanted to, they could have marched right in." There had been some confusion about who would act as Head Councilman after Willem's defection. The laws indicated Malikel, but none of the laws took into account what to do if the second in line was currently under investigation. In the end, Malikel had been given temporary authority until the Edlanese were defeated.

"Why do you think they didn't?" asked Tristam.

"Willem is a man of Forge at heart. He doesn't want to see it looted or damaged."

"Do you think he made it out of the city?"

"I think so. I believe you forced his hand, Tristam. He most likely didn't mean to trigger any attack until after the forest offensive began. He could have picked off or captured our own soldiers in the forest with his own, and we would have blamed the Demon Riders. Once we were sufficiently weakened, he would have sprung his trap. Our position now isn't good, but at least we have our forces intact within the city."

"What do you think Willem wants?" Tristam asked.

"He'll tell us himself, soon enough."

An hour later, several riders rode toward the city, escorted by a contingent of Edlan soldiers. They came to a halt just outside of arrow range and raised a flag of parley.

"Come with me, Tristam," said Malikel.

Malikel assembled a contingent of ten guards, and Tristam took up ranks with them. The gate was pulled open, and they rode out. Tristam did his best to ride proud. Not the easiest thing to do when an entire army was spread out in front of him, but he had to trust his comrades on the wall behind him to watch for signs of betrayal. At least the skies were clear today, and they had an unimpeded view.

As they came closer to the other party, Tristam finally made out their faces. Lord Alvred, the Defense Minister of Edlan, led the party on a giant black war stallion. And next to him was Willem.

Traitor. Tristam looked over at Malikel, trying to see his commander's reaction, but the fur lining of Malikel's cloak blocked his view.

"Alvred," Malikel said pleasantly. "I didn't expect to see you again so soon. Was our hospitality not up to your standards?"

Alvred's mustache twitched humorlessly. "We both serve our cities, Malikel. You know that as well as I."

"If we're dispensing with pleasantries, I'll address my former Head Councilman directly," said Malikel. "What do you want, Willem?" Malikel spoke loud enough to be heard by all nearby, and Tristam wondered whether it hurt his wounded ribs.

Willem, to his credit, didn't look as smug as Tristam had expected him to, though he regarded Malikel with the confidence that came with knowing he had the upper hand. "You know you can't win this, Malikel. We have more troops, and we have the strategic advantage now that we're in position. You have no allies who will come to your help. We can either drag this out and let the people suffer, or we can solve things quickly."

"What are your terms?" asked Malikel.

"You and the rest of the Council will sign a measure ceding power to me as Duke of Forge. I have no wish to harm any of you, though you will be required to live out your lives outside of the three cities."

"Head Councilman wasn't enough, Willem?" An edge finally found its way into Malikel's voice. "You want to wield absolute power?"

"Our Council is fundamentally flawed. We spend most of our time in deadlock or undoing one another's efforts. That's no way to rule a city."

"And, of course, you'll be the one to lead Forge to a glorious future." Malikel looked to Alvred and the Edlan officials behind him. "What are you giving Edlan for their help? Better trade?"

"Among other things."

"And you're confident they won't stab you in the back once their soldiers have breached our walls?"

Willem drew himself to his full height atop his horse. "Do you think me so incompetent? I have safeguards in place."

Tristam wondered what those safeguards might be. Willem must have cultivated favor with Edlan houses as well, enough so that they would support him against any possible double cross from Symon.

"Let's not drag this conversation on," said Willem. "Will you take my terms or not?"

"Of course not," said Malikel.

"Perhaps, then, you will change your mind in a few weeks."

There was an emergency Council meeting that evening. As Red Shields carted off bodies from the battle within the Palace walls, and others scoured the ranks for any remaining Edlan imposters, the nineteen remaining Council members faced off and yelled at each other. Councilman Caldre argued vociferously for a head-on charge against the Edlanese army, while Malikel dismissed this as suicidal. Another Councilman suggested sending for help from Parna, but even Tristam knew that Parna would happily remain neutral while Edlan and Forge weakened themselves. And they'd make plenty of money selling supplies to both parties.

The problem was, there were no good solutions. The Council knew this, but as men used to power, they couldn't come to terms with that fact. So they continued on with their posturing. They wouldn't come to an agreement tonight, and by now, Tristam wished they would simply agree to go to sleep. He supposed he could ask to be excused. He'd given his testimony to the Council hours ago, and they hadn't asked for him since. But tired and disheartened as he was, he couldn't bring himself to leave.

The first time he heard someone knock on the window next to him, he thought he'd just imagined it. But he heard it again, in the silence between Councilman Caldre bringing up another impossible strategy and Councilman Perce ruling it out. A definite tapping—he wasn't deluding himself. He casually stood and made his way over to the window.

"Kyra?" he whispered, still not quite believing it.

There was a soft tap on the shutters in reply.

Tristam's rush of elation was quickly tempered by incredulity over what Kyra had done. She'd been in the forest, hadn't she? Had she snuck past enemy lines and somehow into the city itself? True, she did have the cover of night, and Palace forces had better things to do now than look for her, but it was still reckless. And what was she doing here, anyway?

"Back corridor," he said. "I'll meet you there."

He slipped out of the room and circled around to the servants' corridor. As he'd hoped, it was empty at this hour. There was a small window, and he pushed the shutters open. After a moment, he saw a familiar outline in the darkness and stepped back to let her in.

Kyra jumped in silently, her body taut and her eyes actively searching the corridor for threats. Her hands, when he took them, were ice-cold, and he wrapped them in his own. "I can't believe you snuck in like this."

"I'm just glad you're safe. What happened?"

Tristam recounted the Council meeting and Willem's betrayal. Had it all occurred in one day? Anger built in Kyra's eyes as he spoke. She pulled away from him and started pacing the corridor.

"I didn't think Willem would go this far," said Kyra. "I thought he at least cared for the city."

"Well, the army hasn't attacked yet."

She turned to him, her gaze fierce. "I watched Edlan soldiers kill an old man today. His blood is on Willem's hands, as is the blood of the soldiers who died in the Palace today. Is there any way for us to break the siege?"

"There's posturing and debate in the Council, but no," said Tristam. "We have nothing except for the prospect of a long and drawn-out engagement."

Kyra seemed to waver over some decision before her eyes regained their focus. "I need to talk to Malikel, if he'll speak with me."

"You have news?"

"A proposal. A far-fetched one," she admitted, with an apologetic shrug. "But at this point, I don't see how it could hurt."

When Tristam returned to the Council Room, he found Malikel listening intently to the debate, leaning over his table and looking from speaker to speaker with a gaze that could have bored holes in the wall. It was easy to forget that the man had been stabbed that morning. Malikel shook out of his focus as Tristam came to his side.

"Are you able to leave the Council meeting?" Tristam asked softly. "There's someone who wants to talk to you."

"Is it important?" said Malikel.

"It's Kyra."

The briefest flicker of surprise crossed Malikel's face, and then he nodded and followed Tristam out of the room. The Council debate continued without a pause.

Kyra was visibly nervous when Tristam and Malikel came back. She stood close to the window, and her posture was such that she looked ready to spring back out at the slightest provocation. Malikel seemed to sense this and stopped a good distance away.

"Kyra," he said simply.

"I'm sorry I hid what I was," said Kyra. "I didn't mean for you to pay the price for my secret."

"There's no use dwelling on what has happened already," said Malikel. "Best we can do is move forward."

Malikel's response was so mild that Tristam couldn't help but interrupt. "You knew what Kyra was, didn't you? Why didn't you confront us outright?"

"I took a gamble. True service can't be forced." He fixed his eyes on Kyra. "Tell me if my gamble paid off."

Relief washed over Kyra's countenance, followed by resolve. "I've an idea for breaking the siege. It's a last-ditch effort, but if what Tristam tells me is right, you don't have many choices. I'm now in contact with the Demon Riders. I can carry a petition to them if you'd like."

"Why do you think an appeal to the Demon Riders would work when they wouldn't even talk to us before?" said Malikel.

"Because they've been taking losses. I think they're starting to see that they can't carry on a war against the humans here, even with their increased numbers." Kyra looked in the direction of the Council Room as muted shouts echoed down the corridor. "I also . . . have reason to believe that Leyus may be more kindly disposed toward humans than I first thought."

"How do you know this?" asked Malikel.

Something flickered in Kyra's eyes. "I know you don't like

secrets, and I'll do my best to be honest with you. But let me keep this one."

Malikel leveled a long gaze at Kyra. "Say we attempt this—what's your plan? The Demon Riders will want something in return," said Malikel.

"Peace might appeal to them, now that some of their number have been injured. They want adequate hunting and a place to live." Kyra looked to Tristam as she said this, obviously bracing for an objection from him. When he said nothing, her surprise was more damning than anything Flick or Pashla could have said.

Malikel's brow furrowed in concentration. "We could offer the Demon Riders protected hunting in a portion of our forest, and terms of trade for what they cannot get."

"Can I get the Council's word on this?" asked Kyra. "Will you pass a resolution to negotiate peace with the Demon Riders if they help defeat Edlan?"

"I will need to bring it before them," said Malikel. "This is a decision that must be made by all of us."

TWENTY-NINE

Edlan didn't have enough forces to completely surround Forge. They'd set up their encampment across the main road, and intermittent patrols formed a porous perimeter around the rest of the city. Kyra could have avoided the camp entirely and dealt simply with the patrols, but she wanted to get a better look at what Forge was up against.

She skirted the outer edge of the Edlan camp as she left the city. The soldiers had dug trenches at the borders of their camp and were in the process of fortifying them with sharpened stakes. Kyra saw a few catapults, but not enough to suggest an imminent attack on the walls. Talk and laughter filtered out to Kyra as she passed. There were many soldiers and many campfires, but even from her limited vantage point in the darkness, she could see that activity centered on one central campfire and a large tent set up next to it. Kyra recognized Alvred, the Defense Minister, and Willem holding court there. Pages and squires attended them, and messengers came back and forth from other parts of the camp. She watched for a while and then headed for the safety of the trees.

Kyra ran deeper into the woods until she was absolutely sure that the soldiers were behind her. Then she stopped and cast about in the darkness. What was her plan? She had to find Leyus, somehow persuade him to help, and then lead an attack on the Edlan forces. It had seemed less ludicrous when she'd proposed it to Malikel.

She wandered awhile, calling out a few times, but there was no response. If any Demon Riders watched her, they weren't interested in helping her. Well, there was one other way to find the clan.

Kyra looked around one last time, peeled off her clothes, and tied them as best she could into a bundle. Her fur came easily, but she shuffled from foot to foot after her shape settled, unsure of what exactly to do. She'd made plenty of sounds in her fur before, but never on purpose. She experimented with something that sounded like a mix between a growl and a bark, and then threw her head back.

The roar reverberated through the forest, and Kyra couldn't quite believe that such a sound had come from her throat. She waited, and for a long time there was nothing. But then, in the distance, there came a faint response. It was far away, but Kyra knew immediately which way to go. She carefully picked up her clothes in her teeth and loped off.

Her sense of direction never wavered. Soon enough, she smelled other demon cats nearby and saw movement in the trees ahead of her. Kyra stopped and changed back into her somewhat slobbery clothes. She had just fastened her cloak when she noticed two Demon Riders watching her.

"Is Leyus here?" she asked.

One of the two, a man around Leyus's age, gestured toward the trees to Kyra's left, though his expression conveyed that he was simply answering her question and not extending an invitation. Kyra heard him fall in step behind her.

There was a surprising number of Demon Riders milling about. Kyra counted about twenty-two in their skin and about half that number in their fur. Kyra thought she spotted Adele at the edge of the group, and near the middle of the pack, a tawny-yellow cat looked up sharply at Kyra's arrival. Pashla.

Leyus—*her father*—sat beneath a tree, one arm propped up on his knee. Next to him sat Havel and Zora. There was something about the body language among the three of them as they talked. Kyra could tell that these were old friends, and she found their easy familiarity with one another almost as intimidating as the power they wielded.

Leyus's expression as he watched her come closer was one of controlled impatience. To Kyra's surprise, it wasn't Leyus who spoke first, but Havel, and he spoke the language of the three cities.

"She cannot stay away," he said, his eyes bright with interest. "Blood calls to blood."

"It is of no consequence," said Leyus. "The girl has chosen her loyalties."

Loyalties. Of course. Kyra had a task to do. "I'm here on behalf of the Palace," she said. "They want to offer an alliance."

Leyus exchanged a glance with Havel, as if Kyra had confirmed his words. Kyra looked at Leyus, then Havel and Zora. "I was born of two different groups, raised by a third, and recruited by a fourth. I belong to no one, but I serve those whom I see fit. Right now, I serve the Council. I know you don't think highly of the humans, but you must hear this message if you want your clans to survive."

Zora turned a languid gaze to Leyus. "Are you in the habit of negotiating with humans?"

"Only those who prove useful," said Leyus.

"They are untrustworthy. Remember what happened with Maikana," said Zora.

Kyra momentarily forgot about her mission. "You knew my mother?" she asked, fully aware that her voice came out a breathless whisper.

The three Makvani exchanged looks, and their silence was more telling than anything they could have said.

"What happened?" said Kyra. She was overstepping bounds, she knew it. But she didn't care.

The woman picked up a stick and drove it into the snow, giving Kyra a pointed glance as she did so. "Your mother forced us out of our homeland."

At this, Leyus made a noise in his throat. "Mind your words, Zora. We would have done the same, had we been in her position." Once again Kyra sensed an undercurrent of emotion. Leyus wasn't as hardened toward humans as he pretended to be. He'd loved a human woman once—her *mother*. Kyra had an opening here, if she didn't ruin her opportunity.

"Is it really so unthinkable to make an alliance with the humans? The man whose message I bear, his name is Malikel. He's an honorable man who won't break his word. Wouldn't it be better to help each other rather than destroy each other?"

Leyus looked at her for a long moment. "What does he propose?"

Kyra plunged into an explanation of what had happened around Forge. Not much of it seemed to surprise Leyus. He knew that the troops out here were from the northern city of Edlan and that they were planning an attack on Forge.

"The Edlan forces are settling in for a drawn-out siege. This buys you time against Willem's forest offensive, but it'll only be a matter of days or weeks before these Edlan troops start causing you trouble. They'll be in the same forest, hunting the same game. Truth is, no matter how this fight turns out, the victors will still outnumber you by far. And eventually, they will defeat you too."

She wondered if she was in danger of insulting him again, but Leyus simply regarded her. "And what does Malikel propose instead?"

"He would have your help breaking the siege. Your people are quick and familiar with the forest. If you create enough trouble for the troops, Edlan will retreat. In return, Forge will cede to you a portion of the forest where you can live and hunt undisturbed. He'll also provide help in the form of workmen and supplies to help you make a real home."

Leyus was silent as he weighed her words. "No," he said firmly. "We will not risk our lives for the promises of a human official we do not know."

"But—"

"I've made my decision. I want nothing more from you." When Kyra opened her mouth to protest again, he cut her off. "I think it's time for you to leave."

There was no hint of compromise in his voice, and Kyra's objections died in her throat. Havel and Zora watched her with equally unyielding gazes. As Kyra turned away, she racked her mind for an alternative, some other way to convince Leyus, but she came up with nothing. That was when she noticed Adele coming toward them.

The young clanswoman walked right past Kyra and bowed deeply in the Makvani fashion, running three fingers down the front of her throat. "Forgive me, clan leader," she said. "I couldn't help but overhear the halfblood's request. I would like to help her, if I may."

Leyus sat up straighter. "That is an unusual request, Adele. How do you plan to help her?"

"I would fight for her, against the Edlan troops."

"By yourself? Why lend them your strength?"

Adele lowered her gaze, and Kyra imagined a slight flush on the young woman's cheeks. "I would like to see peace between our people and the humans on this side of the mountain."

"And you want this enough to risk your life for them?"

Adele raised her eyes to Leyus, and her voice was clear when she responded. "I want this enough that I am willing to take this to Challenge if you forbid me to go."

There were gasps and murmurs, and Kyra realized that many of the Makvani had gathered around to listen. The Challenge was a right of anyone of Makvani blood, an opportunity to fight to the death on behalf of a petition. If Adele claimed a Challenge here, it would be against Leyus or someone of his choosing. Kyra had seen Leyus fight. He was almost twice Adele's size, and far stronger. As unfamiliar as she was with Makvani customs, Kyra knew that Adele had just said she would rather die than lose her chance for peace with the humans. Why was she doing this? Was this all for Flick?

"Adele." Pashla's voice rang out from the back. The older woman came to her side, acknowledging Kyra with a nod before she too addressed Leyus. "I also beg permission to help Kyra in her quest. And I too am willing to Challenge for it."

Leyus had risen to his feet by now, his arms crossed over his chest. His brow was furrowed, but he didn't look angry. "The two of you, then. Is there anyone else who wishes permission to go with the halfblood?"

Halfblood, Kyra thought. He still spoke of her as if she were a stranger to him.

"I would," said a new voice. Kyra recognized Mela, Adele's friend. A few others also stepped out, mostly younger clansfolk, several of whom looked familiar.

Leyus looked over each one of them. "You understand that this is no paltry raid. This army comes in great numbers, and they are well armed." There were a few nods. By now, almost all the Demon Riders had gathered around to watch. When Leyus spoke again, his words were to the volunteers, but his voice was loud enough for all gathered to hear. "You have my permission. Fight as you will. And if you succeed in breaking the siege, I will consider negotiating peace with Forge."

All in all, there were twelve of them: Kyra, Pashla, Adele, Mela, three other women, and five men. They were all young. Several were friends of Adele's or had spoken with Flick. Most were from Leyus's clan—three were from the other. When Kyra asked one of them why he was helping, he replied, "We've been sleeping in trees and eating raw meat for over a year now to stay hidden from the human troops. If there's a better way, I would like to find it."

She was grateful for their help, but still, there were only twelve of them against over a thousand troops. What good could they possibly do?

"I'd imagined surprising these soldiers with two hundred demon cats at my back, but we can't do that now," Kyra told Flick. He'd found her in the forest soon after Kyra left Leyus with her recruits. Mercie, Lettie, and Idalee had taken shelter with friends farther from the city, but he chose to stay with Kyra and her band of Makvani fighters. Whenever Flick wasn't talking with Kyra, he was at Adele's side. Kyra wondered if he knew that Adele had been willing to fight a Challenge to win her right to be here. It seemed too personal a thing for Kyra to disclose.

"If you can't attack them directly, mayhap you could weaken their position some other way," said Flick. "Their supplies, perhaps?"

"That might work," said Kyra. "But I know nothing about the Edlan supply caravans."

"What about that trader Craigson? He's from Edlan, in't he?"

Kyra considered his words. Craigson did live close to Edlan, and he bore no particular loyalty to its Duke. "I'll go speak with him."

Though the trader camp lay outside the line of Edlan soldiers, Kyra wasn't surprised to find them readying their wagons to leave. A potential battlefield wasn't exactly the best place to winter. Craigson was bundling up cooking supplies when Kyra arrived, and he beckoned her closer.

"I'm glad you found us," he said. "I was regretting having to leave without a final word with you."

"I'm afraid I'm not here to talk about my past," said Kyra. "Things have become more complicated since then."

"Aye, it has. What might I do for you, then?"

Craigson listened with sharp-eyed intelligence as Kyra told him what had happened. "We'd like to avert a war," she said. "Do you think we could stall the army by stopping their caravans?"

"I reckon you could," he said. "The Edlan army gets its supplies from wagon trains that come down from the north. The trains are heavily armed, of course, but man for man they'd be easier to go up against than actual soldiers. What you really want to do is destroy the wagons along with the supplies in them. That would make it harder for them to recover." Craigson paused to roll a bundle tight. "They're friendly folk, the supply caravanners. I hate to think of them coming to harm, but I suppose they knew that risk when they took the job."

"How big are the wagon trains?" asked Kyra.

"Ten to fifteen wagons, with two to four men manning each wagon."

Kyra did some figuring in her head. One demon cat could probably handle one wagon, especially if they attacked at night. The image of demon cats leaping out of the darkness onto unsuspecting caravanners left an uneasy feeling in her stomach.

Craigson's gaze lingered on her face, though Kyra got the impression that he was actually seeing something in his mind's eye. "You know, your mother once led a small force against a much stronger one."

"Did she win?" asked Kyra.

"She drove the Makvani here, didn't she? Maikana was a strong leader."

Kyra picked up a piece of charcoal from the fire pit and rolled it between her fingers. She knew he meant well, but Craigson's words only made her feel smaller. "To be honest, Craigson, I've got enough people telling me how wonderful my ma was. Please tell me she made mistakes too."

To her surprise, Craigson laughed. "Mistakes? Maidy, your ma's first year as her village Guide was one mistake after another. If she hadn't made mistakes, you wouldn't be here." He paused and lowered his voice. "Though she loved you dearly. It near broke her heart when she had to give you to me, and that was with the understanding that you'd be back when the drought ended."

Kyra latched onto Craigson's final words. "She did love me, then? She didn't hate me, for what I was?"

Craigson's eyes were soft with compassion. "She worried about what you'd become, but it didn't stop her from loving you and hoping for the best. Maikana didn't always know what to do, and she made many, many mistakes. But she loved her village, even when the villagers didn't love her, and when she fell down, she always got up again."

Craigson's words reminded Kyra of the conversation she'd had with Malikel, when the Defense Minister had told her he stayed in Forge because he had work to do, despite the mistrust he faced from some. Kyra wondered about herself. Did she love

Forge that much? There were certainly parts that she loved—the gutter rats, the southwest quadrant, the streets and rooftops that were as familiar to her as Flick's laugh or Lettie's smile. Was that enough to make it worth fighting for?

"Thank you Craigson. For everything," she said.

Craigson took her hand in his own. His skin was callused and dry, but his grip was warm. "I'll likely return to Edlan for the rest of the winter. When this all calms down, come find me, and we'll talk more."

Twelve was too large a number to convene for long, and the Makvani grew restless to disperse. It was decided that they would set scouts farther up the road to watch for the caravans. When one came close, the scout would reconvene them.

Flick pointed out that it wouldn't be enough just to stop the caravans, since stores from nearby farms could feed the army for a few weeks at least. He volunteered to carry a message to those still around and rally them to hide their food stores.

"It's the least I could do," he said, rubbing his bearded chin with his fingers. Between the facial hair and the lengthening curls atop his head, he was starting to look rather wild. "To be honest, I feel rather useless. I'd much rather be taking down wagon trains with the rest of you, if only I had the claws to do it."

"Don't feel guilty," said Kyra, thinking of all the Makvani who had come to her aid because of Flick. "You've already done much more than you realize."

When the signal came the next evening, Kyra was still

half-asleep in her cave. If she'd been in her skin, she might have missed it completely, but she'd slept in her fur, and instinct pulled her awake. Once again Kyra knew exactly where the roar had come from. It was a new thrill, bounding through the trees toward the others and seeing the branches rush by. When she sensed motion in her periphery and her nose picked up the smell of other demon cats, the fur along her spine prickled in recognition. She had never been in her cat form around so many others before, and the unexpected feeling of kinship surprised her.

They gathered in a small clearing. When they had all changed into their skin and dressed, the scout spoke. "There is a caravan on its way. I think they will camp here tonight and meet the army tomorrow."

"They'll be most vulnerable when they sleep," said Kyra. "Pashla and I will go closer and get a better look at how they're positioned. We can attack when the moon sets."

A few of the gathered Makvani bowed to her, running one finger down the front of their necks. Then all except Pashla scattered into the trees.

Kyra stared after them, wondering at this honor they paid her, before she returned her thoughts to the matter at hand. She spoke to Pashla. "I prefer to scout in my skin, if you don't mind."

"You lead the way," said Pashla.

The scout had pointed them toward the road slightly north of them, so Kyra set off in that direction with Pashla walking silently alongside her. It didn't take long for them to hear voices and see campfires in the distance. They slowed and Kyra pointed to a tree. When Pashla nodded, Kyra led the way up.

She wasn't surprised to see that Pashla climbed well in her skin. In a few moments, they were both high enough to get a good view of the wagon train.

Like the scout had said, there were ten wagons, circled now for the night. Armed guards ringed the outside, while those inside tended to animals and prepared food.

"Where will they sleep?" asked Pashla.

"Under the wagons, I'd think," said Kyra. "The wagons themselves are likely too full to fit any people."

Pashla watched the wagons with the sharp gaze of a predator. "We'll fall on the guards from the trees above. They won't be expecting it, and they won't be able to see us coming. But it's still a large number of enemies for the twelve of us. We'll all have to be in our fur, if we want our best chance of surviving to fight again. You too, Kyra."

"I know," she said. The idea didn't sit well with her, but if she was to lead the raid, she would have to fight as the others did.

She and Pashla returned to her crew and made plans to meet again after the moon set. When the rest of the group left, Pashla stayed behind.

"You're not leaving?" asked Kyra.

"I think it's best if you're not alone," said Pashla.

She was grateful for Pashla's company, though the two of them didn't say much. Pashla seemed lost in her own thoughts while Kyra sat against a tree and scribbled diagrams on the ground with a stick. She couldn't stay still and got up frequently to pace.

"Something worries you," said Pashla.

Kyra took a moment to choose her words. "People will die in these raids," she said. "Both ours and theirs."

"Is it really so bad a thing to die in battle?" said Pashla. "There's a saying amongst our people: 'It is better to die honorably and render yourself immortal than live to old age and fade to dust.'"

"It in't quite the same," said Kyra. "You joined the fight because you think it's worth fighting. But most of the soldiers in this war fight under orders. Some might truly care for the cause, but others serve because it's the best way to feed their families, and still others were conscripted. So many lives stand to be lost, and it's all for the ambitions of a few." And there was more. It was becoming clear to Kyra that there would be no turning back from this. If she changed shape and fell on the caravan with the others, there would be no Tristam this time to keep her in line. She would take pleasure in the slaughter. She would lose herself in the act of war, and the men in the caravan would die gruesome, painful deaths.

Pashla laid a hand on her arm. "We have all agreed to follow you. If you've changed your mind about attacking the Edlan troops, then we don't have to continue on with our plans."

It was tempting, but Kyra shook her head. "No, we continue with the plan. I don't see any better way. I do love Forge, and if we hand it over to Willem, more people will be hurt in the long run. More people will go hungry, or lack for medicine..."

Kyra stopped short when she realized that the words coming out of her mouth were not her own. *Did the fire take more than what the Palace would have taken eventually? Lives lost when folk can't buy medicine and food. Homes lost because the fatpurses forever grab for more.* James had been talking about his Demon Rider raid, the one that killed Bella. Kyra had confronted him in a rage, unable to understand how he could have done something that took so many lives. *Oh, James, if you could see me now.* Here she was a few months later, in the forest among her fellow Makvani, orchestrating an attack of her own and justifying it with his words.

Something crunched in the snow around her. Perhaps Kyra was becoming attuned to her kin, because she immediately knew that another Demon Rider had come. Still, it was Pashla who recognized the newcomer first.

"Leyus," she said, and bowed as he came out.

There was something about the clan leader. Wherever he went, he gave the impression that the territory belonged to him and everybody was there at his will. Kyra wondered what kind of greeting she would have given him if she had been raised as his daughter. Was there a different bow?

"I will have a word with Kyra," Leyus said.

"Of course," Pashla said, and retreated.

In the past, being left alone with Leyus would have frightened Kyra, but knowing the truth made her bold. Kyra found that she no longer feared Leyus. Nor did she worry about losing his good opinion. He'd already made it clear that she didn't have it.

Leyus took his time before speaking, gazing down at her like a potter searching a vessel for flaws. "You're planning to raid the army caravan tonight," Leyus said.

"Aye," she said. It was hard not to fidget under his scrutiny.

What was Leyus doing here? "It seemed the best way to hurt the Edlan troops."

He walked a slow arc in the snow in front of her, gazing into the forest beyond. "Had you been raised in a clan, as my heir, I would have trained you to lead your people into battle."

Your people. What would it have been like to grow up as the daughter of a Makvani clan leader? She imagined herself hunting beside Pashla, learning to fight in preparation for her first Challenge. Would she have been friends with Adele? Would she look upon humans as lower beings and despise that part of herself?

"But I wasn't raised your heir, was I?" She'd grown up in the gutter, about as far from leading a desert village or a Makvani clan as she could get. "And I only have eleven fighters to lead into battle."

"Do you pity yourself, that I did not give you more help? A true leader would not rely on the charity of others."

And here it was again, another reminder that she didn't measure up. "And I suppose you'd rather have me kill all the Edlan soldiers with my bare hands," Kyra said bitterly. "Or was I supposed to have inspired more of your people to follow me?"

"I'd rather have you know yourself and your own strengths, and to act with purpose. That is the first lesson I would have taught you, had I raised you." There was no sentimentality in Leyus's voice, just his direct and unflinching words. Anger stirred in Kyra's chest. Would it kill him to express even some scrap of regard for her? Some minuscule hint of happiness to have discovered the daughter he'd lost?

"I'm sorry I wasn't there to learn your lessons," she said. She kept her voice low and cold so it wouldn't quaver. "But I will do my best with the things I've learned in the life I've had. I must ask you to leave now, as we have many preparations to make."

"To have command of eleven of your kin is no small thing. Use your power wisely."

He left her then, and as soon as he was out of sight, Kyra took her frustrations out on a nearby tree, kicking and pummeling it with her fists. What she really wanted to do was scream, but she retained at least the presence of mind to remain quiet. Her shoes were soft leather and the tree was sturdy, so all she managed to do was bruise her toes and send shooting pains up her elbow. At some point during her tantrum, Pashla came to stand next to her and quietly watched until Kyra was still again.

"If this is what it's like to have a father," said Kyra under her breath, "I'd rather go back to being an orphan."

"He does wish you to succeed, Kyra," Pashla said. "He would not have come to speak to you if he did not care."

Pashla's voice was as calm and smooth as a healer's balm, yet Kyra resisted her words. "If he wanted me to succeed, he could have given me more help. Instead, he lists my failures and gives me useless advice."

"To know your strengths and act with purpose is not useless advice," Pashla said. So she'd been eavesdropping.

"I know my strengths, and they're nothing like what I need to see this through. I'm a thief. I climb rooftops, I slip into windows, and I steal things." Her voice got louder as she spoke. "I've no idea how to lead fighters into battle, and with this coming raid, I feel like I'm running headlong toward the edge of a precipice."

"Then perhaps our plan is the wrong one," Pashla said.

Pashla's words surprised her. Kyra supposed she'd expected the clanswoman to be in favor of a raid and nothing else.

"You think so?" Kyra asked. "But what else is there?"

"I don't know. You are not like us."

Well, that was one thing the two of them could agree upon. Kyra sank down into the snow and leaned back against a tree, paying no heed to the cold seeping into her trousers or the rough bark pulling at her hair. She stayed like that for a long while, eyes closed, simply trying to hold on to what sanity she had left. Then she sat bolt upright.

"What is it?" asked Pashla.

"I have an idea," said Kyra. It had come to her suddenly, but as soon as it came to mind, she knew it was the right one. It would be dangerous, but it was something she could attempt with a clear conscience. Perhaps Flick was right. Whatever she was, whatever hidden pasts she discovered, in the end she would always be the thief girl that he met on the streets so long ago.

Kyra turned to Pashla. "Cancel the raid. I've a new plan." Leyus would probably tell her that her decision was driven by fear of what she was, but it wasn't fear that motivated her this time. It was confidence—in what she was, and more importantly, in knowing what she wanted to be. "I'm going into the enemy camp," she said. "And I'm doing it in my skin."

THIRTY

Flick didn't like the idea, of course. He never liked anything that placed Kyra in danger, and this would be far riskier than a caravan raid.

"You know, you don't always have to pick the most fool-hardy way forward," he told her.

"But if it works, it could end it all before it begins," said Kyra.

The plan was simple. The easiest way to control an army was to control its leaders, and the leaders currently resided in a large tent at the center of Edlan's encampment. If someone were to, say, steal the leaders and turn them over to Forge, then Edlan's army would have newfound motivation to retreat.

Of course, an army encampment was perhaps the very defi-nition of "well guarded." Kyra was fairly confident she could get in. She wasn't nearly as confident that she could get back out, but she had to try. They had so much to gain if she succeeded.

She risked a trip back into the city and relayed her plan to Tristam and Malikel. "If all goes well, I'll deliver Willem to your gates tomorrow night. My Demon Riders will be waiting outside the camp to guard my initial retreat, and I'll need troops from Forge stationed by the city to guard the final stretch. If things do not go to plan..." She paused here and avoided Tristam's eyes. "All the Demon Riders with me are dedicated to this task. They can carry out raids on the Edlan supply caravans even if I can't help them."

"I will have a unit by the gates ready to come to your defense," said Malikel.

"Thank you." She finally looked at Tristam then. She could see the effort it took for him not to object to her plan, and his struggle tugged at her chest. Kyra swallowed and met his gaze. "This is war. We do what we must."

She left before her resolve could weaken further.

Kyra tried her best to get plenty of rest the next day, though her nerves didn't allow her to sleep for very long. When she could no longer stay still, she paced the ground in front of her cave. She'd just about churned the snow into mud when Adele and Pashla appeared.

"We will go with you tonight," said Pashla.

Kyra's initial reaction was to refuse. "I can't in good conscience make you run a mission in your skin."

"We have stake in this as well," said Adele.

"You can't subdue both Alvred and Willem by yourself," said Pashla. "And your plan does work better with us in our skin."

Once she gave up trying to dissuade them, Kyra had to admit that they were right.

They set out late that night, after the moon had set. Kyra had Pashla and Adele darken their clothes with mud to blend in. Then they walked silently to the forest edge, where they could see the campfires of the Edlan army. Kyra looked back to check that the other two were still with her, then set off on a slow jog toward the camp. The women fell easily behind her—Kyra's own stealth, after all, was a legacy of their blood. But though the clanswomen were quiet, they still looked to her as they neared the edge of the encampment. As Kyra watched the guards go by, waiting for an opening, she sensed that her companions couldn't read the intention in a sentry's footsteps or predict where he would look next. The clanswomen didn't have Kyra's lifelong experience breaking into guarded places, but they watched her carefully, and Kyra led the way into the camp, trailed by two impossibly graceful shadows.

The ground of the camp was muddy and wet; all the snow had long been trampled away. The muck was slick in some places, while others times it sucked at their shoes. The three of them passed campfires at regular intervals, all burning low. Kyra steered clear of the occasional groggy soldier who got up to feed the flames.

The center of command was a large tent near the physical center of the camp. Kyra could see its shadow looming in the dim moonlight. Little by little, from one patch of darkness to the next, they made their way closer. There was a sentry at the tent flap standing next to one of the few torches around. Kyra motioned to Pashla. They approached him from opposite sides, skirting along the edges of the tent until they stood just outside the light cast by the torch. Kyra could barely see Pashla's form as the clanswoman bent down, picked a rock off the ground, and let it drop. The sentry turned toward the sound, alert but not alarmed. Kyra ran while his back was turned and brought the hilt of her dagger down on the back of his head. He grunted, and Kyra snaked her arms under his armpits as he crumpled to the ground. Adele rushed in to help drag the body out of the torchlight. The sentry had a partner, who circled around from the other side of the tent. When he saw Kyra and Adele, he drew breath to shout but pitched forward before any sound left his mouth. Pashla bear-hugged him from behind and eased him to the ground.

"Ho, what's happening there?" came a shout from across the camp.

Sweat broke out over Kyra's skin. "We have to get them now," she said.

She drew her dagger and rushed into the tent. It was dark inside, and Kyra barely caught the glint of metal as a man charged at her with a blade. Kyra shouted a warning as she sidestepped his swipe. He moved with the clumsiness of someone who'd just woken. When he stumbled, Kyra saw her opening and slashed at his knife arm. He dropped the blade and clutched his arm, swearing.

Kyra pressed her knife to his throat, and for the first time, got a good look at her opponent's face. He'd trimmed his mustache since she last saw him, but there was no mistaking Edlan's Minister of Defense. Lord Alvred's eyes widened in recognition as he took in her features. Around her, the scuffling died down. As Kyra's eyes adjusted to the darkness, she saw that Pashla had Willem facedown on his bedroll, her knee on his spine and her dagger pointed at the base of his skull. Adele stood alert by the tent flap.

"Adele, rope," said Kyra. Her heart pounded so loudly it was a wonder the entire camp couldn't hear it.

Pashla shifted her weight so Adele could bind Willem's wrists. The Head Councilman glared at Kyra as Adele pulled the knots tight. His gray-streaked hair was messy and tangled from the scuffle.

"Do you really expect to get out of here alive?" asked Willem.

"Your fate will be tied to ours," Kyra said. When Adele finished binding Willem's arms, she stepped toward Kyra and Alvred, rope in hand.

"Kyra, take care!" said Pashla as someone threw open the tent flap. Kyra tightened her grip on Alvred as she turned. Three Edlan soldiers stood at the entrance with swords drawn. Several more stood behind them.

"Drop your weapons or your commanders die," she said, her voice sharp in her ears.

"Do as she says," said Alvred in his low, booming shout, and the others obeyed.

Well, it was too late for rope now. "Clear a path," said Kyra. Slowly, the soldiers parted. Kyra turned Alvred around so he faced away from her and nudged him to start moving. She stepped out first, followed by Pashla and Willem, with Adele bringing up the rear. It was awkward progress. He was much larger than she was, and Kyra had to reach up to get her dagger to his throat. Her arm quickly began to get sore, and sweat from his skin soaked into her clothes.

Kyra scanned the soldiers around her as they walked. This couldn't last forever. There were too many soldiers, and too few hostages. Her spine prickled—she expected an arrow in her back any moment. When Alvred lagged, she pressed the blade closer to his throat, nudging him forward. Slowly, ever so slowly, they made their way to the edge of the camp. Her arms burned. She could see the forest now when she peered around Alvred's bulk. Almost there. They just needed the shelter of the trees.

Something whistled through the air, followed by a woman's cry. Kyra turned just in time to see Adele fall to her knees, an arrow shaft sticking out her back.

"Adele!" she shouted. At that moment, Alvred broke free and struck her hard in the stomach. Kyra fell to the ground, retching. Alvred grabbed for her dagger, but she snatched it away just in time.

"Lord Alvred!"

A soldier handed Alvred a mace, an evil-looking club with a steel-coated head. Kyra dove to the side as he raised it high and brought it down. He missed the first time and the second, but his third blow came down squarely on her right hip.

Kyra screamed, and for a moment she couldn't see anything for the pain. When her vision cleared, Alvred was closing in for another blow. She tried to scoot away, and realized with horror that she couldn't move her leg at all.

A roar split the air and a demon cat charged into the fray, coming to a stop protectively above Adele. Two more came after and stood tail-to-tail with the first, fangs bared and snarling dangerously. For a moment, everyone stared. Then the demon cats disappeared behind a wave of soldiers. Alvred raised his mace once more, and Kyra hopelessly threw her arms in front of her face.

"Stand back!" Suddenly, Pashla was next to her, still with Willem firmly in her grasp. How had she managed to hold on to her hostage in all that chaos? Alvred hesitated, and in that moment someone's arms threaded under Kyra's and pulled her to her feet. She cried out again as the movement jarred her leg. Then she realized it was Flick holding her.

"Easy, Kyra." His voice was a safe harbor she could cling to. "Let's get you to safety."

"To the trees," said Pashla, dragging Willem in that direction. Flick threw Kyra over his shoulder and hurried after the clanswoman. Kyra buried her face in his chest to keep from screaming. Every step he took was agony. Two swordsmen gave chase, but a demon cat jumped in front of them, cutting off pursuit.

The sounds of battle followed them into the forest. "Our people won't last long," Kyra said. And Adele. Was she alive?

Pashla forced Willem to his knees in front of her. "We must get him to Forge."

She was right. If the Edlanese recovered Willem, all their efforts would have been in vain. "Pashla," she said. "I can't walk, much less run. You must bring him to the gates."

Pashla's eyes flickered quickly over Kyra, and then she undid her tunic as Flick lowered Kyra to the ground. When Pashla regained her form, Flick hoisted Willem onto her back and secured him with rope. The Head Councilman's attempts to resist met with two solid clouts to the head. Willem swore at Flick but stopped fighting.

Finally, Flick pulled the rope tight. When Pashla bent her

head around to check Flick's progress, he patted her on her flank. "Go," he said. "Run quickly."

Pashla took off with a bound, zigzagging through the trees. Kyra watched her disappear, then turned back toward the battle, trying to see between the trees to the chaos beyond. Demon cat growls split the air. Swords clanged as fur and steel flashed in and out of view.

Kyra drew the deepest breath she could. "Retreat!" she yelled. "Makvani retreat!"

The battle continued on, and she wondered if anyone had heard her. Then a demon cat ran for the trees and knelt in front of Kyra.

"Hang on," said Flick as he lifted her onto its back and climbed on behind her. Another demon cat came on its tail, and Kyra was light-headed with relief to see a very pale Adele clinging to its back. Other demon cats followed, turning around several times to fend off pursuers. The demon cat Kyra was riding looked around at the gathered Makvani and let out a roar. And then, as one, the beasts ran into the forest.

⬚ ⬚ ⬚

Tristam stood at attention outside the city gate, facing the empty road. He might as well have been sitting in a root cellar for all he could discern in the darkness. Tristam knew from Malikel's strategy charts that fifty Red Shields stood to his left, armed with spears. To his right came the occasional whinny and snort from the horses of twenty cavalrymen. Sir Rollan stood in command at the front, while Malikel oversaw everything from the wall.

"Disturbance in the enemy camp," came a lookout's voice from above.

Perhaps it was good that his position required absolute stillness, because otherwise Tristam would have worn down the road with his nervous energy. Of all the schemes Kyra had come up with so far, this had to be the most brazen, and he couldn't quiet the fear that her luck would finally run out. What was this "disturbance" in the enemy camp? Panic at finding their leader gone, or celebration at capturing an intruder?

"Light the torches," Rollan commanded. "Put them in place."

A ripple of readiness went through the troops. All around him, there was the sound of flint striking. A warm glow illuminated the troops as sparks caught on pitch-coated wood. Each cavalry man took two torches and rode down the road to place them in stands before returning to formation. They all waited, growing more and more tense as the shadows formed and dissipated on the newly lit road.

"A rider, sir," came the lookout's voice, sharp now. "No, a demon cat. With a single rider. A man."

"Tristam," said Rollan. "Is it Kyra?"

Tristam squinted down the road. He could make out the rider now, and his steed was definitely a demon cat. As the beast passed the torches though, he saw that the fur was tawny yellow.

"It's not Kyra, sir," he said. "Wrong color." Was it Pashla? "I think it may be one of her allies."

"Spearmen, take formation, but don't attack." Rollan

delivered his orders with confident ease, and his composure seemed to rub off on the troops around him. "Tristam, speak immediately if you see anything untoward."

"Yes, sir," he said. Where was Kyra? A knot formed in his stomach. *Concentrate on your task.*

"It's Willem tied to the beast's back," called the lookout.

The felbeast slowed as it neared them and approached carefully with its head lowered and ears flat. Willem was indeed tied to its back. He must have been captured while he was asleep because he wore only a plain wool tunic and trousers. And though Willem's face was turned partially away, Tristam could clearly see the rage etched in his features. Tristam almost felt sorry for him. What a fall it must be for a Head Councilman to be delivered to his city gates like a sack of flour.

Red Shields formed a half circle around the demon cat and raised their spears as it came closer. The beast stopped and eyed the weapons warily. Tristam was almost certain now that it was Pashla.

"Sir Rollan," said Tristam. "May I cut the hostage from the beast's back?"

"You may."

Pashla knelt as Tristam approached. Willem glared but didn't say anything as Tristam surveyed the ropes and cut the ones that tied him to Pashla. Willem slid to the ground, and several Red Shields lifted him to his feet.

"The cat's changing shape," a man said.

Apparently, Red Shield discipline couldn't match the sight of a demon cat transforming before their eyes, because shouts and exclamations rose up all around. As Pashla shrank down,

Tristam unclasped his cloak and threw it over her shoulders. She gathered the cloak around her and looked calmly at the troops before settling her eyes on Tristam.

"Thank you," she said.

It was on his tongue to ask about Kyra, but the gate opened just then, and Malikel walked out. He was flanked by soldiers, and he looked, every inch of him, like a leader of men. He faced Willem, who stood with his hands bound in front of him. A Red Shield held each arm.

"That was cleverly done, Malikel," said Willem, his voice crisp. "And what happens now?"

"That is something we'll have to discuss." Malikel turned to Pashla. "We are grateful," he said with dignity, "though we'd expected Kyra to come."

"She was injured in the fighting," said Pashla.

"How badly was she wounded?" asked Tristam. His need to know outweighed his adherence to protocol.

"She is alive," said Pashla. "And she is unlikely to die from the wounds she'd received when I left. Beyond that, I do not know."

It was a small relief, but not exactly happy news.

"You are welcome to take shelter within our walls tonight," said Malikel.

Pashla shook her head. "If you have no further need for me, I will return to my clan."

"Very well, then. We are indebted to your people." Malikel addressed the men holding Willem. "Take the prisoner back to the Palace."

As Malikel and Willem disappeared into the city, Pashla stepped back from the soldiers around her. She handed Tristam's cloak to him, her shape blurring. The spearmen around her squared their stances as she fell on all fours, but Pashla simply turned and raced away.

There was a collective release of tension amongst the troops as Pashla left.

"Return to formation," commanded Rollan. "Head back through the gate."

Tristam turned with the rest of his comrades toward the city. He realized now that he should have asked Pashla to take him to Kyra, but it was too late. As the first soldiers started to march, the lookout called down again.

"Sir Rollan," he said. "I see troops riding toward the city. Edlan riders, carrying torches."

Tristam turned, as did the men around him. Dots of torchlight bobbed in the distance, illuminating men on horseback. They were riding down the road to the city, though now they stopped and fanned into a half circle, as if they were surrounding something. A demon cat. Pashla.

"All troops retreat into the city." Rollan's voice rang over the troops. "Close the gates."

Tristam looked to Rollan in disbelief. Were they simply going to leave Pashla to her fate? The soldiers around him started marching again, but Tristam didn't move. When the soldier behind Tristam stepped around him, Tristam broke out of the stream, elbowing his way to Rollan's horse.

"Rollan," he said. "There must be at least ten horsemen out there. Pashla can't face them all."

"We're tasked with securing the city." Rollan barely gave Tristam a sideways glance as he observed the retreat.

Tristam looked back out toward the Edlan soldiers. One horseman lowered a spear and charged Pashla. She jumped aside just in time, then twisted around to rake her claws across the horse's flank. The torchlight played off her fur as the other horsemen formed a loose circle around her, cutting off any escape.

"She just saved our city," said Tristam. "And we leave her now to the enemy?"

A spasm of irritation crossed Rollan's face. "You forget your place, soldier."

Tristam suppressed the urge to pull Rollan off his horse. Not three months ago, he'd have been commanding troops alongside him. But it was clear that Rollan would not have his authority challenged. In the distance, Pashla roared, and the Edlan horses danced apart. Was she limping?

That was when Tristam noticed that the knight next to Rollan was not on his horse. Tristam wasn't sure why the man had dismounted, but an idea came to him. *Well, I suppose there are more important things than regaining my knighthood.*

Tristam pushed his way toward the steed before he could change his mind. The horse's rider stood nearby, still holding his lance. Tristam grabbed the weapon and knocked the man aside. Before anyone realized what was happening, Tristam had pulled himself into the horse's saddle and urged the creature forward with a kick. Over the pounding of his horse's hooves, he heard Rollan yelling after him. He looked over his shoulder to see several Forge cavalrymen giving chase. Were they coming to help him or knock him off his horse? He wasn't about to wait and find out.

The Edlan troops had seen the Forge soldiers coming by now, and five of them turned their horses to face them. Tristam could see Pashla beyond them, definitely limping as she charged her enemies. She roared once, and the sound quickened his blood.

Tristam leveled his spear, shouted a war cry, and braced for impact.

⊘ ⊘ ⊘

The felbeast Kyra rode had a smoother stride than a horse, but every leap it took still sent agony shooting through her limbs. She gritted her teeth and tried to convince herself it didn't hurt. As they ran farther away from the troops, she started to feel lightheaded, as if she had lost a lot of blood. But she wasn't bleeding, was she? Not on the outside at least. Her awareness started to leave her. She began listing to the side, but Flick tightened his arms around her and kept her from falling. She was aware of other demon cats around her, also fleeing, but as time passed, she no longer had the energy to think about them or anything else.

She wasn't sure how long they rode. By the time they slowed, she was drifting in and out of consciousness. She felt a breeze at her back and realized that Flick was no longer behind her. Strong arms lifted her off her steed. Flick? No. It was Leyus who looked down at her, his expression grave. And then she drifted again.

The next thing she knew, she lay on a fur spread over the ground. New hands and voices tended to her. Someone was cutting the clothes from her body. A man spoke. Not Leyus this time, but she couldn't place the voice. "Kyra, change into your fur."

She tried to ignore him at first. Change now? She could hardly lift her head. She closed her eyes and tried to sleep, but someone shook her. She realized she was shivering without her clothes.

"Change into your fur, Kyra," said the voice again, more commanding this time. "Then you can rest."

Kyra obeyed just so that he would leave her alone. The spark of her other form was hard to find by now, and everything around her seemed dim. But finally she grabbed on and coaxed it stronger. Welcome warmth spread through her body. And then it was too much for her, and she slept.

Kyra awoke disoriented. She was in her fur, but not in her cave. There was no strength in her limbs. Pain still radiated from her hip, although it was not nearly as bad as it had been before. Kyra shook the fog out of her mind and climbed slowly to her feet.

She was in the forest, and the angle of the light suggested it was afternoon. Some demon cats lay a stone's throw away, tended by their kin. A few other Makvani stood nearby in human form. Their voices carried easily over the snow, but Kyra couldn't understand the words.

It was too painful to put weight on her back leg, so she hobbled awkwardly forward on three. She'd only made it a few paces when someone approached her. It took her a moment to recognize Havel, the leader of the new clan. He greeted her with a friendly tone and held out a tunic. Kyra understood that he wanted her to change into her skin.

She obeyed. Her weight shifted as she changed, and the resulting pressure on her injured leg would have made her lose her balance if Havel hadn't steadied her shoulder. When Kyra stabilized, he handed her the tunic, and she pulled her arms through, too disoriented to be concerned about modesty.

"How do you feel?" Havel asked.

There was warmth in his voice, and Kyra recognized it as the one who had commanded her to change shape the night before. "Was it you who cared for me last night?"

Havel inclined his head. "I served as a healer for your father long ago. He still asks me for help, in cases that are important to him." He met Kyra's eyes as he said the last part, and the meaning was not lost on her. Nor had she forgotten the worry in Leyus's brow as he'd lifted her off the demon cat last night.

"Is Leyus still here?" asked Kyra.

"No, not at the moment."

Perhaps that was just as well. She'd wished for some sign that her father cared for her, but the thought of facing him and having this new knowledge shaken was too frightening.

Now that she was in her skin, worries came crowding back. Where was she? What was the outcome of the battle last night? And—a new urgency hit her—who had been hurt?

"Flick and Adele, are they safe?"

"Flick is unharmed," said Havel. Maybe it was something about Makvani healers, but Kyra felt at ease with Havel. The edge of aggression carried by most of his kin seemed softened in him. "Adele lost a good deal of blood, but she will live. Flick has been either at her side or yours all day."

Kyra closed her eyes, relieved. "And Pashla? Did she convey Willem to Forge?"

Here, Havel's countenance darkened. "We have no news of Pashla. Our scouts have been watching the Edlan troops, and they say the Defense Minster Malikel met with the Edlan leader this morning. Edlan troops are packing up their camp, so we can only guess that Pashla succeeded. But we do not know where she is."

Kyra thought back to the determination in Pashla's face when she'd changed shape to convey Willem to the city. She would have done her utmost to get him there. A chill went through Kyra, and she looked into the trees, wishing she could somehow see through them to the city.

"How is your leg?" Havel asked.

Kyra realized she'd been silent for a long time. "It doesn't hurt nearly as much as it did last night," she said. "But I can't put weight on it."

"Lord Alvred is a strong man. The blow crushed the bones of your hip and caused you to bleed in your abdomen. We had you change shape so the bone fragments would go back to their proper place, but it does not always work, especially in someone who does not share all our blood. We'll have someone cut you a staff to use while you recover. In the early days, you might find it easier to move around in your fur."

Someone shouted in the distance just then. It didn't sound like an alarm, more like a sentry's report. Havel looked toward the sound. "We may have more news now."

There was someone coming through the trees—someone tall, who walked like a soldier. He carried a long, rolled blanket across his arms, and a horse trailed behind him. Kyra squinted. Was that . . .

"Tristam!" Kyra shouted. Only at the last minute did she remember that she couldn't run to him. His eyes fixed on her, and his entire body sagged with relief.

It was awkward, standing and waiting for him to get to her. She found herself leaning forward, impatient to talk to him. Tristam couldn't walk very quickly because of what he carried, and as he came closer, Kyra felt a rising dread. Tristam's steps were heavy, and his eyes did not signal good news. Kyra turned to Havel, only to realize that the man had slipped away.

Tristam came to a stop in front of Kyra and laid his burden on the ground in front of her. For a long moment, they stared at each other. She longed to throw her arms around him, but it was too strange, with all the Makvani around.

"I heard you were injured," he said.

"Alvred's got a deadly mace arm," she said. "But Flick got me out alive." She gestured weakly toward herself. "I . . . can't walk very well at the moment."

"I'm glad you're alive," said Tristam. He started to reach for her but curled his hand into a fist and lowered it to his side as he stared down at the ground in front of him. When he spoke again, the words came out deliberately, as if he had to push them out before his resolve failed. "We had a unit waiting outside the gate for your arrival." he said, his voice low and even. His eyes were clouded with anguish. "Pashla made it to us with Willem on her back. But when she tried to return to the forest, she ran across a group of Edlan horsemen."

He stopped then, and Kyra felt something cold grip her

chest. She looked down at the rolled blanket on the ground. She'd known what it was. But still she'd hoped…

"I'm sorry, Kyra," Tristam said. "I tried to help her, and several of our knights as well. But we were too late." He kneeled then and pulled up one edge of the blanket to reveal Pashla's face.

Pashla's eyes were closed, her skin pale and bloodless, and Kyra found she couldn't breathe. She started to kneel down beside Pashla but stopped when pain shot through her hip. Tristam reached out to steady her, and slowly, she eased herself onto the snow.

The battle at the enemy camp played over and over in Kyra's mind. The arrow in Adele's back. Lord Alvred's mace coming down on Kyra's hip. The chaos that had led to Pashla taking her place.

"It should have been me," Kyra said. There was a lump in her throat that didn't move when she swallowed.

"The tides of battle cannot be predicted by any of us," said Tristam. "Don't blame yourself for the hand of fate."

He spoke the words as if he knew the grief they addressed. And Kyra supposed he did. His fellow knights had probably told him the same thing when Jack and Martin had died.

Kyra reached out to adjust the blanket around Pashla. Her fingers brushed against Pashla's cheek. The flesh was cold, as icy as the snow around them, and Kyra snatched her hand back with a gasp. The difference between that frozen shell and Pashla's warm, gentle touch was so stark that it felt like a cruel joke.

And that was when it sank in. This body was all that was left of the woman who had saved Kyra's life and nursed her back from near death. The woman who had fought for her, taught her the secrets of her Makvani blood, and forgiven Kyra when she returned to the humans. Kyra felt a burning beneath her eyelids. She fought it for a while, but when Tristam came and placed an arm around her shoulders, Kyra buried her face in his chest and let the tears come. He held her wordlessly through the sobs, occasionally rubbing her back, until finally she wiped her eyes and pulled away.

"Pashla and I," said Tristam, "we had our differences. But it was not my wish to see her fall."

"Did you speak to her before she died?" Kyra asked.

Tristam's nod was so slight that she almost didn't see it. "She asked me to take her body back to the clan."

Kyra stared down at Pashla's face, stern and beautiful, mysterious even in death. *What are you thinking, Pashla?* "She thought it an honor to die in battle for a cause she believed in. I hope she found this fight worthwhile."

"I think she did," said Tristam. "I know she did."

Kyra closed her eyes and breathed a silent thank-you and good-bye. Then she once again covered Pashla with the blanket and let her sleep.

The clan burned Pashla's body, with each member contributing a branch for the fire. In addition to Pashla, they mourned the deaths of two others who had been in Kyra's band of twelve. Those two had perished in the enemy camp, and there was no way to recover their remains.

Over the next few days, Tristam came often with news from Forge. The morning after Willem's capture, messengers had been dispatched to the Edlan troops with orders from the captive Willem to call off the siege. While some of Edlan's commanders might have been tempted to continue their attack even without their original ally, Willem had enough relatives in Edlan, including the Duke himself, who did not wish to see him harmed. The Edlan troops began their long march back a few days later. Malikel dispatched scouts to make sure they had gone, and after a few days, it was declared that the Edlan invaders had returned to their own city. Willem himself would be tried in front of the Council for treason.

"The Council voted to keep Malikel in his position as Head Councilman," said Tristam. "In part, he has Willem to thank for it. When your most vocal enemy turns out to be a traitor to the city, it tends to boost your credibility." Tristam paused. "Malikel requests that you return to Forge to speak with him, and he promises you safe passage into the Palace, should you take his request."

The promise of safe passage was important because Kyra was in no condition for any daring escapes at the moment. Her leg had healed to the point where she could walk with a crutch. It was a relief to be able to get around at all, but rooftop running was going to be out of her repertoire for a while.

Havel told her he wasn't sure what trajectory her recovery would take. "Your bones were crushed severely, and you're of mixed blood," he said. "The pain will lessen with time, but I don't know how far the healing will go. It may never return to the way it was before. You have to be prepared for that."

It was the uncertainty that scared her. Not knowing how the future would look, whether she'd be able to climb or run.

But Kyra also remembered that she was alive, when Pashla and two others had died for a plan that she'd proposed. It wasn't an easy thing to forget. Every conversation with Havel reminded her of Pashla, and how the clanswoman had also nursed Kyra back to health not long ago.

Two weeks after the big battle, Kyra accepted Malikel's invitation, and Tristam brought a cart to convey her to the Palace. It felt strange to be sitting up straight in the back of a wagon, rather than being smuggled under a blanket, as she had done so many times before. Tristam wore plain clothes as he drove, and though she got some curious looks, nobody made a noticeable commotion about recognizing her.

Once they reached the Palace though, things were different. The gate guards looked on her with thinly disguised fear, and Red Shields within sight kept their hands close to their weapons. Tristam stopped the cart near Malikel's building and offered her an arm. Kyra did her best to walk with her chin up the rest of the way.

Malikel looked older than Kyra remembered, or perhaps it was just the circles under his eyes. Kyra thought she saw more gray in his beard as well, but that was impossible in just a few days, wasn't it? The new Head Councilman thanked Tristam and dismissed him, then motioned for Kyra to sit down across from him at his desk.

"The city thanks you for your role in breaking the Edlan siege," he said, folding his hands in front of him. "Without your help, many more would have suffered."

"I heard about the Council vote," said Kyra. "I'm glad you've taken over Willem's position."

"Thank you. Though I'm guessing you've gathered by now that I've not summoned you here to exchange pleasantries."

"No, I suppose not," said Kyra. Had it been any other man who'd invited her back, she might have suspected a trap. But she believed Malikel honorable.

"I won't mince words, Kyra. You've always been a challenge as far as our laws are concerned. You've committed considerable transgressions, yet at the same time, you've performed great services for the city. You're responsible for the death of Santon of Agan and the assassin James. You also wounded many men, including Dalton of Agan and several Red Shields at James's execution. The Council could not simply pardon those crimes, even with your services to the city. Perhaps if you had an otherwise blameless record, but you've already been pardoned for one murder, and now that the truth of your bloodlines is known . . . I'm afraid it's impossible."

Kyra bowed her head at the mention of the murder she'd already been pardoned for, the manservant she'd accidentally killed when she worked for James. Of all she'd ever done, it was the one thing Kyra wished most she could undo, and she suspected it would haunt her for the rest of her life. "Does your promise of safe passage still stand, then?"

Malikel looked her over with an appraising eye. "I assure you, I have no desire to drag you into our dungeons. Nor would I want to take the losses in soldiers and guards should I attempt to do so. My promise of safe passage is sincere."

She waited. There was more. She knew there was more.

Malikel met her eye. "It brings me no joy to do this, but the Council has voted to exile you from Forge. You'll be conveyed out of this city, but after this, you will only be allowed within the city's walls under strict guard."

It took a moment for Malikel's words to sink in. And then she stared at him in disbelief. "You're exiling me from Forge? If it wasn't for me, you wouldn't have a city to exile me from."

"I know Kyra, and I'm sorry—"

She interrupted him angrily. "You're sorry, but you're bound by the decisions of the Council. Just as you were when the magistrate pardoned Santon for beating my sister to near death. This in't about the law, is it? It's about how the Council won't trust a halfblood Makvani in their city." *Not just any halfblood Makvani*, said a traitorous voice in her head. *A halfblood who's killed three men and thrown the city into chaos more than once.* She still thought the Council's decision was motivated by fear, but she couldn't deny that the case against her was substantial.

She collapsed back into her chair. "So nothing's changed," she said. "I'm still a criminal. The Council makes its decisions, and the city continues as before. Somehow I'd thought, with Willem gone and you in his place..."

Malikel pushed a piece of parchment across the table. Kyra had half a mind to throw it back at him, but she grudgingly looked it over. It was a Palace document, from one of the city magistrates. Something about a trial to be planned. And the accused was named...

"Douglass and Dalton of Agan will be tried for assaulting Idalee," said Malikel. "The magistrate conducted a further investigation into the case and determined that the initial ruling was unduly influenced by political factors. In addition, other victims have come forth with complaints against the brothers, and the magistrate is investigating them all.

"The Agan brothers will not be the only ones investigated. Others who enjoyed immunity under Willem are being held accountable as well. It will be a busy season for the magistrates." Malikel waited for Kyra to finish looking over the parchment. "Things are changing, Kyra. Though they progress slowly, in fits and starts. You're not the first to find this frustrating. My predecessor in this position found it so as well, and in fact engineered a plan to change our system of government." Malikel's lips twitched in the slightest of smiles. "I heard that the plan did not go well for him."

Though Kyra couldn't bring herself to smile back, she couldn't deny the irony. "It's funny," she said. "Remember the conversation we had, about serving the city even though not everyone within it would care to have us? What I did to break the siege, I did because I'd finally decided I agreed with you."

"And you can still serve the city, if you wish," said Malikel. "Which brings me to the last thing I wanted to discuss with you. I'm ready to follow through on the promises we made to the Makvani and discuss peace."

That, at least, was good news. "I can convey your message to Leyus."

"Thank you," said Malikel. "Given the times that lie ahead, I see the need for a go-between for our two peoples. An emissary, of sorts, and preferably someone who is familiar with both societies." He glanced significantly at Kyra.

She bristled. "And you would like me to do this? Why should I?"

"There's no reason why you should. I won't try to convince you that you owe it to the city or create some other sense of false responsibility. You owe Forge nothing, but you can do some good if you want to. The choice is yours."

Kyra gazed across the desk at him. It was tempting to throw a refusal in his face, but the less hotheaded part of her urged her to pause. The thought of peace between Forge and the Makvani—cooperation, even—was a good one.

"I'll think on it," said Kyra.

"That's all we can ask," said Malikel.

When Tristam came to convey her back out of the city, she could tell he was curious about what had transpired.

"Malikel didn't tell you why he called me in?" said Kyra.

"No," said Tristam. "He didn't share anything."

She supposed it was no big secret. Tristam would find out about her exile soon enough. "Let's leave the Palace first, and then I'll tell you."

He helped Kyra into the wagon. As he walked to the front, Kyra called to him. "Tristam."

He turned.

"Do you mind if we take a different route out of the city this time?"

"I suppose," he said, looking slightly perplexed. "How would you like to go?"

She let out a slow breath as the full implications of the Council's sentence finally hit her. "Bring the wagon by the southwest quadrant. I'd like to see The Drunken Dog."

Kyra accepted Malikel's offer to act as emissary between the Makvani and Forge. Sometimes the Head Councilman met with her outside the city. Other times, a contingent of Red Shields escorted her from the gate to the Palace. Her first job was to arrange a meeting to begin peace negotiations, and after a few proposals and counterproposals, the leaders agreed to meet on a patch of farmland bordering the forest.

Each group brought a contingent of five. Leyus, Havel, Zora, Adele, and Mela formed the Makvani contingent, while Malikel brought Tristam and three members of the Council. Kyra was there as well, the only person present who was not affiliated with either party. She arrived first and watched nervously as the two groups came to the meeting place, then held her breath as Malikel and Leyus shook hands. The Forge contingent set up a tent for shelter, and the Makvani provided deer hides to sit on. Kyra noticed Adele glancing over her shoulder toward the forest before stepping into the tent. When Kyra followed her gaze, she saw Flick watching from the trees. He winked at Kyra when he saw her looking, and the sight somehow made her more optimistic about the way things would go.

It was a long day, and there were several tense moments, but by the end of it, the two groups had the beginnings of a peace agreement. Malikel and Leyus shook hands one more time before they parted.

"I feel hopeful about this direction," said Malikel. "If any concerns should arise before the next time we meet, have Kyra convey a message to the city. I trust she has been satisfactory thus far as an emissary?"

Leyus looked at Kyra and gave the slightest of nods. "Yes," he said. "She has done well." Their eyes met, and just for a moment, something passed between them, a hint of understanding between father and daughter. It wasn't the stuff of talesinger ballads, but it gave Kyra hope. Perhaps someday she'd come to know him better, learn about his past and the mysterious woman he'd left on the other side of the Aerins. Someday.

Kyra initially took up residence again in her cave, but she eventually found a small cottage near the forest, far enough removed from other houses that they didn't have to worry about fearful neighbors. Lettie and Idalee moved back in with her from Mercie's house. Lettie took to the spot immediately, as it gave her a chance to stay near her new playmates. As spring came, Idalee started a small garden. Though the girl enjoyed tending it, Kyra guessed that Idalee might move back to Forge when she was older. She missed the bustle of the city, as did Kyra.

As was the case with their previous quarters, Flick was still a semipermanent fixture at the cottage. These days, however,

Kyra wasn't sure if he came by their house because she, Lettie, and Idalee were there or because it was convenient to the forest, and to Adele. The Makvani themselves didn't build permanent houses, though they crafted large, sturdy tents that they set up where they wished.

One morning, when Idalee and Lettie had gone to buy seeds for the garden, someone knocked on Kyra's door. Kyra thought it was one of the Makvani, and it was a few seconds before she recognized the human woman who greeted her. Darylene of Forge looked very different than she had when Kyra had seen her last. Her thick chestnut hair was bound back, and she wore an unassuming dress of undyed linen. But though she dressed to blend in, Willem's former mistress was still stunningly beautiful.

"I'm sorry to visit unexpectedly," Darylene said. "May I come in?"

It took Kyra a moment to get over her surprise, but she waved Darylene in and motioned for her to sit down. Kyra offered her a cup of tea, and Darylene accepted.

An awkward silence stretched between them then, and Kyra was grateful that she could busy herself with the stove. She knew by now that she'd been unfair in her initial animosity toward Darylene, and she was also well aware of the girl's role in Willem's overthrow. But still, old impressions were hard to get over, and Kyra didn't know what to say to Darylene, much less why she was here.

"I trust you are well?" Kyra asked when the tea was finally poured.

Darylene nodded. She still moved and held herself like

an elegant lady. Kyra could see why she might have caught Willem's eye. "Things progress well. I no longer work in the Palace. There's too much talk. Half the nobles deem me a traitor, while others treat me like a former trophy of Willem's to be won and flaunted," said Darylene. "As for my fellow servants, they've never had much use for me, and turning Willem in wasn't enough to earn their good opinion. It all grew to be too much."

Kyra could imagine.

Darylene brushed a stray curl from her face, then continued. "It probably won't surprise you that Willem provided for my material needs while I was his companion. And it was a big reason why I hesitated to say anything about Willem's crimes. It was selfish of me, I know, but I had a brother and sister who depend on me, and what I made as a servant in the Palace was not enough." She gave a sad smile. "Why worry about the fate of the city when my own family was fed?"

"You have siblings?" asked Kyra.

"Yes." Darylene's eyes softened when she spoke of them. "Ava is ten and Derek is eight. We're very close, since my ma and pa passed."

Kyra thought of Idalee and Lettie. "They're lucky to have you." And she found that she meant it.

Darylene smiled then and looked down at her tea. "It's . . . hard for us to stay in the city after all that has happened. I think I need to take my family and leave, at least for a while. James said you could help me with supplies, coin, and arrangements."

At first, Kyra thought she'd misheard what Darylene had said. "James?" Kyra asked. "The Head of the Assassins Guild?"

Darylene nodded. "When he escaped from prison, he came to speak with me. He'd somehow found out that I had proof of Willem's misdeeds. He said . . . that if I ever decided to turn Willem in, I could ask you for help getting back on my feet."

Kyra stared at Darylene, unable to respond.

Someday I'll call in a favor from you, and I'll hold you to it.

So he'd decided that Kyra was the best person to help Darylene. Kyra supposed he was right. Compared to Bacchus or even Rand, she was the one most likely to see Darylene safely off to a new life.

"I'll need some time to make arrangements and call in some favors," said Kyra. "But I'll see it done. Come back in three days, and we can talk further."

Darylene took Kyra's hands and squeezed them. "Thank you," she said.

Kyra looked down, wondering if Darylene had any idea how deeply Kyra's distaste for her had run before. "Thank you for what you did," said Kyra. "Who knows where the city would be now if you hadn't come forward."

"I should have done so earlier, but I didn't have the courage." Darylene paused. "I know you must hate him, but Willem was kind to me. I'm not sure I can say I loved him, but I respected him. He was a proud man, with a vision for Forge to be a beacon to the surrounding cities. Willem had the kind of ambition and foresight that few men ever dreamed of, much less acted on." Darylene's gaze went distant for a moment. "But James was persuasive when we spoke. Eventually, I realized I couldn't stay silent."

"He was a very persuasive man," said Kyra.

"Did you . . . know James well?" Darylene asked. "I got the impression that he was a hard man to know."

"I don't think he revealed much of himself to anyone," said Kyra. She once again heard James's whispered words. *Choose your fight.* And Kyra felt something in her chest. Not quite grief, but not far from it either. "James kept his secrets close, and we didn't always agree. But I learned much from him."

Kyra's injuries continued to heal. As the weather grew warmer, she became able to move around without a cane. She almost had a normal stride now, though larger steps pained her, as did the few hours before a coming storm. She experimented a bit with running, but her hip had a troublesome tendency to lock up unexpectedly, forcing her to react quickly to keep from tumbling to the ground.

At Flick's and Idalee's insistence, she didn't try to climb, though as the months passed, she grew restless. Finally, one warm morning when Lettie had gone into the forest and Idalee had gone to the market, Kyra paused while sweeping the doorstep and found herself gazing longingly at the overhanging eave of her roof. She looked around one more time, assuring herself that there was no one nearby, and then jumped for it. She missed by quite a distance—it would have been a stretch even in her uninjured days. But there was always the windowsill, which she climbed by leading with her left leg. From there, it was a precarious moment as she jumped again for the overhang, but this time her fingers caught, and she pulled herself over.

She straightened to her full height and couldn't help but grin. A light breeze blew through her hair, and she turned her face to enjoy the sun.

She walked a leisurely circle around the edge of the roof. Flick would have scolded her, but she knew she could catch herself if she stumbled. After one loop, she climbed to the top and walked along the ridgeline, pausing a few times to readjust her balance when her hip locked. But she didn't fall, and she felt lighter than she had in a long time. Finally, she decided it was enough climbing for the day. Kyra settled down next to the chimney and watched the road. It was a crisp morning, and only the occasional farmer or horseman passed by. She'd been up there almost an hour when she recognized the next person coming down the bend.

It took her a while to be sure it was Tristam. He'd been gone the past couple of months. As soon as Edlan retreated and peace with the Makvani became likely, Lord Brancel had called Tristam home to help rebuild the damage from the Demon Rider attacks. In addition to helping his family, there was another reason for him to leave court for a while. The Council had stripped Tristam of his knighthood for two more years as punishment for disobeying Rollan's orders, and his absence gave the resultant gossip some time to settle down.

As Tristam came closer, his eyes locked on her roof, and he smiled and waved. Kyra waved back.

He came to a stop at the corner of the house. "How's the breeze up there?" he asked.

"Quite nice," said Kyra. She made her way to the edge and lowered herself down, making sure to land on her good leg. He caught her in a big embrace as soon as she touched the ground, and she squeezed him tightly back.

"Are you returned for good now?" she asked.

"Yes," he said. "I've done about all I can back at Brancel."

Kyra pulled back and looked him over. "Home life has agreed with you. You're looking rather handsome." It was true. The shadows that had weighed him down over the past months had lifted, and his eyes were bright. And though he'd lost some weight over the stressful winter, the time at Brancel had filled out his chest and shoulders again.

Tristam's mouth quirked, and his gaze drifted over Kyra's face in a way that made her stomach tingle. "You're looking very well yourself."

Kyra invited him in and offered him tea and a piece of the cake Idalee had baked that morning. The girl's cooking was rivaling Bella's these days.

"Things are much better at the manor," he told Kyra as they sat down at her table. "There's still the occasional raid from the rebellious Demon Rider, but the number has dropped enough so that our family can handle the defense."

"That's good to hear," said Kyra. "And your family, they are well and safe?"

"They are all well," he said. "Henril will be returning to his post in the border patrols. Lorne will stay with Father a while longer." He hesitated for a moment. "I . . . sent a message to Lord Salis in Parna with my regrets. Lady Cecile is a beautiful, intelligent, and amiable woman, but I do not think we would make a good match."

Kyra had been drinking her tea, and she was grateful she

had an excuse not to look at Tristam. She took a long sip while she composed herself behind the mug. "Will they take offense?" she asked.

"The family was not pleased, since we'd spent so much time on the negotiations, though my most recent demotion did make me a less favorable match." He gave a wry smile. "Apparently, even Parnan families care about court reputation if it gets bad enough. As for Cecile..." And here he paused. "I didn't know her well, but I think she might be happy for me. I can only wish her the best."

Kyra wrapped her mug in her hands. It threatened to scald her skin, but she was too distracted to mind. "So that gives you some respite, then, before your da and your ma start thinking about another match for you."

This time it was his turn to look down. He'd eaten his whole piece of cake, and he stirred the crumbs with his fork. "I've been speaking to them about other matches. They've always been reasonable on the subject of marriage, and now that our manor is no longer under direct attack, they were happy to hear my thoughts. We've talked about the new peace agreement with the Demon Riders. We're hopeful that even if things don't go completely smoothly from here on out, there might at least be some basis for coexisting." He paused, and when he spoke again, it was with the expression of a man scaling a cliff without a safety rope. "I... mentioned to them that it might be good, though perhaps unconventional, to think about a match with one of their number."

Kyra let go of her mug and wiped her damp hands on her trousers. Her heart beat strange rhythms against her rib cage.

"Well, don't set your sights on Adele," she said. Her voice didn't sound like her own. "Flick is a decent brawler, even if he doesn't have a knight's training."

Tristam smiled at that, though his eyes were still uncertain. "No, I don't have my sights set on Adele."

It would have been easier to continue teasing him, but as Kyra met his eyes, she found it hard even to breathe, much less say anything clever. "I see..."

She swallowed, but it didn't make her mouth any less dry. A long moment of silence stretched between them. Bits of bird-song drifted in through the windows, and still neither of them spoke.

Tristam cleared his throat. "I'm not asking you to marry me right away, of course. I mean, I've been gone a while, and with everything that has happened...I just thought...well..." He laughed at himself then, and put his fork down to take a deep breath and pull himself together. When he spoke again, his voice was calm but strong. "I love you, Kyra. You know that, don't you? And I'd fight for a future for us, if you'll have me."

What a difference a few words made. The cottage itself seemed to hold its breath, waiting for her reply. "And what about what I am?" she asked quietly. "Would you tie yourself to someone like me?"

Tristam rubbed his jaw. The bruise was gone, but Kyra would always remember striking him there. "I've seen you struggle with your bloodlines, and I will always have tremendous respect for what you can do." He stopped and looked her in the eye. "I also trust you with my life. I hope you can do the same with me."

He spoke the words with conviction, and Kyra found that she believed him. How things had changed since their first encounter, when he'd tackled her in the Palace courtyard. She'd been a common thief, and he had been dead set on destroying her. Kyra reached over and covered his hands with her own. "I do trust you."

They smiled at each other then and stood up at the same time. The table was still between them. Tristam started to walk around to her side, but she stopped him with a touch on the arm. The table's height had caught her eye. Kyra kicked off her shoes and hoisted herself up. She had to put more weight on her arms to accommodate her hip, but she jumped up quickly without knocking any dishes to the ground. From there, it was just a short hop to land in front of Tristam. He ringed her waist with his arms, his touch setting off a pleasant shiver that swept to the tips of her toes. Tristam looked down at her, amused.

She shrugged. "I'm still getting a feel for what I can do."

"And was that a difficult climb, master thief?"

She wrapped her arms around him and pulled him close. He was wonderfully warm. "Horribly difficult, but worth it."

Tristam bent his face down toward hers then, and she closed her eyes. Her skin prickled at his nearness, and she let out a contented sigh. Then, after what seemed like forever, his lips brushed hers, and they put off the rest of their talking until later.

ACKNOWLEDGMENTS

Whisper the word "sequel" into a debut author's ear and she'll likely jump five feet into the air and flee wild-eyed into a corner. Writing *Daughter of Dusk* was a very different experience from *Midnight Thief*, as I made the transition from writing for my own enjoyment to delivering a book under contract while my newfound (and wonderful) readers waited in the wings. Thankfully, I had a fantastic team of people steering me safely into port.

My editor, Rotem Moscovich, shepherded this manuscript from early outlines to final draft, providing insightful guidance the entire way. Julie Moody, Jamie Baker, and the rest of the team at Hyperion were instrumental to the process as well.

My agent, Jim McCarthy, kept me sane and assured me, time after time, that each draft was not as horrible as I believed.

My longtime critique group, Courtyard Critiques, offered encouragement and suggestions on my first draft as it came out, three thousand words at a time: Amitha Knight, Rachal Aronson, Jennifer Barnes, and Emily Terry.

First-round beta readers kindly slogged through the original (boring) beginning and offered key insights for restructuring every plot arc: Lauren James (*Love is not a triangle*), Andrea Lim (jukeboxmuse.com), Anya (*On Starships and Dragonwings*), Stephenie Sheung (*The BiblioSanctum*), Tabitha Jensen (notyetread.com), Summer McDaniel (*Blue Sky Shelf*), Alyssa Susanna (*The Eater of Books!*), and Maja (*The Nocturnal Library*).

Second-round beta readers pushed me to polish every scene and campaigned (successfully) for more sparks between Kyra and Tristam: Faye M. (*The Social Potato*), Jenna DeTrapani, April Choi, Amy Hung, Lianne Crawford, Emily Lo Gibson, Bekah (*Awesome Book Nuts*), Kelsey Olesen, and Lisa Choi, MD.

Thanks to several authors' loops for wisdom and laughs: The Fourteenery, One Four Kidlit, and YA Binders.

And of course, love and gratitude to my husband for being a (captive) sounding board on everything from plot ideas to copy edits (and, to his credit, he was only slightly insufferable when his grammar or vocabulary proved better than mine), and my parents, in-laws, extended family, and friends for their constant excitement and support on this journey. You make a girl feel loved.